To: Donna

WHEN THEY HEAR OF THE FASCINATING WORLDS
MY CAMERA HAS EXPOSED, THEY ALL TELL ME...

YOU OUGHT'A
WRITE A BOOK

... BY GEORGE

Hope You Enjoy My Adventures

George Bayle

WHEN THEY HEAR OF THE FASCINATING WORLDS
MY CAMERA HAS EXPOSED, THEY ALL TELL ME...

YOU OUGHT'A WRITE A BOOK

... BY GEORGE

A WORLD-TRAVELING PHOTOGRAPHER AND
FILM PRODUCER CHRONICLES THE HIGHLIGHTS
AND ADVENTURES OF A UNIQUE AND
THRILLING CAREER

George Boyle

WORD ASSOCIATION PUBLISHERS
www.wordassociation.com
1.800.827.7903

ISBN: 978-1-59571-852-5

Library of Congress Control Number: 2012923504

Designed and published by
Word Association Publishers
205 Fifth Avenue
Tarentum, Pennsylvania 15084

www.wordassociation.com

1.800.827.7903

DEDICATION

This book is dedicated to my parents
George W. Boyle Sr. and Alice E. Boyle
Without whose unwavering encouragement
and support, the circumstances that made
the stories in this book a reality would
never have occurred.
God bless them both.

ABOUT THE AUTHOR

George Boyle has been producing film features for television documentaries and news programs for well over a half century. He was in on the ground floor when the infant medium of television arrived on the scene in the Pittsburgh market. At one time or another throughout his film career, George has done production filming for all three of the network affiliate stations as well as the public broadcasting network. All of the above stations have one or more award plaques adorning their walls in recognition of the excellence in filming and production which he brought to their operations.

Concurrent with his local affiliations, he also maintained a position with UPI Television News, as a cinematographer and film correspondent, and, in this capacity, supplied newsfilm and feature story coverage to independent stations around the country and overseas.

In addition to the television career, a free-lance film production business was also maintained. This was the phase of operations which presented the author with the opportunities to seek out the exciting adventures which are chronicled in the latter chapters of this book.

A unique partnership was established between George's love of photography and his love of the sea. As a Licensed U. S. Coast Guard Captain and a Certified SCUBA Instructor, many opportunities presented themselves in which photography and the marine environment merged into a desirable marriage. Underwater films were the natural offspring of this union and the highlights of some of these endeavors present some unusual story twists.

Beyond his experience in photography, the author's zest for life, love of adventure, and the ability to get along with people from all walks of life, produced the elements necessary to bring about the stories that are chronicled in the pages of "You Oughta' Write a Book" ... by George

CONTENTS

* Denotes photographs of that subject

PREFACE

Author (left): holds "Photographer of the Year" trophy while reviewing award winning film with co-worker.

The room was dark, the only illumination coming from a dull, ambei bulb hanging some distance from the activity below. A young boy slowly slipped a sheet of white paper into a tray containing a liquid chemical formula. He waited patiently, concentrating on the miracle that was about to occur. Just a minute earlier, this paper had been exposed to a white light through an apparatus with a lens that focused the enlarged image of a small photographic negative onto its surface.

Now the miracle was beginning. Ever so slowly and ever so faintly, at first, the weak outlines of the image began to appear in varying shades of gray upon the plain white sheet. As the chemical action progressed, the shades of blacks and grays intensified and the scene that magically appeared on the previously pure white paper now vividly portrayed an identifiable image. Highlights and contrasts of the stonework and architecture of the new house the boy's parents had just constructed were clearly visible even in this dull amber illumination.

The miracle was complete. The picture was just the right intensity. Chemical action of the developing agent was stopped by a water rinse. Immersion into a "hypo" solution fixed the photograph for all time. In a few seconds, the white light could be turned on and the boy's first experience with the magic of photography could be viewed in the bright light of day.

Needless to say, the results were overwhelming to a 10-year-old boy. The mystery of the photographic phenomenon made a profound impression on his young mind. A desire to continue in this field of endeavor remained constant for all the years to come, for no matter how many times he would go into the darkroom to develop, print, and enlarge the thousands of photographs subsequently taken, the fascination of that first miracle never subsided. Each time an image appeared on a previously blank sheet of paper, the memory of that first experience was revived and perpetuated.

When subsequent years advanced the photographic process from black & white to natural color, the original fascination increased manyfold. There was never any question that this science and technology would be this boy's choice for his future profession in life Beyond still photography was the fascination of motion pictures. He learned how to edit these "movie films" into logical stories and programs

Now, add sound capabilities with voice, narration, music and sound effects and the attraction continued to grow. With the infant medium of television just making its beginnings in the local area, the combined set of circumstances were ideal for the launching of a career that could take any direction the future would present.

One other element enters into the formulation of the 10-year-old boy's ultimate lifestyle and activities: WATER. The fascination with water most probably began at an earlier age, but the vivid recollection of the first positive experience involving water occurs during the same age period, 10 years.

New house (remember the first picture), new neighborhood, new friends, and, come summertime, the first unsupervised encounter with a new swimming pool in the neighborhood.

Although loving the feel of water, he'd never had any formal lessons in the art of swimming. Never having been in water above his waist before, the 10-year-old boy was naturally timid in his first venture with playmates to the new public swimming pool.

Entering the shallow part of the pool, he played catch with some fellows who had a rubber ball, and generally enjoyed the play. He made a few feeble attempts at putting his head under water and copying others who were holding their breath. He also made some awkward efforts to imitate the swimming strokes of others in the pool, all to no particular avail.

But the shallow water play was not where the action was. Up in the deep end, fellows were playing a game of tag. Fast paced diving and swift swimming took place as the one who was "it" tried to catch up with other players and tag them. The pace was furious and exciting to watch and the boy was drawn alongside the deeper end of the pool to more closely observe this active fun.

Suddenly, without warning, someone pushed or accidentally bumped into him as he stood too close to the deep end. In an instant, he found himself some distance out from the side of the pool, underwater and not knowing how to swim. To make matters worse, the lifeguard was paying attention to the fury of the game and did not notice one young boy getting pushed into the deep water.

There's something about being the "new kid on the block" that instills in a young boy a false sense of pride. The predicament was serious, even life threatening, but the sense of false pride was so strong that it took over in this drastic situation. The boy summoned all his limited ability and got himself to the surface. He caught a breath of air, and, amid the fury of the tag game, proceeded, as best he could, to mimic the actions of the other swimmers.

To his pleasure and amazement, he found he could navigate his body through the water in some limited fashion. With each stroke, the self-assurance that he could survive in deep water continued to grow. The fear that he had previously experienced melted away and was replaced with an unusual measure of self-confidence that continued to grow at a rapid rate.

Not only did he succeed in saving himself by swimming to an area of the pool where he could touch his feet, now that boyish fear of the unknown deep water was a thing of the past. Little by little, he expanded his efforts and, before the end of the week, found himself participating in the game of tag that had earlier been only a source of passive fascination.

By the middle of that summer, the boy found himself participating in competitive swimming meets. Although not yet a winner, nevertheless making a suitable showing for a novice who would go on to compile an impressive array of ribbons and medals in swimming and diving competitions in subsequent years. The confidence that was built by confronting the first deep-water experience created a foundation for the love of all things related to water that continued to grow throughout the years.

The combination of love of photography and love of water influenced almost all of the future decisions relating to career and professional choices. They are at the heart of most of the following stories.

The rest of this book will consist of a series of chronicles relating to opportunities that presented themselves and the stories that surround them, because almost every time I relate some of these experiences to an audience, the listeners usually tell me, "YOU OUGHTA' WRITE A BOOK."

Sometimes I'll tell it like a story. Sometimes I'll interject my personal feelings and inner thoughts. There'll be no particular pattern to the prose. Thoughts will just spill out however my mind recalls the incidents and events as, of course, you realize that now, many years and many experiences later, I'm that 10-year-old boy, grown up and thankful for those events that shaped my life and career. I hope you enjoy reading of my experiences almost as much as I did living through them. You'll see that basically I'm an ordinary guy who just happened to have some extraordinary adventures that I'd like to share with you. So that makes it time for Chapter One and a start with the early years.

CHAPTER ONE
EARLY YEARS

Family of deceased requested color photo to send to relatives overseas.

I know many people have not experienced the thrill of seeing a photograph come to life in a darkroom. The closest thing to that experience is when you take a Polaroid picture and watch it develop before your eyes. That's close, but not exactly the same because, with a Polaroid, your involvement with the development process is mostly as a spectator. You exercise no control of intensity, contrast or, as with color photography, choice of the wide variety of tints and color saturations that allow the photographer to become an artist as he applies his skills to the making of the final print

As a matter of fact, part of me realizes that I am a frustrated artist and that frustration accelerated my involvement with photography. Since I was unable to draw, sketch, or demonstrate any of the talents that I envied in people with artistic ability, I let my artistry flow and function through my cameras and the follow-up processing and editing.

Its not easy for a boy of grade school age to be taken seriously by his adult neighbors. It takes persistence and perseverance to break through that grown-up barrier and let them know you mean business. Fortunately, I think, a little bit of extra maturity fell upon me because of some accelerated educational opportunities that placed me a couple of grades ahead of others in my same age group. Socially, this was a mistake, but career-wise, perhaps a distinct advantage. I didn't neglect my playtime altogether, but took some time away from ball games and other play to establish a photographic business while not yet out of grade school.

I subsequently convinced a local merchant that I was able to do his photo finishing work. To this day, I don't know how I persuaded him. I didn't undercut the prices he was paying, so I just have to thank him for his confidence in me that allowed a small commercial start to my career. If his customers had any idea that a kid in grade school was responsible for their precious family pictures, they'd probably have had a fit.

There was no commercial processing machine, just hand-dipping each roll up and down in a small enamel tray. No fancy enlarging apparatus either. I couldn't afford such a luxury in those early days. My Aunt Grace graciously permitted me to take her precious Kodak folding-bellows camera and convert it into an enlarger. This I did by removing the camera back and replacing it with a light box and diffusion filter.

Aunt Grace Buxton, in addition to being a staunch supporter of my young career, is also an inspiration to the writing of this book. At the age of 90, she authored a book about her life as a social worker at St. Paul's Orphanage. She was a most positive influence throughout all my life.

Meanwhile, back at the homemade darkroom, the makeshift camera and lightbox were mounted on a 2 x 4 upright board and it was possible to change the size of the projected negative image by carefully moving the camera up or down this board and focusing the bellows extensions. It just took a lot of time and many mistakes to correct by trial and error.

This activity was taking place in the basement of my parents' new home. Their patience was a key ingredient in my early success. Just picture this: My mother's laundry room and clothes lines taken over to hang roll after roll of film to dry on pinch-type clothes pins. Many's the time she wanted to do some of her wash, but had to wait until my films dried on her lines before she could do her own laundry.

Then there was the takeover of the living room and dining room for mass drying of prints. You see, I didn't have the finances to purchase a commercial dryer, so when I branched out into volume printing (like hundreds of school group pictures), the only way I found to get them dry was to spread bedsheets all over the living room and dining room carpets, place all my wet prints across these sheets, and then cover them with another set of bedsheets for a blotter effect. Magazines and books had to be placed over each print to weigh it down and prevent curling during the drying process. My parents should be given a medal for their patience in allowing me to disrupt their home, and I an forever indebted to their indulgence.

I previously mentioned my parents' "new hone" and maybe I'm creating an image of family wealth? Nothing could be further from the truth. Just a decade earlier, my parents, like so many others of that period of time, were unable to keep up with the mortgage payments on another home and fell victims to bank foreclosure and the loss of their house. This occurred at the tail end of the great depression and I was too young to realize the tremendous financial pressures that affected them. I only knew that it wasn't proper to ask for any allowance money like some of my playmates received weekly. So, when this little photographic business was able to provide me with some spending money, the idea of financial independence was probably responsible for adding to my interest in continuing and expanding in the photographic field.

Most of my work in these early years was routine and, at times, even monotonous. But a couple of things left lasting impressions and I'd like to share them with you.

I can particularly recall two incidents in these early days of photography that left profound memories. One is the story of little Raymond.

As the business had now progressed to school group pictures, the next thing that logically came up on the school calendar was First Communion. Arrangements were made to photograph the group of First Communicants, mostly children in the second grade, about 7 years of age. In addition to the group photo, I thought it would be nice to have individual portraits of each child taken at the church altar. There were special floral arrangements on the altar and this made a beautiful background as I photographed each boy and girl individually, standing in front of the altar with their prayer books and rosary beads in their folded hands. They all looked like little angels. The parents were pleased with the results and sales were brisk.

Little did I know, however, that one of these children who looked so angelic this communion day, was soon to be called by the very angels he resembled. Little Raymond had some type of rheumatic heart problem that claimed his young life just shortly after his communion day. Much to my shock, the family contacted me for a special favor. They were so impressed by the way he looked in his portrait in front of the altar in his white communion suit that they asked for an enlarged copy of the photo to have enclosed in a special glass cover that was to be impregnated into Raymond's memorial tombstone for his grave.

It's difficult to explain the feelings that went through my mind as I complied with the request of Raymond's family. At first I didn't even want to think about it. The idea of this beautiful little boy being dead at such an early age really upset me. I had just been involved in one of the happiest moments of his young life, his First Holy Communion day.

Well, there was a job to be done and I couldn't put it off any longer. Reluctantly, I found the proper negative and placed it into the enlarger, focusing the bigger image onto the white easel below. I was having a difficult time focusing a sharp image because tears kept coming into my eyes and making things blurry. Finally, I was able to get it all together and was determined to make the best possible photograph I had ever produced. I finished the process and delivered a beautiful portrait to the grieving family.

I never had any idea that a picture could be so important to a family in this special time of loss. Shocked and saddened as I was at the death of this young boy, still I had a great sense of pride and relief in knowing that my photograph had contributed to easing the family grief and would be a lasting memorial. In all my subsequent years of making pictures, I've never had a similar request.

There was one situation that did come along shortly thereafter that also leaves a unique memory for the unusual nature of the request. A neighboring family of European extraction had been caring for the husband's father who had come over from the "old country" a few years previously. The elderly gentleman subsequently died while residing here with his son. All the proper funeral arrangements were made and visitations were held at a local funeral home. It seemed there were some skeptical members of the family still living in the old country who questioned the care that the old man was given by the son here in America.

In order to alleviate any of their concern about the final care and tributes to their father, the family asked me to make a color photograph of the gentleman in his casket, showing all the floral arrangements, the quality of the casket, and the general decor of his final resting area.

It was a strange feeling to set up the picture in the funeral home and the eerie feeling continued as the film was processed and the color print was made.

But, when the photo was delivered, and the family showed such pleasure in knowing that the family members overseas, who could not be at the funeral, would be able to see, in vivid color, the care given to their father's funeral, I was relieved and gratified that I had played a part in fortifying this family assurance. That's also the only time I have been requested to photograph a person in a casket.

Strange that these two unusual and dramatic requests should come along so early in my career and then never be repeated. I think these incidents made me realize the importance of photography in its effect on people's lives. I'm happy to have had the opportunity to be of service to these two families in their special needs. This helped increase my sensitivity to the importance of pictures in family living.

Nothing else memorable stands out in any special way throughout the remainder of these early years and I proceeded on to high school, which I think should be addressed in Chapter Two.

CHAPTER TWO
HIGH SCHOOL

The "Speed Graphic" press camera that started a professional career in news photography is proudly displayed by the 13 year old author. It was purchased from a $350 loan from Uncle Chuck as related in Chapter 2

I don't think this chapter is going to be very long, because memory doesn't recall any spectacular or particularly interesting events that were much above the ordinary high school curriculum and activities.

Naturally, with my interest in photography already in high gear, as soon as I got going in my freshman year, I wanted to be involved with taking pictures for the school newspaper. There was just one catch. An upperclassman currently held that position and was not about to let some upstart freshman move into his territory.

To make things even worse in my eyes, he possessed a professional "press camera" and really knew how to make the proper use of it. Every time I tried to take some pictures of a school event and submit them for publication, they would be passed over and the editorial staff would choose the pictures taken by the upperclassman. After a number of rejections, my enthusiasm diminished and I began to concentrate my attentions toward my other passion in life, WATER.

The high school that I attended did not have a swimming pool. Therefore, they did not include a swimming team among their sports activities. By fortunate coincidence, a hotel just two blocks from my school did have a swimming pool as a part of their recreational complex. A friend and classmate of mine was employed there in the locker room. Because of his employment, I was able to come over after school and gain admission for an afternoon swim.

On one of these afternoon swimming occasions, the lifeguard and pool director got into a conversation with me about my school. He questioned why we didn't have a swimming team like other high schools in the area. When I informed him of their lack of pool facilities, he suggested that the hotel pool would be available for the school's use if the principal wanted to organize a team. The task of making this presentation to the principal fell upon my shoulders.

Well, here we go again. Picture this little freshman (even smaller than most freshmen because of age difference due to skipping a couple of elementary grades) waiting in the outer office for an appointment with the principal. That's right, I was shivering in my boots. Maybe the little bit of maturity that I had built up through my business contacts with adults in my photography work pulled me through this interview. The results were surprisingly favorable. The principal listened attentively to my proposition, interjecting pertinent questions where necessary, and, when the interview was completed, I had secured his permission to advertise in the school bulletin for tryouts for the school's new swimming team.

A teacher was appointed to be moderator, the hotel lifeguard was hired as coach, and a new sports activity was added to the school's extra-curricular roster: "Competitive Swimming." I was even able to get the principal to commit funds for bathing suits and robes for the team. His only concern was that we form a professional looking team and work ourselves into an organization of which the school could be proud. Subsequently, we did just that and I am happy to have had a principal role in the formation of that team.

An ironic footnote to this swimming team story is the fact that the team continued to grow and gain prominence throughout the years. Then, a generation later, when my eldest son would attend this same school and become a member of the team his father was instrumental in starting, a difficulty with the availability of a suitable coach led to the disbandment of the team in my son's final year.

All the swimmers who were so active in this sport were greatly disappointed and I was sorry to hear that the team had folded. I'm grateful that my son had the opportunity to participate in four great years of competition before it ended. While I was a member of the swim team and competing with other schools in various meets, I managed to take some action photos of the swimming activities that were not covered by the upperclassman photographer. I can remember the glowing feeling of pride and satisfaction when the first picture made it past the editorial board and got published in the school newspaper. There's a certain unexplainable feeling in knowing that something that you did has been accepted and displayed for viewing to the public.

Every person likes to be congratulated for a job well done. Psychologists will all agree that compliments and congratulations are key ingredients in the maintenance of good morale in almost any job situation. I didn't understand any of this psychological mumbo-jumbo. I only knew that it felt good to do something that was worth displaying to the world, and I wanted to continue in these kinds of endeavors.

I finally found my loophole to getting pictures published. The Year Book. This publication required many more photographs than the monthly newspaper and, by my sophomore year, I learned how to submit the right kind of activity pictures that the year book staff would use. Once the pattern was established, I continued to supply them with photos for their publication. My enthusiasm returned .There was a certain amount of envy I had for that upperclassman with his big professional "press" camera. It was a Speed Graphic, the workhorse of the photojournalist trade in that era. The camera that all the big-time newspaper photographers used. Needless to say, I wanted one.

You've heard it said, "People in Hell want ice water." Hell, that's just about how ridiculous my request was at the time. High school sophomore, and a very young sophomore at that, a little pocket money saved from a small photofinishing business, but nowhere near enough to finance the purchase of an expensive Speed Graphic. Parents couldn't help either. Payments on their new house taxed their earnings to the limit. Still, something inside me kept saying, "There has to be a way."

God bless Uncle Chuck. That's right! For everyone there ought to be an Uncle Chuck in their life at some point when things seem critical. My own Uncle Chuck was in business for himself as a distributor of pretzels and potato chips. Throughout my younger years. I had occasionally worked for him in a part-time capacity, assisting with menial tasks in his warehouse and sometimes helping him on his delivery truck when he had medical problems with his legs.

He became my "angel." Somehow I was able to convince him that I was serious in this business of photography and that an investment in a press camera of professional quality would not be money thrown away on a kid, but a good investment in my future. He agreed and advanced me the sum of $350, an enormous amount in those days. I promised to have him paid back within one year, from the proceeds of my photography business.

Believe it or not, that promise was kept. Payments were made every month as I eked out some profit from baby pictures, school groups, weddings and even a payment of a whopping $5.00 for my first real news picture that was published in the local newspaper.

I was traveling through the business section of East Liberty on a streetcar (I wasn't old enough to drive a car yet), carrying my camera en route to a photo session with somebody's kid.) Looking out the window of the trolley, I saw flames coming from the front window of a clothing and shoe store in the heart of the business district. Immediately I asked the conductor to let me off the car and proceeded to shoot some action photos just as the first fire engines arrived.

The front of the store was an inferno when the firemen got first water onto the blaze. The pictures were quite spectacular, but now, what do I do ? The pictures may be action filled and dramatic, but that's no good unless I can do something with them. I telephoned the editor of one of the local newspapers and told him what I had. His instructions were to bring the undeveloped film downtown to the paper and let them develop and print them for possible use in the evening edition.

I didn't tell him my age, or that I didn't drive, I just said "OK" and proceeded to take another streetcar downtown and got my first experience with the operation of a metropolitan newspaper. The veteran photographers seemed a bit surprised and perhaps even a little annoyed with this kid showing up with a press camera and having "scooped" them on a big fire story. Nevertheless, they developed and printed my pictures and the picture editor chose one of them to run with the story. I filled out some kind of a pay voucher form and left in a hurry because I still had a commitment to take pictures of some lady's kid out in East Liberty.

I don't think my mind was on the pictures of the kid. I don't even remember the outcome of that job. I had been exposed to the "big time" and one of my pictures had been used in the daily newspaper. There was probably not a hat in town that would have fit on my head at that moment. Besides, I was getting paid. Five dollars. It seemed like a fortune back then, and it was like hanging a carrot in front of the nose of a racehorse. I was off and running and news pictures were my new target.

Naturally, with this new experience of having a picture published in the paper, a little bragging was in order with my classmates. One of them challenged me. However. It seems that his particular hero of the moment was Primo Carnera, a giant of a man who had been a prizefighter and now had turned professional wrestler. Primo Carnera was appearing at the old Duquesne Gardens arena in a professional wrestling match the following night. My classmate challenged me to get him a picture of his hero and offered to pay me as much as the newspapers paid for a photo ($5).

I was caught between a rock and a hard place. Having taken up his challenge, now what? I lied about having press credentials to impress my classmates. I didn't have any way of getting into the big wrestler's dressing room. What to do? Use your ingenuity, of course. Sneak into the building by a back service entrance. Find a way around all the service area corridors to the area where the dressing rooms were located and, by some stroke of luck, stumble into the big man's dressing room.

Too late to turn back now. The first close-up look at Primo Carnera was absolutely breathtaking. He wasn't big, he was huge. His trainer and assistants wanted to throw me out. I was an annoyance to them as they tried to prepare him for his match. As I pleaded with them to let me take just one picture, the big man took over. He pulled them away from me and said, "Let the kid get his picture." He stood tall in the middle of the room for a quick pose. I got overanxious. Afraid to ask him to move back to the other end of the room so I could get his massive size into one picture, I got as far back as I possibly could, aimed the camera quickly and got the one picture I had been allowed to take. A quick retreat was now necessary before someone asked for some credentials or identification.

I felt very smug on my way back to the darkroom. I'd show my classmate that I had what it takes to get the job done. Besides, he'd owe me $5 and that would be my final coup. The sheet of film was placed in the development tank and processed. I couldn't wait to get it completed and see the results in the white light. Now the fixing process was complete and I opened the tank and lifted the negative up to the light.

Horrors !!! In my fear and haste to get the job done, I had not allowed enough space to get the big man's head entirely into the picture. This magnificent giant was cut off about the middle of his forehead, spoiling an otherwise perfect photograph. The man was so huge that I simply didn't have enough room to back up and get all of his massive height into the picture. Because I was afraid to push my luck any further in his dressing room, my hurried-up shot had missed its mark by a forehead. I had blown my chance to play the role of the "big shot" with my classmate.

This incident, however, taught me a priceless lesson. Never again did I hurry my actions to a point where I might make a similar mistake. I still printed the cutoff picture of Mr. Carnera and gave it to my friend. I did not have the guts to ask him for payment, and that was an important lesson also.

One lesson I really learned the hard way was to thoroughly check my camera before every shot. The painful experience that brought this lesson home with devastating clarity was the wedding of my favorite girl cousin. Antoinette. Even though I was just a schoolboy, she had enough confidence in my professional ability to hire me to shoot her storybook wedding.

Prettiest wedding I ever saw. Set in a garden beneath a rose trellis and blessed with a June day that was weather-perfect. Everything went without a hitch. Beautiful bride, handsome groom, lovely gowns, and a setting that was a photographer's dream. I shot three times as many pictures as I normally would have taken for a wedding album.

The next day, in my darkroom, the dream began turning into a nightmare. My developing tank for the film from my Speed Graphic camera held 12 sheets of cut film at a time. I had carefully mixed fresh chemicals for this special occasion, and had paid particular attention to temperature and time of development.

When the allotted time was completed for the developing and fixing of the first batch of negatives, I anxiously opened the tank and removed the first group for viewing. Oh no!! I couldn't believe my eyes. They were blank! Every one of them. Impossible! I had been so careful. How could this be??

I made a new batch of chemicals. Tested them on other film before starting the next batch of 12 negatives through the processing. When it was time to turn on the lights, again I was horrified at the results. All blank. Not even the slightest trace of an image on any of these 12 pieces of film. It just couldn't be the chemicals. I had to check the camera.

The Speed Graphic is equipped with two shutters. One shutter is located between the lens elements and is generally used for flash synchronization photography. The other shutter is a "focal plane" shutter that consists of a movable curtain, tightly wound on rollers at the back portion of the camera housing.

The focal plane shutter exposes the film by releasing this tightly wound curtain from its spring tension and allowing a small slit-hole in the material to rapidly pass by the unexposed film. This type of shutter adapts the camera to very high speed exposures and is used primarily to freeze sports action and other high speed applications.

To use the focal plane shutter, the between-the-lens shutter must be locked in an open position. Subsequently, to use the between-the-lens shutter, the focal plane curtain must be locked in a position where a large slot in the curtain leaves the film clear for exposure.

In shooting weddings and using flash synchronization photography, I only used the between-the-lens shutter. The focal plane shutter was always locked in the open position. Well, one look at the camera revealed that this was not the case now. The trigger on the focal plane shutter release had been pulled and the back curtain was obscuring the entire film plane and not allowing any exposure whatsoever from the front shutter. It was like leaving the black slide in my filmholder. No light ever reached my films.

Devastated, I tried one more batch of development, hoping for a miracle. I didn't get my wish. Another tankful of blank film. This beautiful wedding would go unrecorded and my cousin's heart would be broken.

There's one more piece of irony to this already tragic story. Rather than waste the remainder of undeveloped wedding films, I decided to salvage what remained and use this film on my next job. You guessed it. Double jeopardy.

My next assignment was photographing a congressman making a speech at my school. A rather important personality and a noteworthy picture for the school newspaper and year book. I used the salvaged film and, upon developing it, got a double shock. Double exposure, that is. Two pictures on the same negative. As I looked again in horror, there was Congressman Fulton giving his speech through the rose trellis at my cousin's wedding. What in the world had happened?

Further investigation revealed that one of my male cousins had tampered with my camera at the wedding without my knowledge. In curiosity, he had meddled with the focal plane shutter trigger and accidentally released the curtain from its locked-open position. He had done this sometime between the wedding and reception activities.

If I had developed all of the film, I would have at least salvaged the most important shots, the actual wedding ceremony in that impressive setting. Instead, I thought all the film was blank and tried to save some money by re-using the already exposed film. Now my anguish was compounded. If I hadn't been so cheap, I could have saved the best part of the wedding pictures and the congressman as well.

Learning is sometimes accompanied by hard knocks. I tried to make up the loss to my cousin by taking special color portraits of her after she returned from her honeymoon. This was only a partial remedy and I feel terrible to this very day about that tragic mistake. You can bet there was never again a time that I did not check every feature on every camera I used. I also have to thank my cousin, Toni, for being so understanding. I think it was contact with people like her that gave me the perseverance to continue.

Color portrait of cousin Antoinette to atone for other lost photos.

Not much else in those high school days rises as being particularly memorable. When I reached the status of upperclassman, my experience with the camera got a great many more pictures published in the newspaper and year book. I had a couple of automobile accident pictures accepted by the local newspaper and published. However, since I was not yet old enough to drive, transportation limitations inhibited the pursuit of a news photographer's career for the time being. But it was far from being out of my mind, I just had to bide my time.

Meanwhile, competitive swimming and diving were not overlooked. Throughout the remainder of high school, I devoted enough time to this sport to become proficient and excel. In the summer months, participation with the City of Pittsburgh Bureau of Recreation swimming team earned me several medals and the attention of the swimming coach from the University of Pittsburgh.

Subsequently, I was offered -- and considered -- a swimming scholarship. However, a thorough review of all the university's catalogues failed to reveal any course of higher education that would advance my photography interests. Reluctantly, I turned down the scholarship. There were those who considered this move a mistake, but this book might not have been written had I accepted the scholarship. Fate took several unique turns after that and placed me in situations that a college student doesn't have the opportunity to accept.

Being only 15 years old in my senior year of high school, I wasn't legally able to learn to drive until just before graduation. As soon as graduation was over, I'd saved enough money to buy a used car and get business off on a full swing. Now it was possible to free-lance news pictures for the paper and have the transportation to get the job done. The $5 checks became more regular. Shortly thereafter, an association with a color film processing lab became quite intriguing. Not only did I gain the additional experience of photography in color, but an interesting side light to this job helped form my future years in photography.

The father-in-law of the owner of the color lab was the football coach at a local college. He needed someone to take motion pictures of his team's games and practice sessions for coaching purposes. Because he was aware that I was heavily interested in photography, he asked me if I did motion picture filming. Now, the truth of the matter is that I had never had a movie camera in my hands prior to his request. The challenge was so exciting that I told him I did do motion picture filming and would be glad to be his coaching movie photographer. Now I had one week to purchase a movie camera, learn how to operate it properly, and be ready for the opening game.

You know I did it, otherwise I wouldn't be telling you this story. Yep, a new avenue of photography opened up with that simple request from the coach. Let's cover the motion picture beginnings in Chapter Three.

Author displays athletic letter for swim team merit.

CHAPTER THREE
MOTION PICTURES

CAPTURED ON CAMERA - Author used high-power telephoto camera
lenses for surveillance work.

In less than a week, I had mastered the basic techniques of movie filming enough to satisfy the coaching needs of the football team. I traveled with the college team all season, shooting their game films and practices. Little by little, the many uses of the motion picture camera began to present themselves.

After shooting the college football coaching films for the second season, I was contacted by one of the alumni, an attorney, about a service that he needed. It seems he represented a company that was being sued by an individual who claimed to have been permanently injured by an accident involving that company's equipment.

Information had come to the attorney that the claimant was neither severely injured nor permanently disabled. He was strongly suspected of faking this disability in order to receive a large monetary verdict in upcoming litigation.

The attorney wanted to get some kind of tangible proof that the claimant was faking his injuries. He wanted motion picture evidence of the man's activities. This request thrust me into an entirely new field of photography.

Its not easy to obtain film of a person's normal activities without his knowledge. It requires infinite patience, skill, sophisticated equipment, and a certain amount of luck as well. People who are trying to give the impression that they are disabled are quite cautious in public. However, when they are not aware that they are being observed, it's amazing the things that they will do, and then deny it when it comes to court testimony.

I don't know if I want to talk about any one particular case or claimant, because they almost all involved litigation. I prefer not to be specific. I'll just mention a few of the situations with which this type of photography got me involved, and the experiences that I had during these endeavors.

Telephoto lenses for the movie camera became a big necessity now. Generally, it was not possible to get close to any of these claimants without having them aware of the camera. It was necessary to conduct surveillance from long distances and be able to produce film with enough clarity to not only recognize the activities being performed, but also to positively identify the person involved.

I purchased big lenses and learned their proper use under fire and by trial and error. You can't have any camera movement with telephoto lenses because the magnification in the size of the image on the film also magnifies the slightest movement of the camera by the same multiplication of power. Judges and juries don't appreciate jumpy or jiggly films shown in their courtrooms. Discipline had to be quickly learned and great patience employed to produce steady and acceptable films.

One of the cases that comes to mind, however, required just the opposite. A super wide-angle lens was needed for this job. The generalities of the story are like this:

A man I'll call Bob was involved in an auto accident in another city. He claimed that injuries to his back and legs prevented him from working. He was looking for a large settlement or was ready to sue for compensation due to his alleged disabilities.

Routine investigation in his neighborhood failed to uncover any evidence of work activity. Residents in the tight little court of party-wall houses where he lived had no knowledge of any employment and never saw him going to or from any job. Nevertheless, there was some subjective inconsistency in his medical reports that led to a suspicion of exaggeration of the disability. A request was made for motion pictures of his activities.

Identification of the subject is of prime importance before any motion pictures are taken of activities. It would be a tremendous waste of time, not to mention how embarrassing it would be to show up in court with film of the wrong person.

In Bob's case, I mentioned that he lived in a closed, party-wall court of row houses. The front of the house was not visible from the front street. These row houses had an exclusive entrance and were isolated from the rest of the area. The back yards of all these houses were protected by a four foot chain-link fence. There seemed to be no way, front or back, to maintain any surveillance to establish positive identification.

There was, however, an old garage building across from the back yards. Investigation of these premises revealed that it was possible to achieve a view of the claimant's back yard and kitchen window from a vantage point atop this old garage roof. Access to this roof was difficult during any daylight hours due to the high density of the neighborhood. Although darkness would not arrive until after 9 p.m. in summer, it was an essential covering if I hoped to gain access to this vantage point without arousing the suspicion of the neighbors.

Patience is as crucial as binoculars in this line of work. I waited for over two hours in silence before there was some activity in the kitchen and heads passed back and forth by the window. At about 11:30 p.m., as I was scanning the kitchen windows for a positive look at Bob, suddenly, the back door opened and "what to my wondering eyes should appear," but Bob, exiting out the back door, dressed in work clothes, and obviously headed for the back fence. There was no gate or exitway of any kind on this four foot chain-link fence. Bob just walked to the end of the yard, placed his hands on the top of the fence and vaulted over it into the pathway beyond. He walked briskly to the next street, which was a block away from his house. From my vantage point I was able to observe him getting into a car and starting the engine.

I was able to descend from the garage roof and get to my own car in time to pick up his trail as he drove around the corner of the back street and continued on towards his destination. I followed at a safe distance without being observed by Bob. He continued five or six miles to another section of the city and parked his car by the warehouse of a large trucking company. I observed him enter just before midnight.

What to do now? Perseverance and luck had placed this man's activities into my view. The job now was to obtain motion picture proof of whatever employment activities he was undertaking within this warehouse and truck terminal.

I didn't hurry. First I circled the building in my car, observing all the entrances, exits, windows, etc.. This was not going to be easy.

From street level, it was not possible to see what activities were going on inside. Across the street from the truck terminal was an old manufacturing building. It had an accessible fire escape which would provide an elevated view of the truck terminal windows. Unfortunately, the manufacturing building also had a night watchman. I observed his rounds carefully and timed my ascent of the fire escape to avoid detection by the watchman.

Placing my movie camera, telephoto lens, and binoculars into an old leather carrying bag, I gained access to the fire escape and climbed to an upper level where I maneuvered into a position to see through the windows of the truck terminal across the street. Once again patience was necessary. I still had to contend with the night watchman in the building where I was perched. I had to carefully pick a spot where I could put my back to a brick wall, not near any of the building's many windows where I might create a silhouette for the watchman to spot.

After an hour or more of not being able to see where Bob was working, my patience was rewarded. Bob appeared through one of the windows in the truck terminal and was observed opening the back door of one of the trailers that were backed up to the warehouse doors. He proceeded to unload all sorts of freight and merchandise from the trailer. By using the telephoto lens from the vantage point of the fire escape, it was possible to film a considerable amount of the work activities that he was performing during the times he could be observed through the window. This was not totally satisfactory, however, for two reasons.

First, the window was somewhat dirty, and although the activity was visible, the clarity was not acceptable by my standards. Furthermore, since I could not carry a tripod support up onto the fire escape, the telephoto lens shots from this position were all hand-held. I balanced the camera against the fire escape railing as well as possible, but could not hold it as perfectly steady as I desired.

Second, although the lighting in the truck unloading area was quite bright, considering the dirt on the windows, it was doubtful that ample light was available to produce court-room quality motion pictures, even with the telephoto lens at maximum aperture.

A further review of the entire circumstances brought me to a daring plan of action. The trucking warehouse and loading platform was very large. There were about 20 or 30 tractor trailers backed in against both sides of the warehouse, where large overhead doors provided access to each trailer. Bob was currently unloading a trailer on the far side of the building. It would be possible to see his activities quite clearly from one of the doors along the near side.

The only trick was to move, undetected, underneath about 15 of the trailer trucks until I could get to the door opposite the dock where he was unloading. By now it was 4 a.m. The streets were deathly still. Nothing was moving in the area. I had seen a police car making rounds within the past half hour. I hoped he would be cruising elsewhere for awhile.

Switching the telephoto lens to a standard and wide-angle lens on the movie camera, I descended the fire escape, narrowly escaping detection by the night watchman again, crossed the street, and carefully made my way, crawling under the tractor trailers until I arrived at the door directly opposite the dock where Bob was unloading his truck. Ever so carefully, I pried up the overhead door from the bottom. To my good fortune, it was unlocked and gave an inch to my tedious prying efforts without making any telltale noise. Then, with more cautious and gentle prying, another inch or so was opened until it was possible to just get the barrel of the wide angle lens under the door and aimed at the activity within.

Fortunately the bustle within the warehouse was; noisy enough to cover the sound of the movie camera as the film passed through the gate and onto the take-up reel. To my ears, in the tomb-like quiet underneath the tractor trailer, it sounded like a coffee grinder in full motion. I wished I had two pillows to cover the camera and muffle the sound. Nevertheless, no one, especially not Bob, heard the camera.

The film clearly depicted his activity in unloading all sorts of machinery, truck tires, appliances, and other sorts of boxed merchandise from the trailer to the sorting floor. It felt to me like my pounding heart was making as much noise as the camera while I loaded a new roll of film and shot a second reel of similar activity.

There was no evidence of any disability in any of Bob's movements or in any of the work activity he performed. To all outward appearances, this was a normal, healthy man, performing his rigorous manual labor with no noticeable difficulty. With my heart still beating like a trip hammer, I carefully lowered the overhead door and began my difficult crawl back out under the 15 parked trailers. I only hoped no truck driver would suddenly appear to start up for a morning run. It was now somewhere between 5 and 6 a.m. and I had had quite an unexpectedly exciting night. There were times during his unloading work that Bob had been as close as three feet away from my camera lens. Needless to say, my nerves were strained to capacity and I just wanted safely out of there, and home to get a well deserved rest.

When the finished film was presented to the attorney, he had all the evidence he needed to effect an amicable settlement with Bob and keep this claim from going to trial. I was informed that Bob received payment for his medical bills and repair of his car for damages that were a result of the accident. The big claim, lost wages and disability allegation, was quickly dropped and the company saved thousands of dollars because of my work.

It was tedious at times, then extremely exciting and challenging. There were times when I was just plain scared. Throughout all of this, my mind was always on the end result and this time it paid off with the proof on film.

There were many other claims cases that I worked on for various attorneys and companies, many of them routine and basic, but a couple still stand out in my mind as unique in their circumstances. Lets take a look at a few.

Like Ollie, for instance. Ollie worked for a railroad and somehow during the course of his employment, Ollie injured his leg. Now railroad employees were under different laws than other workers. If they got hurt on the job, they were not covered by Workmen's Compensation insurance like millworkers, construction people, or truck drivers. Railroad workers either accepted a settlement for medical costs and injury compensation from their company claims department, or they were entitled, under law, to sue for their injuries in Federal Courts.

Somehow, Federal Courts got the reputation of being much more liberal in disbursing awards to injured railroad workers and big money awards received considerable publicity in the media. Now its possible that Ollie had something like a big money award in his mind after he injured his leg. He got an attorney and wouldn't settle with the railroad claims department. Instead, he filed suit in Federal Court for an alleged disability that supposedly left him with a permanent limp.

Seems like Ollie lived in a farm house out in the middle of one of our Midwestern states where he rented his house from the owner of the big farm. The farm owner had moved into the small adjacent town for more convenience in his elder years. By coincidence, he had moved next door to the railroad foreman who had been Ollie's supervisor prior to the leg injury.

Mr. Ramsey, the farm owner, got to talking with the railroad foreman who lived next door and the subject of Ollie's disability came up. It seems that Ollie wasn't as disabled as he'd have liked people to believe, according to the observations of Mr. Ramsey and his sons who saw Ollie on a regular basis when they worked the big farm. The railroad foreman reported this apparent discrepancy to the claims department. That's when their attorney contacted me.

I traveled to the Midwestern state and surveyed the situation. The problems were multiple. Ollie's rented farm house was surrounded by nothing but flat farmland as far as the eye could see. There was a big barn near the house that belonged to Mr. Ramsey. It was used when he worked his fields with his sons. Another smaller barn and some outbuildings stood across the road. No other cover existed for miles in any direction. No place to park a car or truck for any length of time without sticking out like a sore thumb. When attempting a job like this, the fewer people involved, the lower the possibility that the nature of your job will be revealed. The ultimate goal in obtaining motion pictures of a claimant is that they should portray his or her natural activities as performed without knowledge of observation. With this objective in mind, I first set out to tackle this job alone.

People who live on farms start their days very early. In order to get into some position from where I could get a vantage point to use a telephoto lens from a distance, I parked my car a couple of miles away a few hours before daybreak. It was late winter, brisk and cold. I was dressed for the weather, multiple sweaters and jacket, multiple socks, boots, gloves, hat, etc.. With camera, film, and telephoto lens packed into a lunch pail for concealment, and binoculars tucked inside my jacket, I began the predawn trek through the fields to obtain a vantage point near the small barn that was located at the end of a field across the road from Ollie's house.

Not a heck of a lot happened throughout the morning. I realized that I wasn't dressed as warm as I would have liked to be. There was some activity about mid-morning at the far side of Ollie's house, but I couldn't see much of it from my vantage point. Then, around noontime, I decided to seek shelter in the little barn and perhaps get a better point of view for pictures from its upper level.

My patience and efforts were rewarded. A short time later, I was able to observe and photograph a man that I assumed to be Ollie who was engaged in carrying some objects around the yard at his house. My filming was disturbed by a curious phenomenon.

Although it was a cold day, it was clear and the sun was shining brightly. The sun warmed the air across the distant field where I was filming. Heat waves were rising across the field and rising up from the road between me and my subject. These heat waves were magnified manyfold by the power of the telephoto lens. The result was a wavy pattern across the focus plane that blurred the image to the viewing eye and, therefore, onto the film as well. I had recorded the man's activity, but the blurry film would not be sharp enough for positive identification of the subject.

Then I got more than I had bargained for. With pitchfork in hand, Ollie proceeded to walk from his house, across the road in my direction, towards the small barn where I had concealed myself. I shot an entire roll of film as he walked toward me displaying no evidence of a limp or walking disability of any kind.

As I was re-loading the camera, it became obvious that Ollie was coming directly to the barn where I was occupying a small space in a loft on the upper floor. He was carrying the pitchfork. To try leaving the barn without being observed was impossible. There was nothing but open, flat land around for as far as you could see. My only chance at not being observed was to lie behind some bales of hay in that upper loft and keep perfectly still. That's exactly what I did.

I could hear him approach and my mind tried to anticipate what to say if I got caught. I knew he was closer than the blurry heat waves now and I was tempted to try and get some positive identification shots through a crack in the barn wall. But discretion was the better part of valor in this case (or else I was just too cold and frightened to move). Nevertheless, I stayed lying behind the bales of hay and keeping perfectly still.

Now I could hear him inside the barn and the obvious sounds of pitching hay around the lower floor below me. Some cattle had come in from the cold to be fed and he was spreading the hay around for them. Suddenly I was aware of the presence of an animal up in my level of the barn. It was a cat. Apparently Ollie had disturbed him downstairs and he came up to the loft and hopped up onto one of the cross rafters directly above the bales of hay behind which I was lying.

Then, to complicate matters further, I heard Ollie's footsteps on the stairs coming up to my loft. He came up the stairs on the other side of the bales of hay where I was lying and proceeded to use the pitch fork to throw down fork-fuls of hay to the cattle below. He was digging the pitchfork into the bale of hay just opposite the bale where I was hiding. At times the thrusts of his fork were only the width of a bale of hay away from my body. The cat on the crossbeam, meanwhile, would look at him, look over at me, and then look back at Ollie again with a quizzical expression on his face while I just lay there holding my breath and thinking, "Thank God you're not a dog.

After a few more fork-fuls of hay were pitched down to the cattle, Ollie went back down the steps, never knowing how close he had been to me for those couple of minutes (which seemed like a couple of hours). The cat followed him down the stairs and left me alone to my shivering, limp exhaustion. I've never been more scared in my life.

I'd like to have gotten some more film of Ollie as he walked back to the house, but I was so cold, tense, and worn out from the ordeal of that experience that I didn't have the manual dexterity necessary to reload the camera and get set up again. Besides, I had to go to the bathroom "real bad" and could barely wait until he got out of range so I could relieve that pressure. I should have waited until after dark to retreat from that small barn, but I just wanted to get out of there. I was cold, tired, hungry, and had been scared out of my wits. Keeping the small barn between myself and Ollie's house, I retreated through the open fields and made my way slowly back to my car to call it a day.

After taking a day to recover, I devised a new plan.

This time I sought assistance from Mr. Ramsey. Through the intercession of the railroad foreman, who was Ramsey's neighbor, introductions were made and the nature of my business was explained. Mr. Ramsey proved to be most cooperative. He formulated a plan whereby I could ride out with him and his son early the next morning and, with his permission, occupy his big barn that was adjacent to Ollie's house. There I could shoot whatever motion picture film necessary to record Ollie's natural activities and then return with him and his son when they came back to their barn that afternoon.

This plan was agreeable to me and I bundled up with multiple layers of clothing, socks, boots, hat, gloves, and again with the camera, film, and lenses concealed in the lunch pail, traveled with Mr. Ramsey and his son to his barn before sun-up where they left me and went to attend their farming business.

Once safely inside the big barn, I found a vantage point in the second floor loft where a large knothole and a wide crack in the boards afforded an excellent view of Ollie's house and all the adjacent grounds. After a few hours' wait, activity began to stir about the household.

The first activity was Ollie coming out of the house, walking over to a pile of wood, and picking up an armload of logs to carry back inside the house to a log-burning fireplace or stove. All this activity was photographed in continuing sequence with no limp or walking disability of any kind observed. Next he exited the house carrying a large pail of feed for barnyard animals and proceeded to walk around throwing feed about again with no noticeable impairment in his gait.

He then returned to the house and came out awhile later with a rag in his hand. He walked back and forth among several lines that were strung between poles alongside the house. He walked briskly along the lines with the rag overhead as he wiped each length of line clean prior to returning to the house for a load of laundry, which he carried out in a large washbasket. All this activity was filmed with no noticeable disability or difficulty of any kind.

Following this activity, his wife came out to hang up the clothes that Ollie had carried to the lines. Ollie headed out for other work.

I should have been content with the amount of film that I had obtained. It was all shot from an excellent vantage point, clear and identifiable. My presence in the barn was not even suspected. But Ollie was now engaged in heavier work and I stretched my vantage point.

To my left, on the other side of the barn, was a large water trough. Carrying two very large buckets and a pitch fork, Ollie walked over to the water trough. In order to get additional film of this activity, it was necessary for me to move my vantage point in the loft. The left sideboards of the barn were solid. No knotholes or cracks between boards that were big enough to see through with the camera. There was an overhead hay-loading door that was partially open. This door afforded a good view of the water trough. The only trouble was that there was no floor in the vicinity of that door.

To shoot film, I had to stand on a beam and balance myself against the door with the outer hood of the camera lens. This worked OK for awhile. I was able to film Ollie as he used the pitch fork to break away a thick layer of ice from the top level of the water trough, throw the big, heavy pieces of ice aside with the pitch fork, and then scoop up the first big bucket of water from the trough and set it down behind him.

At that point, I tried to adjust my balance slightly. I must have made just enough movement for him to catch a glimpse of sunlight reflecting from my lens as he looked up to the barn door where I was all but concealed. While the camera was still running, a curious thing occurred. Just as Ollie was scooping up a second big bucket of water from the trough, I could detect his sense of awareness that something wasn't right. He stopped scooping the water, let go of the bucket in the trough, and immediately started to walk with an exaggerated limp

He headed toward my vantage point in the big barn. The transformation in his walk was almost comical, but I couldn't shoot any more. I had 30 seconds to hide a camera and prepare for a confrontation.

Hell hath no fury like . . . what? Well, maybe like a man caught malingering.

In the 30 seconds or so that it took Ollie to limp up to the barn from the water trough, I was able to hide the camera and film safely in another part of the loft. When he arrived at the barn door, I was sitting on the steps waiting for him. The confrontation was anything but friendly. He insisted on knowing what I was doing there. I proceeded to tell him that I was there to help his landlord with some chores. He didn't believe me, so I told him to call Mr. Ramsey in town and verify my story. He wanted me to come into his house with him while he called, but I wisely chose to remain in the barn while he made the phone call.

I thought I was in the clear. It's only a five or six minute drive from town to the farm. I expected Ramsey to come right out and take me back. Bad luck! Ramsey's wife was the only one home. Ramsey was on a shopping trip with the boy and she didn't know when they would be back. Ollie returned to the barn to relay this information and to question me further. This time his wife came along.

Hell hath no fury like . . the wife of a man caught malingering.

Ollie's wife was livid. She threatened me in every way, shape, and form. She also agitated Ollie into threatening me. He told her he thought he saw a camera at the upper barn door. She retaliated to my denials by telling Ollie to go back to the house and get his gun and use that to deal with me. She had also telephoned her brother to come out from town and lend them some assistance. In a few more minutes, her brother's car raced up the road and pulled up to the barn. He was no picnic either, a rough character with a foul mouth, and ready to do battle if turned loose.

Meanwhile, Ollie went back into the house for the gun, but decided first to telephone his attorney in Chicago, inform him of the situation, and ask for instructions about what to do with me. I think his talk with the attorney made him a little more cautious. He didn't come back with the gun as I had anticipated. Instead, there were more threats and lots of nasty talk. Meanwhile, I had my eye on a shovel handle that I could use to defend myself against the three of them, who were generating more violent talk each minute. I was also trying to keep my right leg from twitching nervously and revealing my fear. All the while I held steadfast to my story that I was there with Mr. Ramsey's permission and I would wait until he arrived. It seemed like an eternity.

I never saw a tan Pontiac that looked any better in my life. There it came up the road, getting blessedly larger as it approached the barn. Mr. Ramsey and his son had returned from their shopping trip and his wife had told him of Ollie's phone call. They came immediately to the farm. When questioned by Ollie and his wife, the landlord simply stated that he had indeed given me permission to be in his barn. He didn't elaborate. I asked to be taken back to town just as soon as I could get my lunch pail from upstairs in the barn loft. I went up, quickly secreted the camera and lens in the lunch pail and tucked all the exposed film under the bulkiness of my many sweaters. I returned to Mr. Ramsey's car with only the lunch pail. No visible signs of any camera or film as we got into the Pontiac and drove away, leaving three very angry and bewildered people at the farm.

I haven't mentioned how badly I needed to go the bathroom. I'm sure you suspected as much from the way things went poorly for me out there. That's the worst part about being scared, you don't dare let on you have a problem and it hurts like hell.

What about Ollie? To the best of my knowledge, the lawsuit was dropped. His attorney was angry because he let himself be caught. Settlement was made for his leg injury based on medical expenses and lost time up until the day the film was made. As for the movie film, I wish I had it back. It was a graphic example of a psychological change in a person's reactions once he becomes aware that he has been caught. The look on Ollie's face and the change of expression just before he dropped the bucket and started to limp were classic.

I'm just glad I only experienced a few confrontations in this portion of my career, and none as traumatic as this one with Ollie, his wife, and brother-in-law. Many cases, like this one, were settled without the necessity of going to court. Many others, however, required the full treatment. Testimony in court, then cross-examination (often lengthy and venomous), and finally, showing the film to judge and jury in courtroom projection. Some of those moments were quite dramatic and emotional.

The most dramatic was the case of an employee of a tree surgery company who was injured in a fall from a tree. He sustained serious injuries to both of his feet. Workmen's Compensation awarded him total and permanent disability and he was receiving monthly payments in the full amount allowed by law. It was anticipated that he would continue to receive this compensation for life. That adds up to a great amount of money over the course of many years of payments.

This man, however, recovered sufficiently enough to start up a tree surgery business of his own. Through subsequent investigation and surveillance, it was possible to obtain a considerable amount of motion picture footage of his activities. He engaged in tree cutting, climbing trees, using power-driven chain saws, carrying large logs, driving a truck, and many other duties incidental to this business.

After viewing all the film, the company attorney petitioned for a new hearing on this case. Upon interrogation at the hearing, the claimant categorically denied being able to perform the entire list of activities that the attorney had prepared from viewing the film. As soon as the claimant finished his testimony, I was called to be the next witness and then to show the film in court.

Every activity that the man had just denied was portrayed in sharp, clear color on the big movie screen. The pressure was too much. To the surprise of everyone in the hearing room, he broke into tears, told his attorney that this embarrassment was unbearable and then said, "Tell them to keep their money, I'm getting out of here,* as he quickly left the room. Even though the case was a victory for my attorney, I felt very bad about having caused such a severe reaction from the claimant. I started thinking seriously about concentrating on other lines of photographic work.

There were a few other outstanding cases that came my way before I finally retired from the claims photography business. For instance, a man who had been injured in a fight while employed as a deckhand on a riverboat. He sued for damages from the boat company. In his sworn testimony in a deposition prior to trial he stated that his injuries were so bad that: "I can't even bend over to pick up a five-pound bag of sugar."

A week or so later, I traveled to one of our southern states and was able to obtain clear, identifiable motion picture footage of his activities while engaged in working at a saw mill. His work included rolling huge logs from trucks with a log-rolling tool, carrying and stacking large, heavy boards after they were cut by the buzz saw, and various other duties about the mill. I have been continuously amazed at the contradictions in people's sworn statements. All this work exceeded by many times over, the lifting of a five pound bag of sugar.

Two more cases come prominently to mind:

Photography and water again? Of course. The two elements continue to influence almost everything that involves me.

One of the accident claimants from my area had been found to have moved to a southern state and had gainful employment with a laundry company in the capacity of a driverdeliveryman. Before obtaining any employment records from the laundry, the claims attorney wanted some photographic evidence of this man's normal activities incidental to his employment.

So I traveled south to see what I could turn up. With a little bit of unofficial investigating about the laundry, I was able to determine which of the fleet of trucks was driven by the claimant, and where it was parked. You see, the job didn't turn out to be as easy as it seemed. Just taking films of a laundry truck driver making his rounds. Piece of cake? No! In the rural South, it's not possible to follow a vehicle around like you can in a metropolitan area. Roads are narrow and sparsely traveled. A few miles of following and you stick out like a sore thumb. Besides, a laundryman doesn't waste time at his stops. He parks, delivers the clean material, carries out the spoiled laundry in ready made-up bags, and is on his way before it would be possible to maneuver into any vantage point from which to obtain films without being observed.

The approach to this one had to be different. Gain unobserved entry to his truck, copy his route sheet and be able to set up at his various stops in advance of his arrival, get films, and then move on to another stop for a repeat of the same without actually having to follow him. Simple, yes? Well, not exactly, but this is precisely what I did and it was working well from a photography standpoint until water entered into the picture.

Seems like this laundryman's route covered an extensive rural string of small towns and hamlets that lay in a path along the course of a meandering river. With the aid of a map supplied with my rented car, I checked the list of towns I had copied from his routebook and made a plan. My timetable enabled me to get to the towns ahead of his truck, set up, and get good motion picture films of all his activities from arrival, unloading, loading, and departure. It was working well too, except I didn't count on the river.

Following the map from stop 17 to stop 19 (I decided to skip stop 18 to allow enough time to get ahead and properly set up again), the road I was following was quite rural and not well paved. At one point, a branch of the road forked off to my left and went towards the meandering river. I looked over and saw some people washing their cars by the riverbank and paid no more attention. I followed the right fork to an upgrade that led to a lesser paved road. This road ultimately turned into just tire tracks through a field that ran for another mile or two and then made an abrupt left turn and down a steep hill directly to the riverbank.

There was no bridge, just these tire tracks leading downhill to the river bank and I, like a fool, had followed them with no possibility of going back up the steep, soft dirt hill from whence I'd come. Just me and the rented car, parked at the river's edge. Am I supposed to drive across the river? The town I'm heading for is definitely on the other side, according to the map. There were no bridges. No other turn-offs. Boy, if there was ever a time I didn't want or need water in my life, this was it.

But water I had. A whole river-full, and I didn't know what to do about it. I looked at the map again. It definitely showed the road leading from one town to the other and crossing the river. I thought there would be a bridge. No such luck.

Well, lets check the river depth. There was no one around, anywhere. I took off my pants and went wading out into the river in my underwear. Halfway out, it was not too deep, but beyond, the other half of the river, the water definitely got too deep for a car to navigate. Also, the riverbank on the other side was just as steep as where I had just come down and there were no visible tracks or paths where a car might exit.

You bet I was perplexed. My shortcut had backfired. I was going to lose my laundryman and I had taken a huge risk just to get this one day's schedule from his truck. Everything had been going so well, and now ... water ... I just stood there in my underwear, not knowing where to turn, when suddenly !!

Uncle Sam to the rescue. Yes, Uncle Sam in the form of a mailman driving a jeep. He had just driven down the hill to the riverbank and was parked behind me, scratching his head. He couldn't imagine why I was there. When I told him the name of the town I was trying to reach, he informed me that I should have driven across the river two miles back where I saw the people washing their cars. At that point, the road actually passes through the river at a very shallow spot. Up here, he advised, people didn't usually attempt a river crossing until later in the summer, when the water level got much lower. Unless they had a jeep .

However, he pointed out to me that, if I wanted to risk it, I could drive straight out to the center of the river and then make a right turn. Then, I had to drive down the middle of the river for about a half mile or more to a place he pointed out way over on the other side. Over there was a slightly less elevated section of hillside and jeep tire tracks to follow as a guide out of the river.

Not having much choice in the matter, I followed his directions. I drove straight into the water, turned right at midpoint in the river's width and had the strangest feeling driving this rented car down the middle of the river. I never knew whether or not I might hit one deep spot that would flood me out of power. His directions were quite accurate. I reached the area where I could exit at a shallow part of the other side and attempted to negotiate the jeep track path that led uphill, away from the river bank.

I made it halfway. The soft ground gave way under my tires and the wheels just spun. The mailman pulled up behind me in the jeep and attempted to push me up the hill. He could not get enough traction to get my inert car into motion. His next suggestion was another wild one. He backed down onto the river rocks and had me back down into the river again in front of him. Then, together, like a train, we both got forward motion. By keeping moving, he was able to push me the full way to the top of the hill with the jeep in four-wheel drive.

I got to my destination one minute before my laundry driver. Not enough time to get a good vantage point for filming, so I drove back to the laundry and set up to film his return. I got an unexpected display of physical activity.

Parking by the laundry, I found that the main plant had closed for the day. No one was unloading at the regular docks. I figured that the best I would get for the end of the day was the truck returning.

What I didn't know was that the building was equipped with an overhead chute to accommodate late returning drivers. When my man drove into view, he proceeded to the area of that chute, which was located in a good line of sight for my camera view. Then I was astounded when he backed the truck up to a spot below this overhead chute. He proceeded to unload bag after bag of dirty laundry, shooting each one overhead into the receiving chute like a basketball player making foul shots. More activity than I had ever dreamed of filming and making a satisfactory conclusion to an otherwise hectic day.

I'll never forget the day I drove "down" the river, and the "train ride" up the other side. One false move and I'd have been looking for someone to fish me and my rented car out of the water. Instead, it ended up with some of the most dramatic shots I have ever recorded of a claimant's employment activities.

These southern states had no end of surprises and unusual incidents to intrigue me. Take for instance this next case. When a woman in another of our southern states, the owner of a dance studio, was injured in an automobile accident, she claimed she could no longer conduct her business because it required dancing demonstrations, and she was no longer able to do this. A large claim was presented for the loss of business income.

Something about her medical reports made the claims attorney suspicious. I was contacted to see if I could obtain motion picture evidence of her natural physical activity. The best I could come up with after a couple of days observation was some footage taken as she walked to a nearby church. While she attended church, I happened inside and looked at the church bulletin displayed in the vestibule.

By coincidence, I discovered in the church bulletin that the claimant's son was listed in the Bans Of Marriage just recently published. Since I had been taking pictures of weddings from early high school days, the notice of the son's upcoming wedding gave me an idea.

If I could get the job as the son's wedding photographer, that would be a natural intro into the reception where there probably would be dancing. So, the son was contacted, a reasonable price was agreed upon for the wedding photography, and I was hired to shoot the wedding album.

The rest was a piece of cake. I shot the wedding photographs just like any other job. When the time came at the reception for the family to dance, it was only natural for me to switch cameras and start shooting motion pictures of the claimant engaged in dancing with many members of the family, the very activity that she claimed she could not do.

Needless to say, when this case came to trial, there was tremendous cross-examination pressure from the claimant's attorney. I was severely criticized for being a double-crosser, and the attorney also tried to infer that I had cheated the bride and groom of their wedding album. However, I presented them with a most professional album, filled with excellent photographs of their entire wedding day. They were without recourse for a complaint.

Nevertheless, the mental pressures I underwent, both during the wedding and while projecting the film and testifying at the court trial, were significant factors in encouraging me to look to other types of photography to continue my career. Between this dancing case and the guy who broke down and cried in the court room, I just about had my fill of this type of work.

Besides, television was becoming a big thing in my local area now. I found that instead of a $5 fee for a newspaper still photo of a news event, I could now get a $35 fee from television for a reel of newsfilm of the same story. Furthermore, the television lab developed the film and gave me a replacement roll. So my career steered towards the TV films and became much more interesting.

I think that should be another chapter. Don't you?

CHAPTER FOUR

TV

28 Aged Women Made Homeless In Fire Given Shelter at Hospital

Bishop Pardue Lauds Men Who Battled Blaze, Aided Rescue

Twenty-eight women, all over 70, who were made temporarily homeless by a four-alarm fire at the Episcopal Church Home, were being cared for today at St. Margaret Memorial Hospital.

Bishop Austin Pardue, who directs the two Episcopal Church institutions, was lavish in his praise of the Pittsburgh firemen for their fast work in bringing the blaze under control.

He also lauded George W. Boyle Jr., 21, of Dorseyville, for rushing into the four-story home at Fortieth St. and Penn Ave. to warn the women that the roof was on fire.

A well-known amateur photographer, Boyle works for the Retail Credit Co., Keenan Bldg., and was en route to the North Side when he noticed the smoke coming through the roof. He said:

"I shouted to a man standing on the corner to put in the alarm and then rushed into the home to help the elderly ladies. I've taken so much time at the fire that I'm worried about what my boss will say."

LAUDED BY MAYOR

Mayor David L. Lawrence shook Boyle's hand and Bishop Pardue put his arm around Boyle's shoulder. The bishop said:

"Don't worry about your job, son. You're the hero here today. You averted what could have been a major disaster. We hope your boss will give you a raise."

Then a group of women, being cared for temporarily in the city's Arsenal Health Center, gave George a hug and tousled his hair.

It was the first big fire for the new fire chief, Stephen P. Adley. After the fire was under control dozens of persons shook his hand for "a magnificent job." Adley said:

"The firemen did the great job. Flames were shooting through the roof when we arrived. We have the best firemen in the world here in Pittsburgh and when they went to work on that fire it didn't last long. Give the firemen the credit—not me."

Adley said at least 20 firemen fighting the blaze "were off work today but wanted to help out." The chief said:

"You have to admire that kind of team spirit."

CAUSE INVESTIGATED

During the heighth of the fire six nurses from St. Francis Hospital arrived at the scene to offer help. The Salvation Army's mobile canteen was at the fire with doughnuts and coffee before the fourth alarm was sounded.

Police and firemen are still investigating the cause of the blaze, which was confined to the roof and did an estimated $15,000 to $20,000 damage.

Mrs. Spencer Howell, superintendent of the home, said the wiring had been inspected recently and that she "suspected arson." She said:

"If the fire had started in any other part of the building I could understand it. But I don't see how a fire could possibly start in the fourth floor storage room. It's very suspicious."

She added:

"A lot of drunks have been getting on the property. I've called the police but they haven't been much help. I've had to put the drunks off myself and I'm getting awful tired of that."

The Episcopal Church Home

BURNED OUT . . . View of charred roof of the Episcopal Church Home, 4001 Penn Ave., after a four-alarm fire swept the place. The aged residents

Sun-Telegraph Photo by Edwin J. Morgan

Top: Elderly ladies thank author for saving them from a multiple alarm fire that destroyed their home as covered in Chapter 4.

Before I got too heavily involved in TV news filming, circumstances placed me in a position to be a subject in the news coverage instead of a photographer. The situation occurred like this:

I was working in the investigative phase of my employment one day and not carrying the usual photographic equipment in my car. I had detoured from my regular scheduled appointments in order to make a side trip to a local bank to cash a check and make a necessary deposit.

While returning to keep one of my regular appointments, I stopped my car at a traffic light alongside a large brick building. While waiting for the red light to turn green, I noticed a reflection of flames in the polished hood of my car. Looking up to my right, I saw the actual flames shooting out of the upper section of the roof of this four-story building.

Looking across the street to my left, I saw some people standing at a trolley stop, waiting for a streetcar. Next to them was a fire alarm box on a telephone pole and I shouted over to them to pull the fire alarm. At the same time, I pulled my car to the curb and ran up the walkway to the building. I wasn't sure if this was a hospital, an orphanage, or what?

As I approached the building, a middle-aged woman, impeccably dressed, was just exiting the front door, putting on her white gloves as she descended the front steps. I said, "Do you know your roof is on fire?" She was stunned. She looked up at the roof and screamed, "Oh my God, the ladies!"

Then I realized that this was a home for elderly ladies and the woman I had just confronted was the superintendent, departing for a social function and unaware of the tragedy underway on her roof. We entered the front door and proceeded immediately to the top floor to warn the ladies of the impending danger and direct them downstairs to safety. The elevator was the culprit in the fire and the only means of escape was via the stairway.

Some of the ladies were unable to walk, so I carried them down the stairs and quickly returned for others. I tried my best to keep the ladies exiting in a calm fashion without creating undue excitement. The roar of the flames overhead, however, was unnerving, and the superintendent was becoming frantic.

Also, the fire engines had not yet arrived and it was obvious that the fire was spreading rapidly above our heads. Through the windows, I could see pieces of flaming material falling from above and landing on a lower roof at the third-floor level in the rear of the building.

As soon as I had checked every room on the top level, and carried down all the women who couldn't walk, I unraveled a fire hose from its stanchion at the end of the third floor hall. I turned it on and took it to the back window overlooking the sub-roof where the flaming debris was falling. The water pressure coming from this fire hose was not too strong because there were leaks at every bend where the hose had been coiled, probably for several years. Nevertheless, I was getting some water flow and it was extinguishing the pieces of flaming roofing materials that were falling on this lower back roof. I was preventing then from igniting this back roof and giving the fire another place from which to start spreading.

Meanwhile, the fire trucks started arriving, en masse, as multiple alarms had been sounded. But they weren't coming around to the back where the flames were dropping on the lower roof faster than my limited water supply could extinguish them.

The building janitor appeared on the scene and saw the trouble I was having with the sputtering water supply. He advised that there were some large fire extinguishers at a location farther back in the hall. Perhaps they could do a better job of stopping the spread of these falling embers. The only problem was, they were located under a section where the fire was rumbling and roaring just above on the roof. We couldn't be sure if or when the roof might collapse into that area.

In retrospect, I think I was a fool. But at the time, I didn't stop to think about the danger to myself. I just wanted to extinguish that back roof fire before it got a good start and put the entire building in jeopardy. The firemen were attacking the flames at the front of the building, but no company had gotten around to see how bad it was in the rear.

I dashed back down the hall under the roaring and rumbling flames and grabbed two large, liquid type fire extinguishers. Returning to the window, I turned them upside down and got good, strong streams of liquid coming from them. While the janitor used the sputtering hose, I continued to douse the flaming debris with the flow from the extinguishers. We were making some progress and not allowing the other roof to get any flaming start.

Just as I got the second extinguisher down to its final spurt, the regular firemen appeared from an aerial ladder at the side of the back roof. They took over with a full-force water supply that completed the job. Now, my thoughts turned to my own safety and I figured that I'd better get out of there before a roof fell in.

Several aerial ladders were now erected at the front of the building and they were playing huge streams of water onto the fire at roof level. A section of the ceiling did collapse a few minutes later, but we were out of there and no injuries were sustained. All of the upper-floor residence rooms of the ladies were destroyed.

Water from the fire hoses was now cascading down stairwells and through the lower ceilings like waterfalls. Many beautiful pieces of furniture decorated the lower rooms. These were in danger of being ruined, not by the fire, but by the water.

Some of the firemen were carrying tarpaulins into the building to cover and protect the fine couches, chairs and other furniture. I assisted them with this covering until most of the goodIthings were protected. Then I started to think about getting back to my work appointments.

Lots of luck ... My car was completely surrounded by fire hoses laid out in every direction around it. I knew it was against the law to drive over a fire hose, unless given special permission. I wanted to get back to work, so I went looking for a captain or someone in charge who could give me permission to drive away over the hoses.

That's when it happened. While looking for the fire chief, I walked across the street to the command post. That also happened to be the location where the elderly) ladies had been taken for their safety. Several reporters and photographers were engaged in interviews and picture taking when one of the ladies spotted me and shouted, "There he is, there's the man who saved us." I was trapped. The idea of being a hero hadn't occurred to me. I just saw an emergency and did what I] thought best under the circumstances. Now, I was surrounded by reporters and photographers and learning what it's like to be on the other side of the camera.

It turned out that this building was the Episcopal Home For Aged Women. One of the elderly women I had carried downstairs to safety happened to be the mother of the Bishop of the Episcopal Diocese. There was no escaping the reporters and photographers when she pointed her finger at me as her rescuer.

The photographers placed me in the center of a group of these ladies and the flashbulbs started popping. The front page of the evening paper carried a four-column picture of the ladies thanking me for their rescue. The Bishop and the Mayor of the City were on hand to thank me for getting the ladies out.

I never told them about how I stayed up there long after the women were out, extinguishing the flaming, falling debris with my limited water supply. Had they learned about that, I might never have gotten away to get back to my regular work. They were starting to talk about a Carnegie Hero's Medal, but I was just happy that the 28 women were safe and I could get back to business as usual. They never found out about the rest of the story and how the rear of the building was saved from further fire destruction.

The irony of all this was that I was aspiring to be a big-time TV news photographer and, when I came across the biggest story of my career, I was too busily involved with the urgency of the moment to even think of my profession. Television news filming was to come later. Not too much later, as you'll see.

It's hard to determine where to begin with the onset of TV filming. I didn't just jump into it cold. Like "Topsy" in Uncle Tom's Cabin, it sort of "just grew."

You don't just bounce into a television station in a major market city and say, "Here I am." It takes time to be accepted for your work and for its quality to shine through. I spent a couple of years traveling about with a police monitor in my car. I'd listen to broadcasts of all the police happenings and then select stories to cover that my experience proved to be newsworthy. Gradually, as the news editors and assignment men learned they could depend on the quality of the film I would submit, I became a regular free-lance representative of the TV station and started getting limited assignments. They expected me to write copy to accompany any stories that I filmed and it gave me a great sense of satisfaction when my reports were read, unedited, by the TV anchorman.

There were problems with union contract regulations, so the number and nature of assignments were limited. I had to be careful not to interfere with any of the work regularly assigned to the station's full-time news cameraman. To maintain a living income and support my family, I still did claims photography for some of the attorneys that I had been servicing for several years. Although TV work was much more exciting and contained a greater variety of interests, I hesitated to get into it on a full-time basis while still doing other photography work.

But the TV attraction was a powerful magnet. The acclaim of having one's name mentioned on TV for having gotten some spectacular coverage of a fast-breaking news event was all that was necessary to draw roe away from other work. I focused my attention more and more on television filming. After all, positive recognition and acclaim for one's work is a powerful incentive. It sure worked its spell on me. I would do everything in my power to get a scoop, get special angles on a story, and beat the competition whenever possible.

And so I continued filming many fires, accidents, shootings, and various other news events. Later, another turning point in my career presented itself without warning. It seems that the program manager of the TV station had a particular project that he needed filmed, a series of 12 half-hour shows about college life. The series would involve two high school students, covering their travels to numerous colleges in the surrounding area. These students would get a firsthand look at higher education and explore all the areas of interest pertinent to a secondary school student looking to continue on to a college level. This series of programs was designed to answer all the questions that high school students or their parents might have about all aspects of college life.

The opportunity to film this entire series was afforded to me with one stipulation. I must have the capacity to shoot sound-on film. Here I'm presented with a situation that was just like when the football coach needed movie film and I was only a still photographer. Now, a very important job contract was available if only I could shoot sound-on film. Well, like with the football coach, once more I didn't hesitate. I said, "Of course I shoot sound-on film." and accepted the job contract.

Now what ? I had never shot a frame of sound-on film in my life. So, with about a week to make preparations, I went out on another limb. One of the local photographic supply houses had a used Auricon 16mm sound-on motion picture camera for sale. It took all of my savings to invest in this piece of equipment and I was gambling right down to the wire with my family's economic health.

Oh yes, I said my family's economic health. In the period of time that covered the previous chapter, I married a schoolgirl sweetheart and began raising a family. Under these circumstances, the gamble of using all our savings for an expensive sound movie camera was no minor decision. I'm thankful for the support I received from a loving and understanding wife.

The sound camera was purchased and less than a week remained to learn how to use this massive array of equipment. The camera was large and heavy. It also required a large tripod to maintain steadiness in filming. Along with the camera came the sound equipment, a battery-powered amplifier that weighed as much as the camera. It was powered by five large batteries of various voltages and ratings.

There were many elements of technical concentration required to achieve the proper results. Proper exposure of the sound track exciter lamp, care not to over-or-under modulate the volume control for the microphones, proper microphone placement and mixing of volumes during dual usage, and keeping track of all the myriad interconnections of camera and amplifier wires. My poor family, they were guinea pigs for almost a week. I practiced lighting, microphone placing and all types of test situation shootings in my home and back yard. Finally, I mastered the equipment and set off with shaky confidence to do the job.

The TV program manager will never know the icy lump I had in my gut when the first assignment was with the president of one of the local colleges. I had to record sound film of his answers to questions from my high school students about college costs and financial assistance programs. I thanked my lucky stars that I had put my family through all those tests the previous week. The double microphone system with multiple lighting and reverse angle shots were as intricate as most location shots ever get, and I was handling it all by myself.

I soon found out that I was not the only person who could get an icy feeling in my gut from this camera work. The shoe also fits on the other side of the camera. College presidents are human too. I was astonished when a Catholic nun, the president of a large college in Erie, Pa., found it almost impossible to give a 10-minute monologue on camera. She just froze each time she started her dissertation. Finally she confided in me that, although she had no trouble teaching a class or addressing a large assembly, she was terrified with the intimacy of the camera. She became stiff when her thoughts tried to come through. Her mind would just go blank and this was proving to be most embarrassing.

I called for a five-minute break and had a little talk with Sister. I assured her that the camera was not an impersonal object. I'd be at the side of the camera and I cared and was interested in what she was saying. "Just forget about the camera and talk to me," I suggested. Then I rearranged the lights so that some of the side lighting fell onto my face during the shooting. Instead of placing my eye into the viewfinder, I placed my face directly beside the lens and looked at Sister while she talked, giving her human eye contact.

The idea worked and she made it through her 10-minute talk without further difficulty. Most of the time I stayed in eye contact with her and she could see my face because of the change in lighting. I only moved away a few times to change the focal length of the zoom lens so the scene would not remain static throughout the length of her talk. Sister was greatly relieved by my innovative arrangement and I learned that the camera is a great equalizer.

Although the purchase of that sound camera was a big financial risk, the gamble paid off. The series turned out great and no one knew that I had never shot a sound-on production before. All 12 half hour shows worked out satisfactorily except for one thing.

I was so proud of my role in this production that I refused to allow a bout with the flu to stop me from completing the filming of the final segment of the series. I forced myself to go out on the final day of the shooting while suffering a sore throat and fever that would have kept any sensible person in bed.

The results were: a complete show, that unexplainable sense of pride, and ,10 days in the hospital with pneumonia.

That's what I got for neglecting the flu symptoms and pushing myself too far. A high price to pay for my stubbornness, but it was clear to see that the attraction for this work was so strong that I was willing to make this sacrifice to achieve the completion of the project.

The series, by the way, won a "Golden Quill" award in television station competition that year, the first of many that I would achieve in succeeding years of TV Program filming. Once again, when you achieve public recognition and acknowledgement for your work, like winning the Golden Quill, there is an incentive to go on and do better in the future.

Some of these future assignments were quite interesting and unique. I'd like to tell you about the most memorable of them.

Big fires play an important part in the career of a newsfilm cameraman. There have been so many over the years that the details of most fade and one blends into the other. There were, however, two instances of fire tragedy that will never fade away and they merit recall.

RANKIN PA., just two days before Christmas, a fire began in a house situated in the congested area of a lower-income neighborhood.. The fire spread to an adjoining house, and calls for extra help were put in by the department chief. I was called out for newsfilm coverage on the second alarm. In the 10 minutes it took me to arrive in Rankin, a brisk wind had swept the fire to two more adjoining houses and a small store.

Water pressure in the borough was pitifully low. Some of the first films that I shot depict frustrated firefighters in front of the store, watching rolling flames engulf the storefront while the stream of water from their hose wasn't enough to put out a campfire.

There was enough drama here to fill a Hollywood epic. Everywhere I turned, people were frantically trying to save their houses and possessions. The fire was spreading and the wind had picked up in intensity. Sudden gusts would pick up flaming pieces of debris from one house and deposit them onto another, starting new fires as they went. Household residents were desperately trying to wet-down their roofs with trickling dribbling's from garden hoses as chunks of flaming materials blew through the air like pieces of an erupting volcano.

The fire played no favorites. It played "leap-frog" from one street to the next, randomly sparing some houses while destroying others just beyond. I had some idea of what San Francisco must have been like after the earthquake started that historic fire. Rankin was becoming a modern-day San Francisco.

Before the day was over, 27 houses, 3 churches, a large school, and some commercial establishments had been completely destroyed by the devouring flames. In the midst of all this destruction, some houses were miraculously untouched. The mischievous wind had blown flaming debris completely over them and onto other houses on the neighboring street.

Fortunately for me, I was wearing a protective hard-hat while filming all this destruction. I'd decided to put on this protective hat when all the flaming debris started blowing about. While filming the interior of the school building that was ablaze with a furious conflagration destroying its inner staircase, I was standing by a broken window shooting a spectacular view of the action. The heat from the roaring flames caused the rainspout and gutter on the building over my head to break loose. It fell directly onto my head. The hard-hat cushioned the blow and I escaped with nothing more than startled shock. I stayed back a few more steps after that experience.

There's no way I'll ever forget that tragic day. My heart went out to all those people who were losing their homes and life's possessions and who were helpless to prevent that loss. One good thing did cone out of all my films. Besides being a most dramatic television story, later on, the fire departments and local service agencies used copies of my films to help raise funds to assist victims of the fire. I felt relieved that I had made some contribution towards alleviating their loss.

One other fire disaster etched itself permanently into my memory. Unlike Rankin, this was just one large commercial building in the East End section of the city. It was several stories high and filled with industrial equipment and supplies.

The fire had a good start before alarms were sounded, and it quickly went to six alarms as the captains realized the scope of the problem.

I had come on the scene in the early stage of the fire and proceeded to shoot routine news film coverage from various angles. It was obvious that the fire was going to get bigger before it was brought under control. The building was large and some of the entrances were blocked by crates of machinery, limiting the firemens* early access to the interior.

At one point, I had stationed myself in a recessed entranceway at the front of the building. I was filming a fire captain as he placed a breathing mask over his face and prepared to enter the building to direct the activities of his men. Immediately after filming the captain, I heard someone shout that the fire was breaking out in the back of the building. I moved to the back alley for more dramatic shots.

I didn't have to wait long. No sooner was I set up in the alley behind several firemen playing water into the upper windows, when the flames made their violent burst through the roof and lit up the entire area with their intensity. My filming of this drama was suddenly interrupted by a warning shout from the firemen. The impact of the flames bursting through the roof had caused a pressure implosion that toppled the walls of the building.

The firemen in the alley scampered back to the safety of the yards on the other side. I ran right beside them as a cascade of bricks tumbled into the alley where we had just been standing. Another close call, but I was used to this by now.

What I wasn't used to was what happened simultaneously at the front of the building. The captain that I had earlier photographed was not as lucky as I and the rest of the firemen in the back alley. He had been caught under the barrage of falling bricks and was buried beneath the pile.

When I got around to the front, the police superintendent and several of the firemen were pulling red-hot bricks from atop his lifeless body in a frantic attempt to save him. Their efforts were in vain. There was just too much weight that had fallen upon him. When they took him away in the ambulance, we all knew he didn't stand much chance to survive.

Then the realization hit me. I had been in that very spot just a few minutes earlier, when I took his picture as he entered the area. If it hadn't been for someone saying the fire was breaking out around back, I probably would have still been there when the walls collapsed. An indescribable cold chill went right through me. I guess I was in shock and didn't know it.

It was lucky that I had a job to do and the story wasn't over until the processed film was edited and on the air. That gave me something to keep me busy and kept my mind from playing "what if" tricks on me.

The whole incident came back vividly when my film was used at an inquest into the captain's death. I was subpoenaed to testify as to my knowledge of the situation and conditions in that recessed alcove prior to the collapse of the wall. They particularly wanted to know about the crates of machinery that were blocking the doorway and my films clearly showed their presence. Some citations were issued and I think the captain's family received a financial settlement. It couldn't have been enough to take the place of their loss.

I've had enough fire to last two lifetimes. Let's get back to a better element. You know, we haven't mentioned water for awhile. I told you earlier that, along with photography, water was the big interest in my life. The high school years and a few years thereafter, when I worked as a lifeguard, were filled with swimming and diving competitions of all kinds and many ribbons and medals were won during those competitive years.

Marriage, family, and concentrating on making a living, somehow took the place of those earlier competitive years, but the interest in water just takes on another dimension. Somehow, the photography income produced enough extra cash to allow the purchase of a boat. The family's interest turned towards boating, water skiing and, by coincidence, scuba diving.

I had dropped my keys into the river from the boat docks and I needed to retrieve them. One of my fellow competitive swimmers from high school days was now involved in scuba diving. I asked him for the loan of his air tank, mask, and regulator so I could descend to the river bottom and search for my lost keys. He agreed, with one stipulation. First he would instruct me on the basics of diving. That consisted of a lecture about not holding my breath while breathing compressed air and ascending from the bottom. He had enough confidence in my ability as a swimmer to trust my judgement with the use of his equipment. I borrowed his gear, descended to the bottom of the river, and subsequently found my lost keys. At the same time, I was thoroughly fascinated with this new experience of underwater swimming.

Once again, coincidence enters to merge photography and water into the focal point of my life. A short time after this lost keys incident, I was given a television feature assignment to film a seminar that was being conducted by the American Red Cross. They had gathered together many of the underwater scuba instructors from the area in an attempt to study the best methods of underwater rescue of a diver in trouble. They wanted to add a new section to the Red Cross manual on water safety. This clinic was being conducted to compare rescue methods and select the best for reference in the safety manual. Television coverage of the clinic was indicated because this was an innovative approach to a newly developing sport.

Since most of the activity of this clinic was being conducted underwater, I got the idea that underwater filming would be a unique and graphic way to cover this event. I again approached my friend to borrow his diving gear and, in addition, I borrowed a water-tight plexiglass housing for my movie camera. With proper lead weights to make me heavy and steady underwater, it was possible to shoot the activities of the rescuers right down there where the activity was taking place. I was able to produce an unusual piece of film footage which, combined with top-side shots, edited together to make an outstanding feature. That got the attention of the director of another show and was influential in getting me additional television work. The combination of water and photography had worked for me again.

It was ironic that the second time I put on diving equipment was to make a complicated underwater movie feature for television. Since then, I have gone on to complete my scuba education to the level of instructor. Following this, I've educated many students in this rewarding water activity. Also, I've constructed my own water-tight underwater housings for my movie cameras. Subsequently, I went on to film underwater feature films which I intend to mention a little farther along in these chronicles.

Because of the attention received from the underwater feature, assignments started coming from the director of a new show that had a type of magazine format. Film features were varied and different every day. They involved interviews with everyone from visiting celebrities, show business performers, politicians, and newsmakers, to people with just unusual interests or occupations.

The variety of this show's format was unlimited and I looked forward every day to a new and different challenge. For instance, one of the features was called "The Private War of Henry Bursztynowicz."

Henry Bursztynowicz was voted artistsculptor of the year. His award-winning miniature sculptures were of an entire army of authentic soldiers. They were both mounted and on foot and arranged in various scenes of battle. They were on display in the local museum. The assignment seemed routine, even boring, perhaps. Just shooting toy soldiers set up in a museum. But, while setting up my lights to illuminate the scene, I started to observe how various positioning of the lights changed the shadows of the soldiers that played upon various backgrounds.

Imagination began to take over. Let's have some fun with this job. Try moving the lights while shooting the film. It was something new. Something I had never tried before. But I loved the challenge. The host of the TV show was also a lover of innovation. We began to play with the lights and shadows, and to have fun with the sculptured soldiers while making the film. Move the light from a low angle and a little soldier becomes huge on an adjacent wall. Shift the light to one direction and his shadow seems to attack an adjacent enemy soldier. With the proper editing, scene after scene of this exaggerated shadow movement brought an otherwise static scene to life. Combine these eerie shadow attacks with the proper mood music and this little piece became animated, making a most entertaining presentation.

I had many other assignments to shoot art shows and award-winning sculptures. I played with many close-up shots, variations, and zoom effects, but nothing ever approached the fun and delightful results of Henry's "Private War."

Another nice fringe benefit of being involved in a variety-show format is being able to have conversations with a lot of famous and interesting people. I was what was referred to as a "one man band" cinematographer. In other words I did it all by myself. Camera, lights, sound recording, direction, set-up, and break-down. I lugged it all in and carried it all back out again, usually solo. This took some time, and the fortunate by-product of this extra time was the opportunity to converse with all these interesting people.

I got some insight into chicken plucking from rock star Chubbie Checker. Jimmy Durante confessed that he was tired of having cameras focused on his nose every time he did an interview (then he did an Eskimo kiss with the co-star of my show for the film). Jazz trumpeter Louis Armstrong spent almost an hour complaining to me about the problems he had with stomach gas when traveling from city to city with irregular eating times.

Joan Crawford was an absolute princess. Despite the nasty book her children wrote about her, I found her most charming and cooperative. Of course she appreciated the inclusion of a bottle of Pepsi on the coffee table in one of the shooting scenes. She was a promoter of this soft drink.

Neverhteless, she had just come from New York where some TV photographer had experimented with her filmed interview, using some high speed, grainy, black & white film. She said he had made her complexion look like a Persian Lamb coat when she appeared on New York television.

I assured her that her complexion would not be blown out of texture by my filming and we proceeded with an amicable interview about her new movie release. My film aired on local television the next morning.

True to my word, I had used fine-grain film and good lighting. Her complexion looked just fine on the TV screen. Believe it or not, a few days later, I received a personal letter from Joan, thanking me for the special attention I had shown to her, and remarking that she had gotten up early just to see how the interview looked on TV. She thanked me for not making her complexion look like the Persian Lamb coat.

That was the only time that anyone of national stature ever took the time to write a letter of appreciation to me and thank me for my work with them. I'll never believe anything bad about Joan Crawford.

Charlton Heston was nice, and particularly patient with me during the changing of a film. Back then, I only owned one 400-foot film magazine. If the interview went over 10 minutes, it was necessary to change films in a black, light-tight bag. His interview was particularly interesting and ran longer than the usual 10 minutes. He was willing to wait while I made the film change. Well, I ran into trouble.

At that time, most television stations used DuPont motion picture film. It was supplied in 400-foot rolls spooled on a plastic core. Somehow, a batch of that film was manufactured and distributed on cores that were not perfectly round in the center. Right in the middle of Charlton Heston's interview, I was stuck inside a black changing bag with an open magazine of film and a new roll with an off-shaped plastic core that would not fit onto the camera spool. It seemed like an eternity as I tried every way possible to get that darn film onto the spool. Finally, it was necessary to get a spare plastic core from my camera case and remove the defective one from the center of the film roll, being careful not to unravel the roll and get things tangled up inside the camera magazine.

Author films Jimmy Hoffa at Pittsburgh Hilton Hotel.

While this eternity of time was going by, I was agonizing over causing this busy star such a delay. He eased the anxiety of my situation by telling me stories about some of the foul-ups he had experienced with Hollywood cameramen. Their screw-ups made my predicament seem mild by comparison. Fortunately, I was able to show him the defective plastic core after the change was complete. He saw that the problem was caused by a manufacturer's defect, and he was most gracious. Nevertheless, I sweat a gallon of water over that foul-up, even if it wasn't my fault. The only benefit was the opportunity to spend some additional time with Charlton Heston, who, I realized, is also a very nice person.

Jimmy Hoffa, the Teamster's Boss, was another interesting filming assignment that got a bit out of the ordinary. I spent some time with him in his room at the Hilton Hotel and was impressed by our conversations on physical fitness and exercise. He advocated health foods, strict diet, and a program of body-building that would impress most athletic coaches.

He was giving a speech to some transportation people that evening at the Hilton ballroom. I set up a large sound camera in the center of the floor to film his entire speech for use in an upcoming TV program. He astonished me by stopping in the middle of his speech to make a point about how Bobby Kennedy and the Justice Department were on a campaign to get him.

He pointed his finger directly at me and asked the audience if they'd ever had a movie camera in the middle of one of their meetings before. He got very paranoic about the campaign of the Justice Department against him. Then, he accused me of recording his speech to "entrap" him in the event he made any mistakes or slips of the tongue.

Nothing could have been farther from the truth.

I simply had to shoot the entire speech so that the editor could pick out the most pertinent parts for the context of the show. No copy was made for the Justice Department and no such request had been made.

Mr. Hoffa was clutching at straws in his distrust of the government and I was being made his scapegoat.

I felt like denying his accusations right there on the spot. I was making a legitimate film and I was being accused of treachery. My better judgement, however, prompted me to keep my mouth shut and just continue with the filming. I didn't want any trouble with the Teamsters.

It wasn't too much later that Jimmy Hoffa disappeared and hasn't been heard of since. I got cold chills when I heard about his disappearance. That man really had a an effect on my peace of mind.

Political hopefuls and presidential candidates were TV targets at every pass through the viewing area. Once I had the occasion to cover two presidents on the same day.

President Eisenhower was in town for a morning visit and we covered his press conference. Then I filmed a personal interview with Ike and our top TV anchorman. My opinion of Eisenhower: He was like a cold fish, standoffish and very difficult to approach.

He evoked no warmth and showed no charm, just all business, very curt and precise. His interview was no fun.

Then, that same afternoon, the pendulum swung the other way. Harry Truman came to town and the fun began

We set up for an interview in his hotel room. It was a charming and delightful exchange of opinions and he interjected many interesting side lights and anecdotes. Then it was time to leave for a political rally at a nearby auditorium. Just before leaving the hotel room, President Truman turned to me and said, "Listen, I'm going to give you some words of advice from your old president." I thought, "Wow! This is going to be something really important." Then, President Truman gave a twinkle of his eye and said, "Never pass up an opportunity to take a piss." And giving me an impish smile, he skipped off quickly into the bathroom for a quick "pit stop" before leaving the hotel. Those were my important words of advice from my old president. We all laughed and never forgot his humor. What a contrast to the morning with Ike.

John F. Kennedy, on the other hand, simply inspired me. The man had a magnetism that had the power to overwhelm. I met Senator Kennedy and his wife Jackie while doing a promotional film during his campaign visit. I sensed that there was more to this man's future the minute I shook hands with him. Both he and Jackie exuded a warmth and charm that was more than I had seen or experienced in other candidates that I had covered. When they shook your hand, there was a sincerity that seemed to flow beyond political politeness. I would like to have had more time with them for some casual conversation while changing a film or taking down lights, but their visit was on a tight time schedule, and, when the filming was over, they were gone for other appointments.

Then he was elected president and made a tour of our city some months later. I was assigned to cover his tour and I wanted to get especially good coverage. But the Secret Service agents held the media a great distance back at the airport and I had no chance to get any close coverage of his arrival. However, his first stop on the tour was at a rally in a steel-making suburb about 10 miles from the airport. From a friend on the police force, I was able to find out, in advance, where they were taking him to meet the people. With this special information, I was able to get away from the airport and with some extremely fast driving (I'll never tell how fast), I was able to beat the presidential caravan to the location of the rally and start to look for a vantage point that would allow me to obtain the kind of film coverage I wanted.

The town square was jammed with people. A literal sea of heads. The situation started to look hopeless for getting an unobstructed view of the president in this crowd. Then I spied a public telephone booth on the corner of the square. Did I dare climb atop the phone booth? Surely the Secret Service was among the crowd. Local police and plainclothes detectives were also on hand to assure that nothing out of the ordinary occurred.

Obviously, a man climbing atop a phone booth would attract their attention. I risked unpleasant consequences, such as reprimand or restraint just when I wanted to get my pictures. There was no suitable alternative and there wasn't any time to waste. As fast as I had driven here, I was still only a minute ahead of the presidential motorcade. I could hear the motorcycle sirens approaching in the distance.

What the heck, I threw my camera atop the roof of the phone booth and hoisted myself up behind it just as the motorcade pulled up into the square. Wow! I'd rather be lucky than good. The spot was perfect and no Secret Service men or police bothered me at all. I had just the right vantage point and got excellent footage as President Kennedy exited from the car just a few feet from my perch and began mingling with the crowd. I couldn't ask for anything better. The network cameramen, who were traveling with him in the motorcade, were ensconced within the crowd. Their shots were being obscured, while I was just high enough above everybody to see all his activities clearly and get good, human interest film coverage.

A side note to my inner thoughts at this moment:

Something inside me just "burst with pride" when John Kennedy opened the door of that limousine and walked forth into the crowd. Inside myself I said, "That's my President," and I really felt it. The man just radiated personality and he had the complete adulation of that massive crowd. He was handsome and confident in his manner, and he gave the impression that the country was all right and safe in his hands. In later years, when I learned of his assassination in Dallas, I remembered this day in Aliquippa, Pennsylvania, and the loss seemed even greater.

President Johnson's and Richard Nixon's visits to our city were routine and nothing noteworthy stands out in my memory about my TV coverage of either of them. One thing I did learn from extensive coverage of Nixon's campaign tours was how rudely and how arrogantly the network TV crews went about their business. With local TV photographers, or "cinematographers" as we were called, there was a degree of cooperation that made working together on a common story a civilized experience. We would cooperate on setting up lights for a news conference, check a light meter reading so that everyone had the proper exposure, and, if anyone experienced technical difficulty, we'd pool our efforts to help one another.

Not so with the network gangs. Look out brother when they came in. You could be all set up, have a nice location staked out with an unobstructed view, and have your lighting all ready and checked. Then the Nixon entourage would arrive with the network crews, or gangs as I called them. They would just barge onto the scene in full force. Forget courtesy or cooperation. These guys would push right in front of you with big, burly brutes carrying portable lights. They'd stand right in front of you, block your view, turn lights on and off as they pleased, changing exposures at will. Heaven help you if you made any protest. They outnumbered you 10 to 1 and outweighed you by about the same ratio. It was necessary to forget your manners, push and squeeze and get the best possible shot available under the circumstances. That took all the pleasantness out of a day's work, but we all learned to live with it.

Speaking of taking the pleasantness out of a days work, Nikita Khruschev came to town for a two-day visit. It was elbows and shoulder pushing for two solid days without end. If you think the network guys were rough customers, you haven't met the Russian camera crews. They gave no mercy, took all the best spots, and were all built like Hulk Hogan, the wrestling champ. I was never so glad to see an airplane take off as when that Russian jet finally left Greater Pittsburgh Airport.

But, until then, there was a story to cover.

The same policeman friend who had tipped me off about the President Kennedy motorcade also gave me an important tip about the Khruschev entourage. The downtown "Golden Triangle" section of Pittsburgh had turned on the lights in all the office buildings and stores to make an impressive greeting for the Soviet leader. A slight detour in the regular motorcade route was inserted into the agenda. They would swing up to an unscheduled stop along Grandview Avenue at the top of Mount Washington. There, a superb overview of the entire city was afforded.

The policeman's tip gave me the chance to drive at top speed, outrun the motorcade, and get into a position along Grandview Avenue from where I could film this unscheduled stop. Chairman Khruschev was truly impressed and I was able to film his reaction to that magnificent panorama of city lights that signified Pittsburgh's welcome. I was the only cinematographer who was set up to record this scene for the TV audience. I considered it a significant "scoop" of the other media and the glow I got from this accomplishment helped ease the exasperation that followed with the hectic pace imposed by the remainder of his visit and the discourtesy of the Russian camera crews.

There was one other moment of respite amid the two day: of hustle and bustle with Khruschev. A luncheon in his honor was given at the University of Pittsburgh and hosted by Pennsylvania Governor David L. Lawrence. I was selected as "pool" photographer for the local TV stations. That means that, due to the excessive numbe: of photographers, only one would be allowed to cover the luncheon, and his film would be shared by all the other stations. I was honored to be chosen and was determined to get good coverage for all the stations. I was given just five minutes to get the job done.

Chairman Khruschev, however, was not cooperative. He was seated next to Governor Lawrence at the head table, but he was ignoring the governor. He had his back turned to him and was in private conversation with his interpreter. The scene looked stupid. The governor was his host, but he was obviously being ignored. Fortunately, Governor Lawrence had grown up in the same neighborhood with my father. (His mother and my grandmother were church bingo companions.) The governor knew me from previous filming contacts. I was able to quickly explain my predicament to him. He immediately invented some question for Chairman Khruschev and attracted his attention and response just long enough for me to get the proper perspective, close-up shots, and all the coverage necessary to provide each station with suitable footage from this pool film. I was able to make my retreat within the allotted time. Little things can mean a lot in tight situations. Thanks, Governor, for the small favor. The pool film turned out just fine.

Jimmy Carter was a different story. I was hired directly by his campaign organization to cover his visit to Pittsburgh. The mayor of Pittsburgh was going to be the first important public official to formally endorse his candidacy for President of the United States. The Carter campaign people wanted to get all the coverage they could of that first endorsement. They also wanted as much footage as possible of Jimmy Carter interacting with the people of Pittsburgh.

My oldest son was in high school at this time, and I brought him along to assist with my lights and be a general helper on the job. I thought this would be a good experience for a young man, to see politics in action.

Well, we covered his visit all right. Filmed him mingling with the people. We even slipped in the back door of a restaurantbar where he stopped for a fish sandwich and a drink. We filmed Carter and the mayor "face-on" while they ate, drank, and conversed with the patrons. Other photographers, who used the front door, only got a view of the backs of their heads.

Then we went up to Democratic headquarters and set up the sound camera and lights for the endorsement speech. When Jimmy Carter came into that room, he took off his coat and tie, rolled up his shirt sleeves, and stepped briskly up to the microphone. He had so much vitality about him that I nudged my son with my elbow and whispered, "Take a good look, son. There's your next president." I had some sixth-sense about him, even then, in the very beginning of his campaign. My son was amazed at my intuition when Carter was actually elected. He thinks I knew a lot about politics. I think I just had a funny feeling about the man and was right, for once. Anyhow, I'll never tell my son, unless he reads this book.

You know, having a movie camera under the seat of your car can be a big help in an emergency.

I was traveling at the speed limit along the parkway one day when the line of traffic in front of me stopped for some reason. I made the stop with the rest of the line, but looking in my rear view mirror, I observed that the car behind me was coming too fast to stop in time. As I realized he was going to hit me, I instinctively reached down for the camera I had under the front seat. The position of my body as I reached down for the camera saved me from a "whiplash" neck injury from the impact of the collision. Much to the surprise of the driver of the other car, I was out of the car, camera in hand, and filming a record of this collision before the dust had settled. He was flabbergasted, and never was a damage claim settled so fast. My repair bill was paid immediately and without question.

On another occasion, it took a bit more doing. I was teaching my wife how to drive. She was coming around a sharp curve on a two-lane road when the driver of a tractor-trailer rig, hauling a bulldozer, rounded the curve from the opposite direction. He cut the curve over onto her side of the road. The bracket for the chain that holds the bulldozer to the trailer managed to catch her left front headlight and just peeled back an entire section of the side of the car from front to back.

He denied being at fault and thought he could get away with it because she was only driving on a learner's permit. His insurance company denied my claims for damage repairs, so I had to fight them the only way I knew how, with my camera (and a little investigation.)

Taking my camera to the scene of the accident, I photographed dual-tire skid-marks that were on the wrong side of the white dividing line on the road. I also used a tape measure to gauge the width of the road at this point. My investigation uncovered witnesses who gave statements to the effect that these skid-marks were made by the truck that hit my wife.

One other point. I had smelled the odor of beer on the driver's breath when he talked following the accident. The only tavern in the area was about a half mile down the road from the accident scene. I made inquiries at the bar and learned that the driver was a regular patron and had indeed been in the tavern the evening of the accident.

The case went to court and, at the trial, I acted as my own attorney. I thought, since I had been cross-examined so many times myself, perhaps I could do it on my own behalf.

The photographs were introduced into evidence and, along with the signed statements of the witnesses, clearly showed that he had operated his truck on the wrong side of the road coming around the curve. Another photograph revealed that there was no suitable place to turn off to avoid him at this bend. The fact that my wife was a student driver didn't alter the fact that she would have collided with a row of mailboxes had she tried to evade the oncoming truck. The pictures and the testimony seemed to be weighing the case in my favor, but the final coup was the driver's own testimony under my cross-examination.

I started to feel like Perry Mason. I had this man in a witness chair, duly sworn, and I began to question him about the drinking. I asked the driver if he was familiar with the tavern that was down the road from the accident site. He admitted that he was. I asked him if he had been in the bar prior to the accident. He admitted that he had been there. The next question asked how long he had been in the bar prior to driving up the road to the accident site. His reply was "half an hour."

When I asked if he consumed any alcoholic beverages while in the bar, he denied doing so. When I reminded him that I had smelled beer on his breath at the scene, he admitted to having one beer. The crucial question came when I asked how long before the accident did you have this one beer. He answered that it was at least an hour before the accident, whereupon I immediately queried "But you said you were only in the bar for a half hour." He replied, "Well, maybe I was there an hour and a half."

At that point, the judge banged the gavel down on the bench and said, "I've heard enough, verdict for the plaintiff". The case was over and I had won. A combination of photography plus experience gained from other courtroom appearances helped me obtain justice for myself and my wife.

I guess my little performance became the talk of the courthouse that day. A reporter for a local magazine ran a small article about the trial and my success. I gained a little notoriety for awhile. That was a good thing because in this business, getting your name mentioned in public can lead to more work.

An added note of irony was the fact that the attorney for the insurance company was so impressed by my presentation of the case and my actions in the courtroom that he hired me to work on several cases for his law firm in the following years. Some of them were quite a challenge.

But you've heard enough about this insurance work. I'd rather move on to some more interesting things and get to a new chapter Ill call "Fun and Excitement".

CHAPTER FIVE
FUN & EXCITEMENT

The "Gateway Clipper" excursion boat showing rear view and paddlewheel
which was lost as related in Chapter 5.

The last chapter started to get too serious towards the end. I don't intend to do the same with this one. More fun and exciting things to tell about, so let's get started.

Candid Camera ... That's right. Alan Funt and his crew decided to circulate around the CBS viewing area. He took the production of his popular show on the road to visit many of the major cities where they enjoyed a good percentage of the viewing audience. Pittsburgh was one of these cities, and KDKA-TV was the local CBS affiliate here.

By innocent coincidence, I happened to overhear some conversation in the hallway one day, indicating that the Candid Camera operation was soon to set up some of their operations in our area. The idea of "turning the tables" on the Candid Camera show suddenly intrigued me. "Why not?" I thought. "If anyone can do it, I've got the skill and equipment necessary to get the job done."

At this time, I was regularly producing features for Don Riggs "Daybreak" show, which aired each morning on KDKA-TV. The only one I shared my idea with was Don Riggs. He encouraged me, although unofficially, because he was directly employed by the station. He was required to respect the sanctity of the network show and their pattern of working in extreme secrecy. So, I was encouraged, but left on my own to come up with a game-plan of how to accomplish this feat.

First, it was necessary to find out where Alan Funt and his crew would be staying. Timing was imminent, apparently they were coming that very night. Tactful conversation with an executive secretary revealed a slip in her secrecy preparedness. I was able to learn that the crew was checking into the Sewickley Motor Inn in a suburban town about 15 miles outside of Pittsburgh.

Unable to obtain any further information from the unwitting secretary, I proceeded to travel to Sewickley and see what I could find out at the Motor Inn. The Inn had a restaurant, lounge, and bar. The first thing I did was to become a patron of the restaurant, try to blend in with the regular patrons and keep my eyes and ears open for any clues. I knew what Alan Funt looked like, but the identities of the cameramen, producers and crew were a mystery. My first break came after dinner, when I noticed comedian Allen King at the bar, smoking a large cigar and nursing a drink. I was able to order a drink and remain in close proximity without being obvious.

Throughout his stay at the bar, a few members of the crew joined him. I was able to pick up enough bits and pieces of their conversations to enable me to determine some of their plans for the next two days of Candid Camera skits. I was also able to tactfully observe and identify some of the members of the production crew, as well as to note which rooms they occupied and their respective vehicles and license plate numbers. Across the highway from the Sewickley Motor Inn was a large apartment complex. Some of the front windows of this complex afforded an excellent, unobstructive view of the activities at the Motor Inn.

Through careful conversation, I was able to secure the cooperation of the superintendent of the apartment building and gain access to a superb vantage point in a front window. I could see almost everything that was going on around the motel.

Very early the next morning, I was set up and waiting with an array of cameras and telephoto lenses, ready for whatever activity was going to take place. I didn't have to wait long. Alan Funt appeared on the scene in a vigorous and very hurried manner. He was giving all kinds of orders and admonishing everyone to hustle in their set-up preparations for their first trick. Throughout all of this activity, I used a high-powered telephoto lens to film all of this activity of giving orders and obviously being the boss. The big lens brought every action into close-up focus and made the film look like it was being shot from right beside him. Alan King also came in and out of the scene a few times.

They were setting up in the motel office for a stunt wherein they would call local laundries in for a pick-up. When the laundryman would come into their set-up, Alan King would pose as a businessman who had a batch of old, dirty money that he wanted to have dry cleaned, pressed and made to look like new money again. Their candid cameras filmed the comical reactions of the various laundrymen.

I filmed all the hectic outside activity of Funt and the crew rushing around to get everything prepared for their shooting inside the motel office. Once they began their skit, all the activity was taking place inside the office and the only shots that I could get were through the plate glass front window. These were not clear enough to be satisfactory.

I made a couple of casual trips into the motel through another entrance in an attempt to figure out a way to reveal how they were operating. I was out of luck here, they had taken over all the good places to hide and were using them for their own cameras. I thought about requesting some assistance from the motel management to obtain permission to hide behind a diningroom door, but I decided against risking my own secrecy at this point. I'd heard other conversations at the bar the previous night that indicated they also had something planned for the Greater Pittsburgh Airport. I decided not to risk being discovered at this point but to wait for better luck with the airport skit.

My patience was rewarded manyfold. After the motel gimmick ran its course, they loaded up vans and station wagons and headed for the airport. I was able to maintain an unobserved pursuit and determine their destination within the airport terminal.

One of the fringe benefits of being involved with TV filming in a community over a long period of time is the many contacts you pick up along the way. One of the most valuable contacts for me this particular day was my previous association with the director of aviation at the airport and also his public relations officer. I immediately used these contacts to my advantage, informing them of my idea to turn the tables on Candid Camera. They were excited about my idea and their cooperation was superb. They were willing to go along with any reasonable request that I made to put myself into position for secretive filming of the Candid Camera activities. The public relations officer went along with me to smooth the way with any airport personnel.

In my parallel capacity as an investigative photographer for claims attorneys, experience proved that it was helpful to carry along several changes of clothing, uniforms and methods of concealing camera equipment. I had all of my gear along for this difficult and impromptu job.

Changing into a dark green uniform appropriate for a working electrician, I secreted the necessary camera, lenses and film into a tool kit and lunch box. The public relations officer accompanied me to the area where the Candid Camera crew was setting up.

The location they had chosen was a telephone booth alcove that was located behind the airline ticket counters in a restroom and service area. Two phone booths were isolated and signs were placed on them reading "Men" and "Women" just like the restroom doors. They were also using two actors, a male and a female, to assist them with this set-up.

The trick worked like this: From their artificial wall that hid the camera from view, they could observe any passenger coming towards the phone booths to make a call. If a male passenger was coming, they placed the male actor in the booth marked "Men." He pretended to be making a call and tying up this booth. The only remaining booth was marked "Women." There was a psychological experiment at work to see if the male passenger would ignore the "Women" sign and make his call anyway, or patiently wait for the man in the "Men's" booth to complete his call and relinquish the phone. The opposite plan went into effect if a female passenger was observed coming to use the telephone.

As soon as I realized what they were doing, I got another great idea. Not only was I going to catch them in the act on my film, wouldn't it also be fun to involve our Daybreak co-hostess in their stunt without their knowledge? I made a quick telephone call to the director of the Daybreak show. When he heard my plan, he was eager for the chance to get a great feature for the show. He immediately drove co-hostess Marcy Lynn to the airport to become clandestinely involved in the Candid Camera skit according to my instructions.

Timing was the next most important item. I couldn't remain in the alcove area for any lengthy period of time without arousing the suspicion of some member of Funt's crew. I estimated the progress of the producer: and crew in completing their set-up and synchronized the arrival of Marcy Lynn (posing as an airline passenger wanting to make a phone call) with my appearance on the scene in the electrician's uniform.

I pretended to be involved with an electrical maintenance problem within a large panel at the rear of the telephone alcove. It was necessary to open and reset some electrical breakers in order to make it look like I belonged there. This caused some disruption at the airline counters out front, but they were pacified by the public relations officer for the duration of my masquerade.

I said once before, "I'd rather be lucky than good." A little bit of each was working for me this day. The crew had just started operating their skit and had pulled the stunt on a real passenger. I was able to slip the camera out of the tool box and obtain good film coverage of their entire operation from behind the electrical panel door. They were never aware of my activity and I continued my charade of maintenance activity until Marcy appeared on the scene, following my instructions to the letter. She played her role perfectly and Alan Funt thought he had just another gullible female caught in his little scheme.

Little did they know that all the while they were filming her at the phone booths and going through their own deception, I was grinding out footage of all their activities from a safe vantage point behind the electrical panel. And from my vantage point, I revealed their hiding place and filming activity, as well as the phone booth area where Marcy was putting or such a smooth performance.

I had succeeded in obtaining great footage of their activities without their knowledge. Now, the big question was, "What to do with it?"

After Alan Funt completed all his stunts on the road, he remained in Pittsburgh to produce two of his network programs from the local KDKA-TV studios. In conjunction with his Pittsburgh stay, a luncheon was held in his honor at the Variety Club.

This was our opportunity. Special preparations were made for an interview with Alan Funt after the luncheon. These preparations included a movie projector and screen set up in the interview room. After a delightful lunch, where he received many accolades from the local media, Mr. Funt was ushered into our interview room, where Don Riggs proceeded to discuss the Candid Camera mystique with him as I shot the sound-on film.

In the middle of this seemingly routine interview, Don casually inquired, "By the way, Alan, has anyone ever turned the tables on you?" The casual reply came back, "Nah, Don, lots of people have tried over the years, but we were always able to spot them or hear a camera running in the next room. No one has ever gotten away with catching us." Riggs just got a twinkle in his eye and said, "Would you mind taking a look at this film we have set up for you?" With that cue, the movie projectionist rolled the motel and airport footage and Alan Funt sat there, speechless.

At the end of the airport telephone booth scene, he asked, "Who is that girl?" When Don advised that she was Marcy Lynn, the co-host on his Daybreak show, Funt requested that she be a live guest on his network program that coming week. Marcy appeared on Candid Camera and the story of our escapade was revealed. Because she was a member of the American Federation of Television and Radio Artists union, she received a royalty check for her appearance every time the show had a re-run.

Funt was puzzled as to how we had obtained all that footage without his knowledge. He was introduced to the man behind the sound-on film camera who was shooting his interview with Riggs. We had quite an extensive talk after the interview and he was amazed at the methods I employed to get my film and the equipment that I used. There was some casual talk of a job offer, but I jokingly suggested that, after seeing the way he drove his employees like a taskmaster, I would respectfully decline.

I had a lot of fun getting this job done. Although exhausting and time consuming, I found it exciting and one of my best challenges. The local management of KDKA, however, didn't appreciate the effort. The assistant program manager even refused to honor an $87 bill for my extraordinary expenses. Maybe he was jealous because it wasn't his idea. Don Riggs ultimately paid me out of his own pocket. This was a very narrow-minded position for station management, especially when their Daybreak show received so much newspaper publicity and got the lion's share of the credit for pulling off the Candid Camera reversal. I just shrugged my shoulders and recalled the fun of the challenge.

What other fun things come to mind? Let me see. I suppose I'm about due to include some water back into the story, so let's tell about the Gateway Clipper and the lost paddlewheel.

Pittsburgh currently has a fleet of half a dozen large, passenger-carrying pleasure boats that ply the three rivers daily on excursions. They do sightseeing, dinner, and dancing trips and passenger shuttle to ball games and other events at Three Rivers Stadium. They are known as the Gateway Clipper fleet.

Their owner is an old personal friend of mine, whose association goes back to the early days of our respective beginnings, when we served together as volunteer firemen. Shortly thereafter, he began to operate his boat service with his initial vessel, the original Gateway Clipper. This excursion boat was rigged to look like an old-time sternwheeler. Its real propulsion, however, was from a diesel engine with a regular screw propeller beneath the ship.

The Gateway Clipper soon became a popular attraction and a familiar sight on the water with its stern wheel turning like riverboats of old. One night an unfortunate thing happened. While on a routine dinnerdance cruise up the Allegheny River, the Gateway Clipper suddenly lost its paddlewheel. There was no navigational problem, the wheel was an elaborate ornament that only appeared to be propelling the boat. The loss was aesthetic. The boat looked lost and awkward without the stern wheel. The architectural lines were chopped off, and the appeal of the old-time riverboat was lost.

Coincidental with the timing of the paddlewheel loss, a reporter from the Pittsburgh Press, Ruth Heimbuecher, was involved in a tongue-in-cheek newspaper article about Pittsburgh having a river monster, akin to the Loch Ness stories from Scotland. We had previously lost a full-sized B-25 Air Force bomber in the relatively narrow and shallow Monongahela River.

Now the Gateway Clipper's huge paddlewheel had mysteriously disappeared in the Allegheny. Scores of divers had searched both rivers for the missing airplane and the paddlewheel. They all came up empty handed. The newspaper was having great fun with the story. They even instituted an amateur artist's contest with prizes to be awarded for the best drawing of. the river monster. The Sunday Roto section carried an entire feature, with color pictures of the winning monster drawings. Curiously enough, all of the winning drawings of the monster had paddlewheels incorporated into their features in some fashion. Some had it attached to the tail, others wore paddlewheels for earrings, still more held it in their mouth or claws. Every winning picture showed the monster with the paddlewheel.

The Sunday that this Roto section came out, I had just finished an extensive photographic project and I was itching to do some scuba diving for relaxation. The monster story and accompanying pictures piqued my interest. Some inner voice told me that, if I approached this problem properly, I might just be able to find the missing paddlewheel, even though many other divers had been unsuccessful in the past.

Contacting my friend, John Connolly, who owned the boat, I was provided with cooperation from his captain and given information necessary to narrow my search area. Direction of travel, distance from shore, location of the boat when wheel was first noted missing, all these facts helped eliminate a

Author (in diving gear) leaps into the water to desend to bottom and attach a heavy line to the paddlewheel that he found. Workman on the salvage barge strongly resembled president Kennedy (Chapter 5).

considerable amount of river from my search plan, but still left a lot of river bottom to be investigated. The next day, I filled all my scuba tanks and set out in my small boat to search the area.

The plan was simple. Starting with the uppermost section of the river where the captain first noticed the paddlewheel missing, I would systematically work my way down current towards the point where it was last known that the wheel was attached. I would drag a line with a small anchor affixed, to scrape along the bottom and relay a signal to my hand whenever any underwater obstruction was snagged.

Each time the drag anchor would bump into some obstruction on the river bottom, I would stop the boat, attach the line and dive down to the bottom to locate and identify the object below. Each time I also took an additional sweep around the 25 foot radius of another line that was attached to the anchor. Time after time after time I descended, only to find the obstructions to be large river rocks that covered the bottom in this area. I used up all my diving air as Monday came to an unsuccessful end. I was tired, disappointed and thinking about quitting.

I only said "thinking" about quitting. Actually, that word is almost foreign to my vocabulary. I couldn't quit. Something inside me knew that darn wheel was down there in that area and it would be only a matter of time until I found it. I went back Tuesday morning and used up three of my five tanks of air on the morning diving, all to no avail. Continuing into late Tuesday afternoon, tank number four was gone, and I was well into tank number five, which was my last supply of air.

Every time I hit something with the anchor, I went down as described before. Except for an occasional waterlogged tree or a sunken 55-gallon drum, most of the obstructions were found to be the big river rocks. Each time I'd dive down and find another set of river rocks the efforts became more exasperating. Almost at the end of the final tank of air, another obstruction hit the anchor. Again I descended into the dull, brown water with visibility becoming even less due to the lateness of the afternoon and the oblique angle of the sunlight. Another dive, another rock, another swim around the 25 foot radius of the search line. Then something different happened.

My flipper hit something off in the darkness, beyond the extension of the line. It was not the same feeling as when I hit a river rock. Only trouble was, it was a full body length beyond the outer extension of the search line. "Why bother," I thought at first, "just another rock or piece of debris, and I'm getting tired, cold, hungry, and almost out of air." But something made me tug on that line enough to move the anchor another body length in that direction. I groped out in that murky-brown bottom water to locate the object that my flipper had struck. It was a board, that's all, just a board with its end barely visible 6 inches away in this awful darkness. But wait, this board's not lying down flat, it's standing on edge. Feel around some more. It's attached to something, a spoke. diagonally ascending out of the murky bottom to an area where the water color is now a deep yellow. As I followed this spoke upward, the water became clearer and brighter. It led to a clearly visible hub and now I could see many visible spokes radiating outward from this hub. Hallelujah! I found it. I had come close to passing by this area thinking it was just another rock.

Quickly I attached the search line to one of the spokes and made it back to my boat just in time to need the reserve air supply on my last tank. Drat, I had the wheel located, but was almost out of air. I needed to properly mark the wheel for recovery. There was just enough air left for a bounce dive to the bottom and immediate re-ascent. No time to follow down the anchor line and swim along the search line to the hub.

What the heck, I had gambled this far and made it. What's one more chance? Taking a long section of ski line, I mentally calculated the location of the wheel from the position of my boat. Swimming out to that position, I put the Scuba regulator in my mouth and surface-dived to the river bottom with the ski line and a clip hook I almost landed right on the paddlewheel, missing it by only a foot or two. Close enough to discern its murky outline and attach the ski line with the clip hook. I had just enough time to untie my search line and get back to the surface before exhausting my air supply.

I now had an identifying line attached with a float bobbing on the surface to mark its location. The only problem now was recovering the wheel. Well, that wasn't the only problem. What if a tow boat and barges passed over my identifying line and snagged it ? If I leave the float, maybe some passing boater would remove it without knowing what he was doing. The only thing I could safely do was to submerge the line along the river bottom and string it over to the nearest shore and hide it where only I could find it again. Using my anchor and all my scuba weights, I utilized every inch of anchor line available to just barely reach the shore, where I secreted the end and left to notify the Gateway Clipper owner of the happy news.

Coincidence plays a significant part in the story's ending. Adjacent to the docks of the Gateway Clipper fleet, a large floating barge was moored. Atop this barge a Russian building contractor had erected a model home, typical of the houses being built in Russia at that time. A grand-opening tour of the model Russian house was being conducted and there was considerable media coverage of this event by both the newspapers and television reporters and cameramen.

As I approached the Gateway Clipper docks in my small boat, I observed many of these newspaper and television cameramen at the Russian house exhibit. I was in a mood of great excitement. Thrilled and exuberant at my success in finding the paddlewheel, I shouted to my fellow photographers and told them of my find. The excitement was contagious and they all wanted in on covering the story of the paddlewheel recovery. Realizing that it would soon be dark and not suitable for photography, I stalled the plans for immediate recovery. Arrangements were made to go out the next morning and bring the big wheel up from the bottom.

The Pittsburgh Press and KDKA-TV bargained for exclusive coverage. I secretly made plans to pick up their reporters and photographers Wednesday morning in a small boat. They were taken to the location of the sunken paddlewheel. Fully re-supplied with diving air, I accompanied the salvage boat to the anchorage over my previously marked spot. Then, assisting the salvage operator, I took the heavy lines from the crane and descended to the bottom of the river. There, I attached a line to each side of the paddlewheel and gave the signal to lift it from the bottom.

Taking a firm hold on the lines, and standing on the upper blades of the wheel, I rode that darn thing up to the surface. The TV cameraman and Press photographer were provided with a dramatic scene as the huge paddlewheel broke through the surface of the water with me riding atop, gesturing triumphantly.

I know I "hammed it up" for the camera, but what the heck, I knew they wanted something extraordinary and I supplied it for them. I had earned my

"Hamming it up" for the camera, author triumphantly rides up with the paddlewheel as it is recovered from the river bottom.

fun and recognition and now I was getting it. Movie cameras whirred and press cameras clicked. They were having a ball and so was I.

The Pittsburgh Press ran a four-column picture on the front page, showing the paddlewheel being recovered. I stood atop in full scuba gear, giving that triumphant wave. In the background water, their artist had sketched a picture of the prize-winning river monster looking on dejectedly, as we took away his treasure.

The TV coverage that evening made an interesting story too. They showed me taking the lines down below the surface and then breaking through the water with the recovered paddlewheel. Once again, I was on the other side of the camera, but this time I was enjoying the limelight as a reward for my successful efforts.

The Gateway Clipper owner was most pleased and most generous. His substantial check more than covered the lost income I had sustained in three days of search and recovery.

One interesting side-note to this story .. I noticed that the man who operated the salvage crane to recover the paddlewheel bore a striking resemblance to President John F. Kennedy. Sometime later, I was able to produce another TV feature that was predicated on this resemblance.

Did I say, "Never let your work interfere with your fun." That's right. Would you like to know how I got that expression for my motto? The story again involves photography and water.

I was involved in a lengthy and tedious film production involving electric arc welding and how it is accomplished. Many series of shots were taken through varying densities of welding glass, and many sets of test exposures were made in order to arrive at the best results. The editing of all these shots and selection of the best ones for final production became monotonous and boring. Working with the advertising manager of this welding company on a day in mid-July, I looked outside around 11 a.m. to see an exceptionally beautiful day. There was a crystal blue sky, some white puffy clouds, and the temperature was in the 80s.

I came back to the editing table and remarked, "You know, Don, you can edit film when it rains." He didn't know exactly what I meant, but I quickly showed him. We left the editing office and drove to my boat club. I supplied him with a bathing suit and we spent the remainder of the day boating, swimming, water-skiing, and properly enjoying this beautiful day with a relaxing meal and a couple of good drinks.

Next day, Don arrived at my editing lab with a package wrapped in brown paper. He presented it to me, and when I opened it, I found a sign that his art director had prepared for me. "Never Let Your Work Interfere With Your Fun." That sign was immediately placed over the editing table and has remained there ever since. I think it has been an inspiration to more than one overworked producer in the succeeding years.

This was a most pleasurable mingling of water and photography. Those elements are still together in the involvements of my life, exerting their respective attractions. One of their attractions did interfere with my fun, however, and I'll explain in the following chapter. Let's call it "More Excitement."

CHAPTER SIX
MORE EXCITEMENT

SOUND ONE FOR BRIDGE LEAPS
ONE GATEWAY CENTER PITTSBURGH PENNSYLVANIA 15222
REPRESENTED BY AM RADIO SALES COMPANY

Rege Cordic, KDKA Radio's wake-up personality, places a bumper sticker for the Cordic and Company Bridge Leap on the car that started it all by making the plunge from Pittsburgh's Fort Duquesne Bridge. The "Bridge to Nowhere" was "completed" three years ago, still has no roads to connect with on one side. It's been a subject of fun on the Cordic show.

Top: Author (left) and fellow scuba diver, prepare to go underwater and place the "Bridge Lean" sticker on a submerged car.

Bottom: Promotional pamphlet from Cordic & Company Bridge Leap contest.

There are times when fun and excitement can turn into more than you bargain for:

A kooky contest, originated by KDKA-Radio personality Rege Cordic became a big topic in Pittsburgh. It generated a great deal of enthusiasm among his thousands of listeners.

A teen-aged motorist accidentally drove his car off the end of an unfinished bridge, flipped upside-down into the Allegheny river, and escaped without serious injury. Mr. Cordic did a tongue-in-cheek report of this incident on his morning radio show. He called this new sport, "Bridge Leaping."

The gag caught on with his many fans. The radio station made up bumper stickers that read, "This car entered in the Cordic & Company Bridge Leap." The fad grew out of all proportions and a contest was organized. Whoever put one of these bumper stickers in the most unusual place would be the winner. First prize was a trip to San Francisco. This is where I come into the picture.

As a scuba diver, I knew of a rock-quarry pool just north of Pittsburgh, where someone had driven a car off the cliff and into the water. The car lay upside-down on the bottom, in about 25 feet of water and looked very much like it ended up in this watery grave as a result of a "bridge leap."

My idea was to take an underwater camera and photograph a fellow diver placing a bridge-leap bumper sticker on this submerged car. This, I think you'll agree, was as unusual a place as any, and quite possibly a contest winner.

On the afternoon of March 13th, I picked up fellow diver Jack Waite. We proceeded to drive the two-hour trip to the quarry pool. It was here that a series of circumstances combined to bring me within an inch of the pearly gates.

Upon arriving at the quarry pool, we were surprised to find that it was covered with a layer of ice. We had not anticipated this. The waterways in the Pittsburgh area were not frozen. This pool, however, was shaded from the sun by high cliffs. It had not been affected by the recent thaw.

OK, so it's frozen ... We climbed down the hill and tested the thickness of the ice. Two inches! That's not so bad. You can stand on it, but it breaks if you jump or bring your weight down on it hard. That doesn't seem to present any major problem. We donned our wet suits and prepared the diving gear. While I was fixing the underwater camera housing, Jack made a hole in the ice and went under.

As I was placing the 35mm camera in the housing and checking the flash attachments and controls, Jack went out about 20 feet under the ice and was testing it from beneath. In the length of time it took me to prepare the camera, he had used his diver's knife to chop a hole that was large enough to permit his head to poke through. He was standing there, waiting for me to enter.

Now everything was ready for a last minute check of the camera. I put the underwater housing up to my eye to check the sights. My snorkel, which was hanging from my mask by a rubber strap, seemed to be an unnecessary annoyance. I removed it and left it lying on the shore as I entered the water. All right Jack, let's go find that car and take the picture. I don't want to be in this freezing water any longer than necessary.

Jack put his head under the ice and started off toward the direction of the car. I submerged and followed close behind. The initial shock of the cold water against the face plate of my mask caused a fogging on the inside due to the warm air within. It was necessary for me to slow up for a few seconds, fill the mask with water and purge to clear it. This brief delay allowed Jack to increase the distance between us, I continued after him, but lost contact somehow and became confused as to my sense of direction.

Well, I thought, "There's no particular problem. I'll just come up to the surface, cut a hole in the ice, get my bearings and then continue." OK, try it sometime, in deep water, with a bulky camera housing in one hand. You try to chop a knife hole up through the ice and you don't have any leverage. As you thrust the knife upward into the ice, the motion of your arm has a tendency to move your body down. This diminishes the force of the impact. It took me several minutes to chop a hole the size of a silver dollar. I realized that I was just wasting my time in this effort. Also, I noticed that the ice was considerably thicker here than it was at the point where we had entered.

Look around some more, can't see any sign of Jack, and I'm completely confused about direction. Another minor detail flashes through my mind ... Last night, when I went to the compressor room to fill my tank, the pump was being repaired and the only air available was from a cascade storage tank. This was down to 1700 pounds of air pressure and did not supply a full capacity of air to my 72 cubic foot tank. Also, that 1700 psi was measured when the tank was warm. Now, in this icy water, that 1700 pounds had responded to Boyle's Law and the air volume diminished with the temperature. It's funny how little facts like this come to you at these times.

I realized that I had been breathing a little faster than usual, due to the cold and the exertion of digging. I decided I had better get the heck out of here without too much further delay. Try to find the entry hole ... Which way? Everything looks the same, top and bottom. Funny how your exhaled air bubbles spread across the underside of the ice, looking like mercury or quicksilver, and then just disappear. That story about Houdini finding air pockets between the water and the ice baloney! Not in a non-tidal lake or pool, there's no air space whatsoever. Well, now I've used up more time trying to find the entry hole and all to no avail. Now what?

I know what I'll do, simply swim to any shore, get as close as I can, stand up and push against the ice with my back or shoulder and just break through. It'll be easy. I made my way to within ten feet of the shore where the water was about four feet deep under the ice. Standing up, with my back against the ice, I began to push with all my might. Nothing budged ... I moved in closer to shore so that I could bend my legs a little more for additional thrust.

C'mon George, you're over 200 pounds with powerful legs and body. Surely you can break through a little layer of ice. Push! Strain It won't budge. Oh! Here comes a twinge of panic. Now what? Drop the camera, it's suddenly unimportant. Use the knife ... Hurry! Dig fast, chop out of here before that air tank runs dry.

Now you've done it. Exerting yourself so much in this cold water, you're starting to pant and gasp for each breath. Get control of yourself. Don't let this panic get the best of you. Relax, stop work for a minute and get your breath and your senses. That's better, lie still for a few more seconds and get your composure. Now start digging again, not so fast, and twisting the knife with each stroke. There, the hole's getting bigger. I can get my arm through now. Time to start another hole next to this one and then connect the two. Boy, this ice sure is a lot thicker than it was at the spot where we went in. Keep digging, steady and even, the second hole is progressing nicely. Aw no, now it's getting hard to breathe. I'm starting to have to suck for each breath. My right arm is getting so tired from all this chopping, I can hardly grip the knife handle anymore. Well, at least I have my reserve air supply. I'd better pull the "J" valve now.

Good Lord, No ! ! It can't be true. The "J" valve is already down. While pushing against the ice with my back, I had accidentally pushed the reserve valve into the down position. All this time, I have been breathing my emergency air supply. Nothing left in the tank but a few difficult sucks of air and I'm finished. Panic? Yes. Frantic? Of course. In desperation, I grasped the knife with both hands and, with all my remaining strength, I chopped, twisted and pried at the space of ice between the two holes. It gave way, and with a few final chops, I was able to make a hole large enough to allow my head to push through. Discarding my mask and regulator, I squeezed my head up through the hole to where my nose cleared the water. My mouth was still in the cold water, but I could get a precious breath of fresh air through my nose. Needless to say, I was thoroughly exhausted and in a mild state of shock, but so glad to be alive that I didn't mind, just as long as I could breathe that open air.

After a minute or two, I regained enough strength and composure to continue enlarging the hole. It was necessary to hold a breath, duck down into the water again and take a few more whacks with the knife before pushing back through for another couple of breaths. This procedure was repeated several times until I had the hole large enough for my head and shoulders to exit. I was now able to turn around, and that's when I spotted Jack, or rather his knife. He was on the opposite side of the lake and was digging out also. He had been looking for me and lost his sense of direction too. He had to resort to using the knife to escape the same as I did. Only difference was, he had double tanks and plenty of air.

Once he extricated himself, he walked across the ice to my location and proceeded to help me. As I pushed against the ice in an effort to get out of the hole, blood poured out of slices in the rubber glove on my left hand. We found that, in my last frantic efforts to dig out, when I held the knife in both hands, the left hand was against the serrated edge of the blade. I had sawed and cut through the rubber glove and into my fingers and hand several times. The one laceration on my index finger was large and deep and required immediate medical attention with a trip to the hospital emergency room and several sutures. I didn't mind. I considered it a small price to pay for my freedom from that icy grave.

What about the camera and the picture of the car and bumper-sticker for the contest? Well, Jack had to dive through my hole in the ice and rescue the camera. I was out of air and badly cut. We had to give up the project and make a trip to the hospital instead. Did that stop us? Of course not. We made a trip back to the quarry the following Saturday. This time, we were equipped with all kinds of safety rope, digging tools, and extra helpers. I got the picture and entered the contest just at the deadline. Too bad there can't be a happier ending to this story. The judges selected a photograph submitted by a contestant who placed a bumper sticker on the limousine belonging to the Mayor of Pittsburgh. Our efforts gained us nothing except an unforgettable experience of a dive under ice and its related hazards.

When I look back on the combination of circumstances that nearly totaled up to disaster for me, I begin to wonder about the superstitions surrounding the 13th. I know I'll surely double check everything before diving on the 13th again, or any other date for that matter.

I have always considered myself to be a careful diver, not a reckless or haphazard type. Sometimes a person can get so wrapped up in attaining a specific goal that he overlooks some of the pitfalls along the way. Just look at one particularly stupid thing that I did. I removed my snorkel just before diving under the ice. I never considered becoming trapped, and the snorkel seemed to be in the way of the camera viewfinder. Now I realize that this little accessory could have been the article that saved my life. Had I been unable to push my head through that hole, I could have used the snorkel to get fresh breathing air while I continued digging at the ice until the hole was large enough to exit.

Interesting too, is the fact that the thickness of the ice at one area of a body of water is not necessarily the gauge for the entire lake. The ice at the spot where I dug out was twice as thick as the ice at the spot where we entered. It was protected from the thawing rays of the sun by the shadows of the high cliffs.

The most important thing that I learned, however, is that panic is the worst enemy of a diver in a tight situation. It is impossible to describe the feeling that wants to overpower you at a time like this. I can only suggest that every person who wants to dive be aware that panic can strike anyone. I though I was immune to panic, since I have kept a level head in other tense situations. Everyone has his moment of truth, however, and I would suggest that any diver at least think about this story and remember that overcoming panic may very well save his life sometime.

In another adventure, the Scuba Diver's Club decided to embark on a thrilling ride down the white water rapids and hydraulics of the Youghiogheny River at Ohiopyle, Pennsylvania. We joined with members of the Greensburg YMCA on an annual outing to ride the rapids, not in boats or rafts like ordinary people, but with our bodies.

Water and photography again. I decided that this sport was unusual enough to merit a feature film for TV.

Members of the Greensburg club had been shooting the rapids in this manner for many years and were old hands at the technique. We were advised to wear a wet-suit and then protect it with a pair of coveralls. That was so the rubber suit wouldn't get ripped to pieces from rubbing against the rocks. Next, you take an inflated automobile innertube and place it inside a burlap sack This is used for a bumper. You also tie it to your body with a length of nylon safety line to prevent accidental loss. Additional uses are made of the innertube and burlap sack. They serve as a vehicle to carry your lunch and any other supplies that you may want to carry down river with you. Simply place the lunch or other equipment inside plastic containers and carry them in the inside portion of the tube. I used this space as a method of carrying my camera equipment One of the movie cameras was also enclosed in a water-tight housing.

In the beginning, I shot regular footage of this activity from various vantage points along the river bank. The cover shots showed the action of the body-rafters taking exciting rides through the white water at the upper section of the river. After I obtained enough footage to establish a feature film the land cameras were stashed and I prepared to shoot the action sequence, using the water-protected camera as I actually rode the rapids with my body. They call this "cinema-verite. The viewer actually feels like he is experiencing the activity because the camera is a participant in the action.

I joined a group of rapids riders, placing myself in the middle of the action. The camera was grinding out some spectacular footage as, one by one, we popped over the hydraulics and into the swirling waters below. Sometimes I shot the person in front of me. Then, after letting the camera run while I descended, I turned it around to record the people coming through the rapids from behind. The action was fast and furious and it didn't take long to use up the film supply. Now I could tuck the camera away inside the innertube center and concentrate on enjoying the rest of this thrilling ride without having to bother with any more filming. I had more than enough exciting footage for my feature. It was going to be my turn to just enjoy.

I spoke too soon. That's when it happened. One of the fellows from the Greensburg group was a couple of bodies in front of me. We dropped and twisted through a particularly intricate minor waterfall. Somehow, he got his leg caught between two rocks. The force of the swirling water snapped his leg bone in a nasty fracture. Fortunately for him, there were four of us nearby when the accident occurred. We were able to pull him over to the riverbank. An emergency splint was applied to his leg and we made a survey of the situation.

The white water rapids of the Youghiogheny River run an eight mile course between Ohiopyle and the village of Mill Run. The river cuts through a stretch of wilderness with no houses or cabins of any kind along the banks. The man was in extreme pain and badly in need of professional medical attention. To attempt to continue downstream with him in the water was out of the question. The worst part of the rapids and the heaviest white water were yet to come.

About 100 feet above the river bank, the B & 0 Railroad paralleled the river. We opted to carry him up to the tracks and attempt to flag down a train. We had no idea what train schedule (if any) operated along these lines on Sunday. We further opted to carry him along the tracks, on our shoulders, towards some civilization, rather than wait in this wilderness for a train that might not come.

So, here we are, four of us, carrying this injured man on our shoulders along the railroad tracks when, lo and behold, along comes a train. We waved and flailed our arms in the air to signal the engineer that we needed assistance. The train did not stop. It would be improper, in this book, to quote the intensity of the language that this pass-up provoked. We just couldn't believe that any human being, train engineer or whatever, could pass by such an obvious emergency and not stop. My God, he could clearly see that we were carrying this man on our backs and that he was hurt.

Well, the train passed out of sight and we had no recourse but to continue carrying him along the tracks.

The nearest civilization was about four miles away. We were tired and greatly discouraged. We walked for what seemed like an eternity (it might have been only 10 minutes) when we heard another train coming from the opposite direction. We tried to hold up the injured man in such a position that the engineer could not possibly misunderstand that we had an emergency. We waved and hollered for help. The train passed us by.

We couldn't believe our eyes. I remember a whole lot more swearing and cursing coming from everyone. But then, something began to happen. As the cars of this long train passed by us, one by one they started to slow down. By the time the caboose was coming into sight, the train was proceeding at a crawl. When the caboose got directly alongside us, the train came to a complete stop. The brakeman came out and helped us get the injured man aboard.

The engineer of the first train had radioed to this engineer advising him of our trouble. He was headed in the direction of better medical facilities in Connellsville, just a few more miles down the tracks. We all felt like fools for our lack of faith and our foul language.

Two of the divers accompanied the man on the train to Connellsville. Another diver and I returned along the railroad tracks to the spot where we had left all our gear. Now we had a problem. There were five sets of gear. Five innertubes and burlap sacks with all the attached paraphernalia, and only two of us to transport all this through the worst part of the rapids.

We divided the equipment equally between us and headed back into the water to continue the trip. My principal concern was for my camera and the precious action footage that I had obtained earlier. I didn't want anything to happen to this film. Hanging on to everything for dear life, I followed the other diver over, under, down, around and through some of the roughest water of the trip. In the back of my mind was the man with the broken leg. It had happened to him so quickly, and in water not nearly as rough as this. Here I am, trying to hold on to everything and bump off the big rocks with whatever innertube I can get my hands on. I was beginning to think my fascination with water was about to come to an end.

What did come to an end, fortunately, was the rough part of the white water rapids. The river settled down to a fast but smooth pace for the remainder of the half mile or so leading up to the exit spot. For once in my life, I'd had enough water for one day and was happy to get back on dry land.

My efforts in making the film feature really paid off. The film received good critical acclaim after it aired on TV. I entered it into the television film competition sponsored by the Press Photographers Association and won the "Motion Picture Photographer of the Year" award for this feature and another called "Spirit of an Amusement Park."

"The Spirit of an Amusement Park" feature was produced at Kennywood Park and incorporated inside and outside shots of all the major thrill rides. What I did was take the movie camera onto each ride and film the action of the ride from the view of the participant. When you viewed the film, you had that "cinema-verite" experience of actually taking part in the ride. The film was a great success, but I ended up a dizzy puddle of jelly-flesh by the time I finished the filming. No one should have to torture himself like I did on all those diving, twisting, spinning, whirling rides while still trying to shoot film.

No one forced me to make this film, it was my own idea. Why then did I torture myself like this? The need for acclaim, I think. After the award was presented, Kennywood Park displayed my huge trophy in a special pavilion for the entire season. I can't adequately describe the feeling of pride and the sense of accomplishment that recognition like this can bring.

It also brings a determination to continue on and do other things that will bring some measure of acclaim. That's what I found kept me going toward more interesting film features.

One sidelight to the Shooting the Rapids film: Later on this same season, the Burt Reynolds movie "Deliverance" was released to local motion picture theaters. When I went to see this movie, I didn't just view it, I lived through all the scenes of those actors shooting the rapids in the movie. When I came out of the theater, I felt like I had gone through all of the action with them. All the memories of my recent experiences with the white water came rushing back to the forefront of my mind. I got double my money's worth from that film. Photography and water ... they just never let go of me.

Let's see if I can get away from them in the next chapter... It's called "Scooping the Networks".

CHAPTER SEVEN
SCOOPING THE NETWORKS

Top: Maurice and Maralyn Bailey survive 117 days adrift on the Pacific in small life rafts.

Bottom: Maurice & Maralyn Bailey arrive safely in Honolulu aboard Korean Fishing vessel.

Water and photography again. I can't get away from them. They keep combining to dominate the forces forging my career. This time the forces were violent, even deadly.

In the small mining town of Hominy Falls, West Virginia, a group of coal miners were busily engaged in their daily activity of bringing coal from the mine several hundred feet below the town. They were not aware that they were digging too close to the support wall of an adjacent, abandoned mine. Suddenly, and without warning, the adjoining wall collapsed. Millions of gallons of water from the flooded, abandoned mine cascaded in upon the unsuspecting miners. They were engulfed by the onrushing water and swept away by its force.

Several of the men, unfortunate enough to have been near the face of the break, were drowned immediately. Others who were working in more remote sections of the mine found themselves trapped as the rising waters filled the mine shafts and escape tunnels. A total of 25 men were deep in the mine on that shift. Rescue workers had no idea whether or not any of them survived the flooding. A few lucky workers had been near the mouth of the escape shaft when the waters hit. They were able to scramble to safety before the rising water blocked their exitway. They said that some of their co-workers did survive, but were trapped by the flood water that blocked the main shaft. The story took on national importance and brought network news coverage to this little West Virginia town.

I found myself wearing two hats for this story. Hat #1 placed me in the role of a competent scuba diver and instructor, bringing numerous air tanks and diving equipment to the scene. Volunteering my services in that capacity, the plan was to go into the mine, underwater, if necessary, and take extra diving equipment to the trapped miners to effect an underwater rescue. That hat was the one related to water.

Hat #2 belongs to United Press International Television News. I had been the local cinematographernews correspondent for UPI-TV News for a couple of years. This mine tragedy represented a national network news story that I was assigned to cover. That was the hat related to photography.

When intra-mine communications were re-established, it was determined that there were at least 15 known survivors out of the total of 25 men who were on that shift. Thirteen of the men were together in a side room, about one mile deep into the mine. They could not get out because interconnecting shafts were below water level and completely flooded. Two other men, a foreman and one worker, were known to be in another side room some one and one half miles within the main shaft. They were isolated from the 13 others and unable to escape for the same reason. The remaining 10 men, it was reported, were on the front line of the work force, at a much lower level, and directly in the path of the onrushing water. Their fate was unknown and little hope was held out for their survival.

As a diving volunteer, I participated in several meetings with the mine safety officials and company supervisors. Every conceivable plan of action was discussed and all options taken into consideration. Huge pumps had been placed into operation, but their progress was painfully slow in the face of the enormous volume of water that had flooded into the mine.

We were given the opportunity to study detailed charts and blueprints of the passageways and shafts within the interior of the mine. My own plan was given intense consideration. I proposed that we first take spools of bright yellow nylon line underwater along the flooded shafts to establish a guide line for further operations. Once this guide line was in place, we could form a shuttle line of divers to take in air, food, and other needed supplies.

Once the guide line was in place and an underwater relay established, we could approach the next level of rescue, getting the miners out. I proposed to outfit them with air tanks, regulators, and rubber protection suits and have a team of divers escort each man along the yellow line to safety.

This approach to the rescue received a veto from the safety team. Their fear was that these miners were not known to be swimmers. The risk of trying to teach then to use diving gear and placing them in an unfamiliar underwater environment might prove too taxing for their physical conditions. Besides, they explained, all these men had some level of coal dust in their lungs. They would be prone to coughing and perhaps choking during an attempt at underwater exit. All the while we were meeting and planning, the pumps kept running, day and night. The water level was receding ever so slowly. Days passed and concern for the ability of the men to survive mounted with each passing hour.

In addition to my diving volunteer position, I passed some of the hours wearing the other hat, UPI-TV News. Shots of the continuing rescue efforts were filmed and interviews with the families of the men were conducted. There was also the daily press conference held by the company spokesman to be covered. All these stories were sent via air express to the UPI assignment desk in New York This was continuing, front-page news.

An alternate plan was formulated by myself and some of the other volunteer divers who were on the scene. We proposed to take rubberized canvass bags (the type used by coroners for body bags), and, if we could string the aforementioned guide line into the area where the miners were trapped, we proposed to dress the men in rubber suits, provide them with air tanks and breathing regulators, and then place them inside these rubberized bags where they could be transported out by a team of divers without coming in direct contact with the water.

We figured on using sufficient lead weights to neutralize the flotation buoyancy of each man within the bag. All we would have to do would be to relay each bag-enclosed man along the line to safety. If he coughed or choked while breathing the compressed air, he wouldn't be in direct contact with the water and would have an ambient supply of air around him and be able to continue breathing until out of the mine. This plan was not vetoed, but given serious consideration at the next safety meeting. Preparations were made to obtain the necessary supply of rubber-canvas bags from local coroners' offices. Meanwhile, days were passing and hopes were getting slim. Then a breakthrough occurred. A larger pump had been installed at the abandoned mine and great quantities of water were being pumped out of that area. That had its effect on the mine where the men were trapped.

The first good news that we received was that the water level had receded enough to allow the foreman and the other miner to join the group of 13 men. Now we knew there were 15 of them, together in one location. With a considerable amount of pumping still continuing, finally, headroom was established in the escape shaft and voice contact was made. The men were tired, cold and hungry, but alive and anxious to get out of there.

The body-bag plan was abandoned. It was now only a matter of time until the water could be pumped low enough for the men to be able to walk out of the mine. That hour finally arrived, five days after the accident. An army of news media was amassed on the hillside overlooking the mine entrance. Lights, cameras, photoflashes, onrushing reporters, and network crews descended upon the scene, overwhelming the families who had waited patiently these many days for the rescue of their loved ones.

I was almost ashamed to be a part of this crush, as the media rushed to cover the exit of the rescued miners. Nevertheless, I did my job,, obtained the necessary film coverage of the rescue with lots of close-up shots of faces of the men that reflected their ordeal. I was even able to get one sound-on film interview with one of the rescued miners before he was whisked away for medical check-up. UPI-TV News was pleased with the film coverage that I sent to them and they were of the opinion that the story had come to an end.

But there were 10 more men still down inside that flooded mine, and 10 families keeping a vigil above. We had looked carefully at the blueprints. The area where those 10 remaining men had been working was much deeper down into the mine. All the experts were in agreement that no hope could be held out for the survival of any of these men.

Once again, we divers volunteered to go into the depths of the mine to check on the situation and recover bodies, if necessary. This plan was also vetoed and the only work that continued at the face of the mine was the endless running of the big pumps that slowly lowered the level of the water hour by hour.

It was time to say good-bye to people I had met at the mine and head back home for other work. One mine safety supervisor had been particularly cooperative with me throughout all these many days. We had spent considerable time together in various meetings and discussions. As I said good-bye to this man, I handed him my business card and told him, "If you ever get the chance to come to Pittsburgh, give me a call and I'll show you the town from one of our best restaurants." I would have liked to return some of the hospitality that he had shown to me during a rough and lengthy vigil at the mine. He had even seen to it that I got a supply of clean underwear while I kept that long and tedious wait in that remote location.

I didn't give much thought to the mine superintendent after I arrived home. The next couple of days were hectic. Important other work had been put aside to wait until the priority job in West Virginia was done.

Sometimes the biggest things happen when you least expect them. At 4 a.m., some five days after the story was seemingly over, the telephone at my bedside rang loudly in my ear. I answered to the excited voice of my friend, the mine safety supervisor. "George," he shouted, "I just thought you'd like to know that we found six more of those miners alive. We're going in to get them out right now." I had the presence of mind to realize that I was over 100 miles away and couldn't get to the mine site in an instant. I quickly questioned him about the timetable for the rescue and where the men would be taken for medical attention. He replied that they would be out in an hour or two and would be taken to the closest hospital, which was in Summersvilie, West Virginia.

Fortified with this tremendous information, I immediately called the assignment editor at UPI-TV News in New York. The person who answered at 4 a.m. was a night man with no particular executive authority. He did not know me personally and was skeptical about my excited call. Fortunately, I have an excellent memory for numbers. I recalled the phone number of the mine safety shack and gave it to him so that he could check out my report firsthand.

He called me back within two minutes, now all excited himself. "Charter a plane, get there as fast as possible," he directed and left the remaining details in my hands.

My sleepy pilot answered the phone on the second ring. When I told him of the fast-breaking story, he advised that, by the time I got to the airport with the camera equipment, he would have the plane warmed-up and ready for take-off.

I decided not to try to fly to the mine site. The time element was not in my favor to catch the men exiting from the mine. I directed the pilot to fly to Summersvilie. There, I paid a local mechanic to be our chauffeur. He drove his old car along those mountain roads like a prohibition rum-runner avoiding the sheriff. We arrived at the hospital in Summersville just as the men were being admitted to rooms for medical check-ups. I was able to get some general footage of the hospital activity and medical check-up work with all the related hustle and bustle of medical personnel and technicians. Then I concentrated on obtaining a sound-on film interview with one particular miner in his hospital room.

He proceeded to tell his incredible story of cold-water terror, miraculous survival, and the drama of the long days waiting for rescue.

The fury of the rushing water behind the collapsed wall of the shaft had hurled him and his fellow crewmembers in a helter-skelter path of hydraulic force along the mine shaft corridor. They were choking and gasping for air, with mouths and noses filled with water. The thrust of the flow had miraculously deposited him and five others into a side room. This room did not become flooded because of a pocket of air that prevented the water level from pressuring into the cavity. The other members of his crew were not so lucky. They were pushed further down the corridor and were drowned.

I was filming this incredible story in the man's hospital room. It was hard to keep the camera focused properly because tears were filling my eyes from the emotion of the tale. My pilot was holding my portable lights, and a reporter from a Charleston newspaper was holding my microphone and getting the story for both of us at the same time. I became aware of a slight commotion behind me.

The miner's family had just arrived at the hospital and were about to enter the room. The man's little daughter had tried to rush up to his bed, but the wife and parents, seeing that our interview was in progress, were trying to be polite and hold the little girl back.

Without stopping the camera, I turned to the family and said, "Let her go, she's waited to see her daddy long enough." I gestured for them to turn the little girl loose and encouraged them to join her at the man's bedside. Well ... the film continued to roll and the sound continued to record, but I couldn't see it. I was crying full-tilt at this point and so filled up with emotion that I was lucky I could keep track of the direction in which the camera was aimed.

These people had been making funeral arrangements and were waiting for the dead body of their beloved to be brought out of the mine. The joy and exuberance of this reunion was beyond description. I just left the camera on wide-angle and kept recording this drama until I ran out of film.

Rather than re-load and follow up with anti-climactic footage, I made the decision to get what film I had back to New York as quickly as possible. We grabbed everything from the room, gave our best wishes to the man and his family, and raced back to the airport with that crazy, wild driver.

Once back at the airport, I telephoned the UPI newsdesk to inform them of the great footage that I had obtained. My excitement was contagious. They asked if my pilot had enough fuel to fly to Washington, D.C. They had facilities in Washington to feed a satellite relay broadcast for worldwide distribution. A motorcycle courier would meet our plane at National Airport and rush the film for processing and editing in time for the satellite broadcast deadline. We had sufficient fuel and so we set off for Washington.

Late in the morning, the sky above Washington D.C. is a sight to behold. There were airplanes everywhere you looked. Jet passenger planes military aircraft, helicopters, corporate jets, you name it and they were there. They all wanted to get on the ground and be on with their business, but had to comply with directions from air traffic controllers and wait their turn according to various priorities.

My pilot was placed in a circling stack of planes waiting to land. We continued to circle round and around the airport, waiting our turn to descend to landing level. I started getting anxious about the time delay. Here I had the scoop of the decade. I knew I had the jump on any network coverage because the CBS, NBC and ABC camera crews were only in the process of arriving at the Summersville airport as we departed for Washington with the film already in the can. If I could just get my footage to that motorcycle courier in time. The thought of scooping all the networks with my dramatic footage of that family reunion in the hospital had my nerves tingling. I just had to get this plane on the ground.

I pleaded with my pilot to contact the air traffic control and inform them of the nature of my story and the deadline pressure. He was hesitant to make any such radio contact, advising me that this would be a breach of communications protocol and he might be reprimanded. So we flew another couple of circles around the airport and precious time continued to tick away. Finally, I just demanded that he get on the radio and at least advise them of our situation. The worst they could do would be to refuse our request. Reluctantly, he picked up the microphone and reported our situation to the air traffic controller below.

To the delightful surprise of both of us, he was given immediate clearance to descend to landing level and come in on the first available approach. Now our position at this time just happened to be slightly beyond the Pentagon building. In other words, between our position and the airport runway, the huge Pentagon building, headquarters for all the military branches of our government, lay ahead in our path.

The air space above the Pentagon is strictly a prohibited zone. No aircraft is permitted to fly over the building without special military permission. We didn't have any choice. We had just been cleared for landing and were coming in directly over the middle of this massive, five-sided building. I wasn't sure if we'd encounter anti-aircraft fire or a rocket attack, but it was too late to turn back now. We passed directly over the building and proceeded to land at National Airport and taxi to the general aviation area.

I honestly expected military police or the FBI to intercept us before our approach to the gate, but the only vehicle that was involved with our arrival was the blessed motorcycle courier. I tossed him the unprocessed film and he took off for the lab. I had just made the deadline. Scenes of the dramatic reuniting of the miner and his family were broadcast via satellite communications relay. Independent TV stations all across this country, Europe, and other parts of the world, had my film on the air before any of the network crews were able to complete their stories back in Summersville.

The commendations I received were great. This scoop placed me high in the line of priority with the New York assignment editors at UPI. When it came time to choose a cinematographer for an important story, I was now at the top of their list. I didn't have to wait long.

The next big assignment that came up was so much associated with photography and water that I ought to call it "Camera across the ocean." There was lots of water associated with this story. Too much, I'm sure, for Mr. and Mrs. Maurice Bailey of London, England. This British couple had set out from England to sail around the world in their small sailing vessel. Their cruise came to an abrupt end on the 4th of March, some 400 miles off the coast of Acapulco, Mexico. Their 37 foot sailboat was rammed by a crazed whale and sank into the depths of the Pacific.

The Baileys had completed a long leg of their journey. From London, across the Atlantic, through the Panama Canal, and up the Pacific coast of Central America. They were approaching a good location for a cross-over to Asia when the shipwreck occurred.

In less than a minute, the sailboat was gone, leaving the Baileys with only two small rubber liferafts for survival. Some plastic bottles floated on the surface and one of the liferafts was equipped with a first-aid kit and some limited K-ration provisions. One of the rafts was oval in shape and just large enough for one person to extend their legs in a sitting position. The other raft was of similar size, but round. It had an arching tube extending across its middle from which there was attached a canvas cover to provide protection from the sun and weather. One person could fit reasonably well under this cover. Two people crowded the area and made for rather cramped quarters.

I mentioned that the accident occurred on the 4th of March. Mr. and Mrs. Bailey had no idea that they would drift, undetected, on the vast surface of the Pacific Ocean until the 30th of June. One hundred and seventeen days adrift at sea in just those two little life rafts. They had no provisions other than what they could obtain for themselves with the help of nature.

This was survival at its ultimate level. Every once in awhile, an errant seagull would land on one of their rafts. They quickly learned how to catch the bird before it had a chance to fly away. The raw meat from the captured birds helped sustain their nutritional needs. They caught rain water and stored it in the few plastic jugs to satisfy their thirst. Bits and pieces of the seagull gizzards were used as bait to catch fish. They bent safety pins taken from the first-aid kit and used them for fish hooks. Fish were caught and eaten raw, with only rain water for a thirst-quenching rinse. Some of the fish and seagull meat was dried in the sun to preserve some food for days when there were no birds or fish to catch. Other parts of the fish were used for bait to catch more fish.

Endless days passed into more endless days. They had unknowingly drifted more than one thousand miles from the point where their sailboat had been demolished. Seven large ships had been sighted on the horizon, each time raising the hope of a rescue. Seven times the ships passed by, too far away to notice two small life rafts floating in the distance. Hope was turning to despair. Even the sea turtle they were able to capture gave them only enough food for a few more days. Chances of a rescue seemed more and more remote. Their physical condition was deteriorating. Muscles were weakened by the inability to assume an upright position for 117 days.

On June 30th, an eighth ship appeared on the horizon, once again very far away from their position. It was a Korean trawler, plying the Pacific waters on a fishing cruise and slowly returning to Seoul with its catch. The captain had noted some debris floating off his starboard bow some distance away but had not attached very much importance to it. The first mate, fortunately was a little bit more curious. He urged the captain to change course for a closer look.

They couldn't believe their eyes when they got close enough to observe Mr. and Mrs. Bailey adrift in their rafts. The Baileys were so weak and dehydrated that they could barely wave to the ship as it approached. The job of getting these half-dead people aboard in a surging sea was a difficult task. The Koreans however, were excellent seamen. They accomplished the rescue without further damage to the frail and weakened couple. When they were safe aboard the trawler, the Baileys could not stand. All they could do was crawl on their backs, in a crab-like fashion, across the deck. This June 30th, the world first learned of this unbelievable odyssey and dramatic rescue, from a simple morse-code telegraph message received in Seoul, Korea.

WORLD-TRAVELING PHOTOGRAPHER'S HIGHLIGHTS

Word inevitably got out to the news bureaus of the world. Stories about survival at sea are especially noteworthy in England. Because this was a British couple, the news bureaus of the United Kingdom were ripe for the story and ready to hotly compete with each other for exclusive publishing rights.

The Independent Television News Network of Great Britain (ITN), was a regular client of UPI Television News services. When it was learned that the Korean vessel was heading for Honolulu, Hawaii to discharge their rescued passengers, ITN asked UPI to provide them with coverage of this dramatic story.

This all happened just shortly after I had gotten the scoop for UPI on the Hominy Palls mine rescue. I was at the top of their list for any assignments requiring extra enthusiastic attention. I was assigned to fly to Honolulu and meet with a British journalist/reporter. He was flying from London to work with me on the story. No timetable had been established for the arrival of the Korean ship in Honolulu.

I met with the British journalist on July 2nd. We checked with various officials on the island for information concerning the arrival of the Korean ship and learned that they would definitely not be arriving in port for a few days due to their reported location and speed.

I was left with time on my hands in Honolulu and I put it to good use. The first problem I had was some damage to my sound camera that had occurred in transit. I made friends with TV cameramen and news personnel at one of the local Honolulu TV stations. They were very helpful in assisting me with the camera repair. However, one piece of equipment, a drive-motor for the camera take-up spool, required replacement. There was no such motor to be found on the island of Oahu. It was a specialty item that would have to be purchased in New York. Just when I thought I was going to be greatly handicapped by the loss of my sound camera, one of the Hawaiian cinematographers came to my rescue. He offered me the use of one of the station's spare cameras, a piece of equipment worth several thousand dollars.

Here I was, a total stranger on this island, and they were willing to let me walk out with an expensive camera in a true spirit of cooperation. What a contrast to the network gangs and the way they operated.

Now that I was back in business with a working camera to use, I tried to occupy my self in Hawaii until the arrival of the Korean ship. There was water, of course, the greatest ocean water anyone could ever want to see. Body surfing was a particular passion of mine. The huge waves at Macapu Point were irresistible. But I couldn't just spend the intervening time on nothing but swimming and surfing. There ought to be something I could do to earn my pay while I was waiting for the ship to arrive.

A telephone call to New York solved that dilemma. Inflation and high prices were the economic headlines of that era. The editors wanted me to produce a story about the economy in Hawaii. I was to focus special attention on how the island people managed to cope with the necessity of having all their essential commodities shipped to them either by boat or air cargo.

The reason I'm telling this side-light tale is because the pursuance of this feature proved to be a great help in attaining another "scoop" in the shipwreck story. The particulars were like this:

In order to visualize the volume of cargo entering the island of Oahu daily, both by ship and by air, it was necessary for me to find my way around the port of Honolulu and also to make contacts at the airport. I needed permission to go out onto the tarmac and film the big cargo planes as they unloaded. Both of these efforts paid off later, when the big story broke.

A couple of days filming around the Port of Honolulu and I got to know my way around the docks and terminal buildings reasonably well. That was some help, but the big assistance came from making friends with the public relations director of United Airlines. I contacted him for permission to film the big planes and the unloading activities at United's terminal. In the course of our conversation. I informed him of my principal mission in Hawaii and the impending arrival of the Korean boat with the British survivors.

He was fascinated by this story and became most cooperative. I informed him that I had important deadlines to meet in Los Angeles as soon as the film of the Baileys was completed here in Hawaii. The UPI-TV News Bureau in L.A. had facilities for satellite transmission back to England. There, ITN people were anxiously awaiting any footage for their TV news shows.

The United Airlines man was more than just cooperative. He promised to hold a seat on any plane leaving for Los Angeles after the time the Baileys arrived in Honolulu. All he wanted from me in return was assurance that I would include the "United" logo in my shots. No problem . . . I completed the economic feature story, including several shots of United Airlines planes and their logo, and shipped the film and accompanying story back to New York on one of his flights.

I now had some more time to kill in Honolulu while waiting for the arrival of the Korean fishing boat.

So, instead of more photography, I reverted to my other basic instinct and devoted this time to water. Big water ... The huge waves that roll in from the Pacific Ocean to Oahu's North shore are the delight of anyone who loves the thrill of surfing. Some people like to surf with a board. Then there are purists, like me, who get their surfing thrills from using their body as a projectile.

Words are insufficient to describe the incredible feelings that are experienced when your body becomes a part of a massive, breaking wave. You are catapulted forward with the speed of an express train, joining in the force and exhilaration of the incoming roller.

All my body-surfing experience, heretofore, was in the Atlantic, where five or six foot waves are considered giants. In Hawaii, however, a six foot wave is an ordinary occurrence. Waves of 12 to 15 feet are not uncommon. I thought I truly was in Paradise.

Paradise, however, had some eye-opening surprises. When you body-surf in an Atlantic wave, you take the breaking crest of the wave with your body extended forward. The force of the wave propels the body in a horizontal position towards the shore. When I applied this technique to my first Pacific wave, I got the surprise of my life and almost broke my neck in the bargain.

These Pacific waves are so huge, and their breaking point so high, the direction of force at the crest is not horizontal towards the shore, but vertical, towards the ocean bottom. In trying to ride this first big wave in the manner to which I had become accustomed in the Atlantic, I put my body in position atop this big breaker, unaware that I was about to be plunged some 12 feet or so, straight down to the ocean bottom with tremendous force.

Fortunately for me, I had some gymnastic tumbling experience in my younger years. It took all that experience to save my neck (literally) in this forceful plummet to the ocean floor. As soon as I realized what wad going to happen, I prepared myself for a forward roll. This prevented serious injury, but didn't protect me from the following force of this massive wave as it tossed and rolled me around like a leaf in a windstorm.

I took a noseful of sand and saltwater and ended on the beach, coughing, choking, and feeling thoroughly beat-up. This ocean was something different and was not about to be easily conquered.

After a 15-minute rest, I made another venture out into the breakers. Ducking under the close-breaking waves, I made my way out to where the big ones were cresting. My strategy, this time, was a little bit different. Instead of trying to become a part of the full breaking crest, I settled for what the Hawaiians call, "shooting the curl." Now I used the force of the center of the wave for my propulsion. Instead of trying to ride to shore in a straight line, I took a diagonal path along the breaking curl and discovered a sensational new way of body surfing.

You know I loved it. Not only did I not get slammed down to the bottom, but now I was able to get a much longer and more satisfying ride. The roar of the big wave, breaking over my head just behind me, was an added thrill as I kept just ahead of it on the ride in to the beach. A dozen rides like this provided enough thrills to fill a lifetime. Fighting that huge surf to get back out again for another ride was an exhausting battle. I slept like a baby that night.

Wouldn't you know, just when I needed a day to rest up from all that great surfing fun and exertion, the big story began to break. It was time to get back to serious photography. Thank goodness I wasn't injured in that first encounter with the big wave. I'll need all my strength and agility to handle the rigors of this news coverage with both silent and sound-on film. The danger of a broken neck from that plunge to the bottom of the ocean briefly flashed through my mind. It wasn't until several week later, after I returned home, that a news story brought this reality home with a bang. One of the Pittsburgh Penguin professional hockey players had been vacationing in Hawaii and had actually broken his neck while attempting the same type of body surfing that I had done. I thanked my lucky stars that a freak accident had not prevented me from doing the job that I had traveled so far to accomplish. Now, on with the tale of its unfolding.

The big day arrived. We got word that the Korean ship was approaching Honolulu and would be in port that afternoon. The event became a media circus. The American representative from the State Department was on hand with a British Consular agent, a Korean Consular agent, and all their related diplomatic staffs. The representatives of the Hawaiian Islands were not to be outdone. Governor and Mayor were present with various deputies and aides, heading group: of official greeters. Then this scrubby looking, rusty old Korean fishing trawler steamed into the harbor. You'd have thought it was the Queen Mary.

Thank goodness for big telephoto "zoom" lenses. The one I had really did the job on this story. In the wide-angle position, I was able to encompass the entire dock area with all the dignitaries awaiting the arrival. Then, a pan out into the harbor revealed the ship slowly approaching the docks. With a slow and steady "zoom-in" maneuver, I was able to arrive at a close-up view of the ship's bridge. There stood the little Korean captain with Mr.and Mrs. Bailey at his side. They were joyfully waving greetings to the assembled crowd. I'd waited all this time for this one dramatic shot, and it was worth it. Thirteen days of good, wholesome food aboard the Korean ship had returned the Baileys to fairly good health.

My journalist was able to work his way through the mob of media personnel and obtain a special interview with the Baileys right there on the dock. The story of their survival was pouring out in an excellent interview when an abrupt interruption came from a representative of a London newspaper. This surly brute broke right into the middle of our interview and said to them, "Remember, the more you tell the TV, the less your story's going to be worth." He was referring to his offer of a large sum of money for the exclusive rights to their story.

We managed to complete the interview without further interruption from this rude person. I obtained some additional footage aboard the Korean ship showing the little life rafts and survival gear that was displayed on the front deck. We then obtained an excellent interview with the Korean officer who had spotted them. With this much of the story "in the can," we took off in my car for the Honolulu airport.

This is where filming the previous economic story paid off. There was a tremendous traffic jam of official cars and media vehicles at the dock where the boat had arrived. Trying to get through there would have meant considerable delay. However, having been in the dock area several other days while filming the economic feature, I knew my way around another exit and got out of there with no problem.

Then, at the airport, true to his word, my friend with United Airlines had held a priority seat open for the British journalist and the unprocessed film. He was off to Los Angeles within the hour. I phoned ahead, and as soon as he arrived, a motorcycle courier met him and took the film for processing. It was edited and transmitted via satellite broadcast to England and the rest of the world, as well as throughout the United States.

Once again, my film broke the story far ahead of the other media, except for the local Hawaiian stations, of course. What tickled me was that we had satellite broadcasts on the air in Great Britain before the London newspapers hit the streets with their pictures and stories. I later heard that the brute who interrupted our interview was unsuccessful in his attempt to get exclusive rights from the Baileys. They had opted to deal with a more civilized representative of a more conservative paper and had reportedly gotten even more money for their story.

The last I heard, the Baileys were using the money obtained from exclusive rights to their story to finance the purchase of a new sailboat and continue with their lifelong dream of sailing around the world. I wished them nothing but luck. They had certainly earned it.

Before I depart from Hawaii, I have one more interesting observation. I visited Pearl Harbor and went out to the U.S.S. Arizona Memorial for some personal photography. As I approached the memorial in the navy launch, a curious sidelight presented itself. There were Japanese tourists aboard the boat. They, too, were making a pilgrimage to the memorial of the battleship that their countrymen had sunk in that sneak attack on December 7th, 1941.

I couldn't take my eyes away from observing their face: as we approached the monument. They displayed many forms of emotion and I continued to study their faces in intense wonder as we entered the area where the names of the men still entombed beneath the water are inscribed. I seemed to detect shame, humility, curiosity, apology, and an uncomfortable fear about their mannerisms that I'm having difficulty in putting into words. I would like to have been able to secretly record these emotions on film, but that opportunity did not present itself. I gained some unusual insight into the nature of the modern-day Japanese and just thought I'd try and share that insight with you.

As I say "Aloha" to these beautiful islands, it's time to continue with a new chapter. This one I'll call "Sports and Humor."

CHAPTER EIGHT
SPORTS AND HUMOR

Author with Bill Mazeroski at 50th Anniversary celebration of World Series
Winning Home Run.

When I told some of my scuba diving friends that I was writing a book, they asked, "Is it gonna be funny?" Perhaps they see me in a different light. There hasn't been much in the way of humor so far in these previous chapters.

Well, this chapter was supposed to be about sports, but I think I can interject a humorous story connected with one of the greatest sports moments of all times in the City of Pittsburgh. Winning the 1960 World Series.

The baseball season of 1960 was one of the greatest years for the Pittsburgh Pirates. All during this season, I was shooting newsfilm for KDKA-TV. A lot of my assignments included Pirate baseball game coverage. When they won the National League pennant and went into the World Series, I got just as excited as any other Pirate fan. Tickets for the series went on sale to the general public on a lottery basis. The rules stated that you send your check or money order to the ball club in the correct amount. They would have a drawing from the many thousands of requests to select the entries that would receive tickets.

I sent my check and self-addressed, stamped envelope along with the multitude of other requests for tickets. Lo and behold, a few days later, I received two tickets in the mail. They were for game seven, the final game, if the series went that far.

My friends scoffed. People at the television station laughed. Pittsburgh was pitted against the mighty New York Yankees. They all said that the Yankees would clean up the series in much less than the allotted seven games. Everyone told me that my tickets were worthless. They didn't dampen my enthusiasm. I went so far as to tell the news director that, if the series! went the full seven games, I wasn't going to work. Instead, I intended to take my wife to the ball game and be a regular spectator. He laughed and said, "Oh sure, you do that," and dismissed the subject.

Nevertheless, the series did come down to the seventh game and the series was tied up at three games apiece.

Assignments were being made the night before the final game when I reminded the news director about my tickets and that I intended to take my wife to the ball game. "OK," he replied, but he continued to hand me a fistful of special passes. Locker room pass, field pass, roving pass, press box pass, etc. He was persistent. I was instructed to take my camera along to the game and, in case the Pirates pulled off a miracle win, I was to start covering any celebration that might occur.

So I attended this all-important game as a spectator, taking my wife along for the enjoyment of the day. Our seats were excellent. Section one, row A, front row in right field, directly behind the play of the fabulous Roberto Clemente. For me, this was a special treat. My wife was a devoted Pirate fan and I was just enjoying the relief of not being required to keep a camera trained on all the action. This was a day I was really going to appreciate.

Then it started to happen, in the late innings. Yankee shortstop Tony Kubec was fielding a hard-hit ground ball. It took an unfortunate bounce and struck him sharply in the throat. He fell to the ground, seriously injured, and I automatically reached for my camera case. Extracting the camera, I replaced the normal lenses with a 10 power telephoto and proceeded to film the action as Kubec received medical attention on the field. I didn't have a tripod, but by carefully bracing the camera on top of the leather case that I had placed on the concrete wall in front of me, I was able to hold the camera steady enough to obtain good, close-up footage of the emergency activity on the field.

Now, I was no longer a regular spectator. I had put the camera into action and the pace of the game was getting furious. There was no stopping now. I braced that camera as best as I could with the emergency setup that I had rigged, and continued filming every pitch.

I don't suppose there is anyone reading this that doesn't know the super dramatic outcome of that game. Bill Mazeroski came to the plate at 3:36 p.m. that October 13th. It was the bottom of the ninth inning and the score was tied at nine runs each. There had been a hectic, see-saw battle with the score to this point. "Maz" connected with a fast ball from pitcher Ralph Terry. A thundering crack of the bat sent the ball over the left-field Scoreboard for the home run that won the game and the World Series. Never before had a World Series been won by a home run. Pandemonium broke loose. When Mazeroski rounded third base, he had most of the fans from the front rows of the stadium running along with him on his approach to home plate.

What most people don't know was that the very first film footage of that famous home run that hit the air on local television was shot under the most adverse conditions.

When the bedlam erupted as the ball cleared the Scoreboard, my wife lost all control of her emotions. I mentioned that she was an avid Pirate fan, now she became fanatical. In her wild excitement, she began beating on my back with both her fists and screaming. "We did it, we did it!" At the same time, I'm trying desperately to follow Mazeroski around the bases with a 10-power telephoto lens trained on his close-up image. I'm shooting the highlight of the entire series.

As I explained earlier, I had no tripod. The camera and powerful lens were just braced on the leather case that was atop the concrete wall in front of my stadium seat. I had things pretty well under control and was filming extreme close-ups from the time the Yankee pitcher began his wind-up. I followed his pitch to the plate and then stayed close-up on Maz as he started his historic, game-winning run around the bases.

Today I can laugh at the situation. I was doing my best to follow his path around the bases. A high-powered lens was providing an excellent close-up view. My back was being pummeled by both my wife's fists with rapid and reverberating blows as she was unable to control her excitement. This "once in a lifetime" action was taking place on the field and I had to stick with it. I couldn't stop shooting to tell her to quit pounding my back. I just had to absorb the blows and continue filming.

Needless to say, the film was not perfectly steady. I did my best to keep it from looking like it was shot during the San Francisco earthquake, but it was still a bit shaky. When people first viewed the film, some of them would accuse me of being drunk. Nonetheless, I had the action on film and time was now of the essence. I broke through the crowd to the street outside the stadium. Luck was with me. I found a taxi and gave the driver a $20 tip to get that film to the station immediately so that it could be processed in time to lead off the evening news. I did get a good laugh when I saw that shaky film on the air and remembered the beating I had taken while filming it.

The rest of the night was spent in such celebration that the fiasco of the unsteady film was soon forgotten. Other, more professionally shot footage, replaced my film in later coverage of the game, but mine was the first to hit the air, and I still laugh each time I remember that day.

While I'm on funny things, let me try to relate another film project that had me laughing throughout the entire shooting session.

I was producing a sales promotional film for Calgon Corp., makers of all types of water softeners and bath products. The film was to be shown to a group of brokers at a convention in Chicago. It had to be incorporated into a Sunday morning presentation. Many of the brokers who would view this film would be coming in from a Saturday night of celebrating in the Chicago night spots. It was anticipated that they would not be in any particular mood to view a serious presentation on Sunday morning, but that was the only time available for Calgon's sales pitch. So a slapstick, gag type of film was needed to keep their attention during the show.

Since we were in Chicago, we used a gangster type format for our skits. Using company sales managers and personnel as "corny" actors, they overplayed cops and robbers roles in a phony raid on a warehouse where a mobster was hoarding a new Calqon bath product. This got a few laughs and loosened up the audience for the ultimate piece, a spoof of Calgon's expensively produced TV commercial promoting their new bubble bath product.

The real commercial was entitled, "Little girls like to live in Mommy's world." It featured a beautiful little girl trying her mother's Calgon Bubble Bath in a luxurious bathroom setting.

To spoof this commercial, I mimicked every scene, but instead of using a little girl, I used Red Barnard, Calgon's big, burly, red headed sales manager. He was well known and liked by most of the brokers in this Sunday morning audience.

Instead of filming in a fancy bathroom setting, we picked a tenement house with an old fashioned bath tub that stood up on legs. Whereas the little girl in the real commercial played delicately with the bubbles in her ornate tub, Red Barnard sloshed and splashed irreverently in that old antique tub and had soap bubbles flying everywhere. He piled a mass of bubbles on his head and let them run down all over his face. We were all laughing so hard at his crazy antics that it was once again difficult to keep the film steady, even with a tripod. I couldn't keep a straight face during the entire shoot.

Enlargement of 16mm file frame showing Calgon sales manager spoofing
their regular tv commercial for "gag" presentation on the
Johnny Carson Show.

The way that the spoof film was shown to the audience was the key to its
success. First, the real commercial, in all its loveliness, was shown. Then,
using the same sound track and narration, the spoof version was presented
without any forewarning. We brought the house down with Red's antics being
such a complete opposite to the original commercial.

The response was so great among the brokers that the advertising manager
got another idea. He decided to run the two commercials, regular and spoof,
back to back, in a time slot purchased on the Johnny Carson show. It was a
fun experience. Both Johnny Carson and Ed McMahon got a kick out of
the spoof. They had a good laugh at my gag film and also made some clever
comments about it afterwards, on the regular portion of their show. My
motto, "Never Let Your Work Interfere With Your Fun," was right on the
mark for this job.

The Calgon spoof received so much good publicity that we decided to try it
again with their next real television ad.

Their next stylish commercial depicted a wealthy, beautiful woman, being driven down a winding road in the South of France to Monte Carlo in a chauffeur-driven limousine. As the limo continued along the road, she pushed a button on the rear panel. Curtains automatically closed between the passenger section and the chauffeur's seat. Simultaneously, a sliding panel in the floor drew back to reveal a small bath tub recessed in the floor of the limousine. The fashionable woman proceeded to undress and take a sumptuous bath, using Calgon Bath Oil Beads for total relaxation. When the limousine arrives in front of the Casino at Monte Carlo, the chauffeur opens the rear door and she emerges bathed, refreshed, and re-dressed in evening clothes. She is met by a handsome, tuxedo-clad escort and they enter the casino for an evening of entertainment.

For the spoof, all I did was change a few things. Instead of the fancy, white limousine, I obtained a white Cadillac of questionable vintage. Oil was mixed with the gasoline so that it would have a heavy smoke exhaust when driven. In place of the South of France, I used a winding road down the back of Mt. Washington, overlooking a part of Pittsburgh. Of course, instead of the stylish woman, once again I used our star, Red Barnard. The ad executive for Calgon's advertising agency played the role of the chauffeur.

Searching through all the old World Surplus stores, I finally found an apartment-sized, mini bath tub that actually fit into the floor of the old Cadillac. Trashy curtains were rigged up between the back seat and the driver. We spoofed every scene, with Red actually taking a sloshing bath as that old Cadillac wound down the side of the mountain, smoke pouring from the exhaust.

The finale had an unexpected twist that money couldn't buy. Instead of arriving at the Monte Carlo Casino, our star arrived at a weird looking fraternity house on the campus of Carnegie Mellon University. It resembled Monte Carlo in an off-beat fashion. The smoking Cadillac stopped in the front driveway and our bogus chauffeur opened the rear door as Red emerged, re-dressed in an outlandish, out-of-style suit and was greeted by a girl dressed like a "bimbo."

The unexpected kicker to end all this spoofing was a mongrel dog that appeared out of nowhere. Just as I was filming the final scene, where Red and his bimbo stroll into the bogus casino, this little dog took a dislike to Red and began nipping at his heels and biting his pants leg. The final scene wrapped up with Red and the girl walking into the casino, dragging the mongrel dog who was chewing at his leg.

It was the ultimate twist to this already hilarious spoof. Everyone connected with the filming just doubled up with laughter at the sight of this little dog stealing the show. Lucky for me, I was able to control my laughter and hold it inside long enough to complete the scene. This priceless and unpredictable footage was recorded without the telltale shaking of laughter to spoil the scene. For this unusual finale, I have to go back to my other slogan, "I'd rather be lucky than good." Once again, the real film and the gag film played back to back on the Carson show and the network audience joined with Johnny and Ed in a good laugh.

One other film that I did for a company sales presentation was also a lot of fun to make. The result was so unique that it bears telling about.

Rockwell Inc. had a sales meeting in Minneapolis and were involved in a similar problem with a Sunday morning time spot. They had to entertain a group of customers who would probably not be in any mood for a serious presentation. I had to come up with something that would hold their attention.

It was the bicentennial year, and the "Spirit of 76" was a familiar motto everywhere you went. In keeping with this motto, I took the company sales manager, the vice president, and one of the top salesmen to the site of a Revolutionary War fort. We obtained authentic costumes and props for the Spirit of 76 pageantry that we were about to film. The fife, drum, continental flag, and bloody bandage across the head of the flag bearer were typical of the familiar portrait.

A clever script was written for the film. It incorporated barrages of sales type questions that synchronized with actual barrages of revolutionary war type cannon fire at the fort. As the Rockwell executives, fully costumed, carried the flag through this cannonade, they made forward progress towards my camera. They were shouting words of encouragement and company sales slogans as they marched through exploding shells and cannon fire, continuing to come directly into the camera location, marching straight by the camera in exaggerated, close-up approach.

Filming of Calgon "gag" commercial in old car using burly sales manager in place of a stylish woman.

The purpose of this march directly into the camera and the exaggerated close-up shots was to set up the audience for the final surprise at the screening in the meeting room. The auditorium and banquet hall of this large Minneapolis hotel were transformed into a combination stage and movie house. A full-length movie screen was extended from ceiling to floor. Instead of being one solid screen, however, it was made up of a series of vertical strips, slightly overlapping each other and giving the appearance of one, large, solid screen.

When the film was shown, a lot of fun and excitement built up among the customers because they recognized the "Spirit of 76" actors as Rockwell's vice president, salesmanager, and top salesman. What they didn't know, or even suspect, was that these very men were "live," in the same costumes, positioned behind that split screen and waiting for their proper cue to act. They had the fife, drum, flag, and all the regalia that was displayed in the movie. At the very moment that the movie showed them coming towards audience and approaching life size on the giant screen, on cue, they marched through the slits in the screen as the movie lights went down and the house lights came up. They continued marching "live" through the audience, shouting the same words of encouragement and sales slogans that they were saying in the movie.

They stirred up a pandemonium of fun and surprised excitement among the delighted customers.

Imagine watching a scene on a full-sized movie screen and then having the actors in the movie burst "live" through the screen and continue the action before your very eyes. The results were most rewarding and that Sunday morning audience really sat up and took notice. I didn't let my work interfere with my fun.

As for anything else humorous, locker room antics of various athletic teams are filled with jokes and gags. Most of them you can't film. For instance, right in the middle of an interview with some sport's star, one of his teammates will walk naked through the background and ruin the shot, just for a joke.

Ball players are always playing tricks on each other and being in the locker room makes the cameraman a target too.

Teams who win Super Bowls and World Series championships don't care where the champagne spurts when the celebrations begin. Their revelry can sometimes ruin expensive camera equipment. They think it's funny. It's all in the game, and if you can't take the heat, they'll tell you to keep out of the clubhouse. I've had my fill of that kind of fun and I'll leave that bedlam to the ball players.

Jack Benny was usually good for a laugh. My involvement with him was a bit different. It definitely was not funny for Mr. Benny.

Every time a celebrity came to town, we would do some kind of a film feature andor interview for a spot on the Daybreak show. Jack was no exception. He was in town for an appearance with the Pittsburgh Symphony Orchestra. I was assigned to shoot a 2 p.m. film feature and interview at the Hilton Hotel the day before the concert.

Since lighting, preparation, and sound camera set-ups take a considerable amount of time, I arrived at the Hilton a few hours earlier than the appointed time. I wanted to be ready for the filming without the panic oi a last minute rush. The show director only instructed me to film Mr. Benny at the Hilton. No further directions were given.

When I arrived at the Hilton, I asked the bell captain for the number of Mr. Benny's room. Seeing all the camera equipment, he assumed that this was a legitimate request and gave me the proper room number.

I took all my camera and lighting gear up to the room and stood outside his door, ringing the bell for entrance. There was no answer, so, after a moderate wait, I proceeded to knock on the door. Time passed and I knocked again, perhaps a little louder. After what seemed to be an eternity, the door finally opened I knew I was in some kind of trouble.

The man who opened the door was in no mood for polite conversation. It was Jack Benny all right, but not the Jack Benny anyone was accustomed to seeing. I had awakened him from a deep sleep. His hair was disheveled and he was fumbling with the belt of a robe that had been hastily put on. He had no make-up and his face revealed the lines of age with stark clarity.

All I could do was apologize for my intrusion on his privacy and make a feeble attempt to explain the mix-up in the directions that I had been given. He accepted my explanation and his hostility subsided. He directed me to another room down the hall, where his music director was available to help me prepare for the filming. A very old looking man retreated back inside his hotel room.

Two hours later, after everything was set up and ready to roll in the other room, a vibrant and robust Jack Benny made his appearance for the interview. I couldn't believe the change in his appearance. He looked 20 years younger. His sense of humor was keen and his conversation was witty. During changes of film, we had an opportunity to laugh a little over my early morning interruption of his sleep. I was forgiven and we went on to make a good film.

As a token of his forgiveness, he presented me with two passes for the following night's concert. I saw a very funny man, who is also a talented violinist, put on a very entertaining and humorous performance.

Sometimes something absolutely innocent can become humerous just by the timing of the circumstances. For instance, I was shooting a film on a large cruise ship enroute to Jamaica. I had just completed the last frame of a 100 ft. roll of film taken of scenes on the ship's sundeck. The action that I wanted to save was on the very end of the reel. To save it, I had to remove the film from the camera in total darkness.

Not wanting to go three decks down to my cabin to locate a dark room, I opted for a quick substitute on the sundeck level. The Men's Toilet Room, near the pool, had a double door. The first room contained sinks and mirrors for washing and grooming. the room beyond the sinks was separated by another door and contained the toilets. I found that, by turning off the lights in the two rooms, and closing both doors, I could go into the toilet compartment and have no sunlight or artificial light filtering into the room.

Just as I had the camera open in the completely dark toilet room, two men walked into the outer room. Concerned that my film might be ruined, I shouted in panic, "Don't open the door and don't turn on the lights!"

Before I realized what that sounded like, being shouted from inside a dark toilet, I heard one of the men remark to the other, "Oh Oh, we've got one of those kind aboard." They retreated before I had a chance to explain. I couldn't stop laughing for the next 10 minutes. My companions thought it was even more funny because we never found out who those two men were. To this day, we laugh to think that two guys believe that there was something fishy going on in the toilet when it was merely a changing of film.

Mixing water and photography again, this time for humor. If you could see some of my first attempts to go over the water-ski jump, you'd laugh. The first time that I approached that jump, it seemed to get bigger and steeper as the boat drew nearer. I don't know what I thought I was doing. I never had any instructions on how to take this jump. My skis edged sideways as I started up the ramp. I went off the end of the jump ramp on my shoulder. I could have broken some bones, but instead, all I did was make the most hilarious, splattering landing that was ever filmed. I made the mistake of setting up my camera at the ski jump and allowing my brother to shoot films of my fiasco. He got a couple of other splash-down wipeouts recorded on film before

I finally learned to jump without falling. Something funny has to be in the family films, might as well be me.

Author going over water-ski jump.

Another water-skiing debacle proved pretty funny to a fellow boater. The scenario goes like this:

One of the members of my boat club had just purchased a very fast boat. He challenged my ability to ski behind it at top speed. I took him up on his challenge and went slalom skiing behind his boat as fast as he could go. It was an exciting challenge and I found it thrilling. How thrilling, I had no idea, until he made a tight U-turn. For an extra thrill, I took the full outside arc radius on the turn, "cracking the whip," as they say, to increase my speed to more than the speed of the boat.

Just as I approached the widest part of the arc and was leaning outward at a sharp angle, the tow-rope harness at the back of his boat broke. All the force and speed of that turn now combined to propel me, horizontally, across the water, out of control. I first skipped across the surface of the water on my back, like a flat stone. My feet came out of the ski as I shot across the surface of the water. When I slowed down and started into a tumbling motion, the ski was still traveling at a higher speed. It caught up with me and struck me in the back, leaving a long welt about the thickness of my thumb.

Another boat club member, in a 19 foot sailboat, had been sailing a course just below where we made the turn. Had the harness broken just a second earlier, the path of my body flying across the water would have placed me on a direct-hit route into the side of his boat. As it happened, I skimmed alongside him, flipping and tumbling as I went by.

One of the tumbles forced my ski safety belt away from my waist and pushed it upward around my upper chest, expanding the rubber and forcing my arms into a position that looked like a surrendering soldier. That's how I ended up when I finally stopped rolling and came to rest in the water. The force of the fall had jammed this belt up around my chest and arms so tight that I couldn't move. I just floated in the water, arms forced upward and laughing uncontrollably.

Author about to have a spectacular wipe-out in missed landing after water-ski jump.

The man in the sailboat and the driver of my boat had a difficult time coming to my assistance because they were laughing so hard. Even with the pain of the welt on my back where the ski hit me, I couldn't stop laughing for quite some time. I'd give anything if I could have had that spill on film. It was spectacular.

Some of my earlier attempts at skiing barefoot resulted in some good spills too, but nothing could compare with that harness-break spill. I'm re-living it again as I write this story.

While my mind is on water skiing and re-living these experiences, I'd like to mention the ski kite. This wasn't anything humorous, I just would like to tell of the incredible feeling I experienced in flying this contraption.

The Golden Triangle Water Ski Club purchased a ski kite, made of aluminum alloy frame in the shape of a real kite, with nylon material for a sailing surface. Very few members of the club were interested in flying this kite, but it fascinated me. Once I tried it, I was hooked. I flew it every time I could find a reliable boat driver and safety man to assist me.

Author flying water-ski kite soaring some 200 feet above the tree tops.

I don't know if I can adequately describe the feelings that I had in flying this kite, but I'll try.

Author water skiing by the tips of his toes.

First of all, the framework, harness and nylon sail material all combined to make a rather heavy apparatus. It was necessary to support all that extra weight on your skis until the boat speed increased enough to start to get you airborne. You were skiing heavy and it felt like someone was on your shoulders.

Then, when the boat picked up more speed, you could feel the sail material fill with air and start its lifting effect. The extra weight became lighter and lighter. Then your own weight on the skis started to diminish. For a few seconds, just before lift-off, there is a sensation of almost weightlessness. It feels like your skis are gliding across velvet.

Then you're airborne. Two hundred and fifty feet of tow rope permits you to climb about half that height and soar behind the boat at speeds of 35 to 40 mph. By shifting your weight from one side to the other you have some control of the sideways motion and positioning of the kite. It's possible to correct for the effects of sudden cross-winds. Flying is fun, but the biggest thrill is the take-off and the landing. A good boat driver can decrease the speed at just the right rate to permit you to land with that same velvet skiing for a few seconds, until you take the weight of the kite apparatus again.

I loved flying that kite, making ski jumps over the ramp, and skiing barefoot. Then I had to go and spoil it all by traveling to Bermuda for a film and getting involved in a motorcycle wreck.

One of the KDKA Radio personalities, Bob Tracey, hosted a trip to Bermuda through a radio promotion. I made a deal with his

Author doing headstand on water ski board.

travel agency to go along free of charge, in exchange for producing a travel film of Bermuda that was to be shown on local television after our return.

Bermuda is a lovely, tropical island, situated in the warm gulfstream waters some 600 miles east of Nags Head, N.C. British culture and native charm combine to make this little paradise in the Atlantic most enjoyable.

British traffic rules also apply here. Drive on the left side of the road. Automobile rental is prohibited on this tiny island and the only means of motorized transportation available is the small motorcycle. Mr. Tracey and I rented two of these and proceeded to drive from Castle Harbour to the capitol city, Hamilton, for some filming scenes.

In Hamilton, we happened upon some other members of our tour and -Joined them for lunch. Food service on island is not speedy. Looking at his watch, Bob realized he hadn't much time to get back to Castle Harbour and make tee-off time for his golf match. Since I needed to obtain film of this golfing activity, I followed him back along the winding roads on the motorcycle.

Tracey, in addition to being a radio personality, also had a motorcycle sales business in Pittsburgh. He was very accustomed to driving two-wheeled vehicles. I'd never driven one of these machines, but I was a good bicycle rider and found myself adapting quite well to the operation of these little cycles. I also adjusted favorably to the British traffic patterns, keeping to the left in traffic lanes.

Everything went well until we hit a section of winding road at Pink Beach. The roadway was cut through a section of coral rocks when we came to a place where there were three sharp bends in the road, a right, left and then another sharp right curve. Bob was pushing the speed limit coming into those bends and, being more experienced, he knew how to lean in to each curve.

Trying to keep up with him, perhaps I got a little bit overconfident of my own ability. Coming into the third curve, there was some sand along the edge of the roadway. I took the curve with less of a leaning angle because I was afraid I would skid on the sand.

That was a big mistake. The centrifugal force of my speed around the bend caused me to be pulled outward, towards the jagged coral wall on the left side of the road.

I was wearing sun glasses, a short sleeved shirt, Bermuda shorts and tennis shoes. My camera was wrapped in a beach towel and secured in a small basket attached to the left rear fender of the motorcycle. I could feel myself being pulled in the direction of that sharp coral hillside. I had less than two seconds to decide what to do. Instinct told me to protect my head and face. I made the decision to lean the cycle hard to the right and let the wheels of the cycle take the brunt of the crash.

I guess I picked the lesser of two evils, but it was still an evil choice. When the wheels hit the coral wall, I went sprawling across the road. My bare hands and legs made abrasive contact with the crushed coral that is the construction material for the Bermuda highways. My right hand and arm took the brunt of the scraping and, if that wasn't bad enough, the cycle bounced off the wall, onto my right ankle, fracturing the bones in three places.

Bob turned back and scraped what was left of me from the road. He flagged down a limousine that was coming by. It was being driven by some millionaire's chauffeur. He agreed to transport me to the island's hospital. I'll never forget the poor guy handing me some beach towels and asking me to please bleed on them and not his employer's upholstery. (You might call that humorous?)

The hospital personnel cleaned my wounds, dug out the ground-in coral and, after X-rays revealed three minor fractures of the ankle bones, they put me in a walking cast. I was given a set of crutches and sent on my way, impaired but still functioning. I guess this story qualifies to be in this chapter about humor, because for the remainder of that trip, it was a riot. First of all, the other members of this tour group insisted on buying me drinks at every turn. I think they tried to outdo each other. I seldom had less than two tropical drinks in front of me at any one time.

Every time the group would go somewhere or engage in some activity, there I'd be, showing up in a golf cart, hobbling around on crutches, but still getting the travel documentary filmed. Between taxis, golf carts and those darn crutches, I covered almost every foot of that island and succeeded in making the film that I had set out to produce. I made a fairly comic sight, but I got the job done and that's all that mattered to me.

Once back in Pittsburgh, I had a good time with the edited film, making the circuit of local television shows with leg in cast and on crutches. That kind of humor I'd rather not see too much of. It was funny until I realized one very important fact. This injury to my ankle made ski jumping, kite flying, and barefoot skiing a thing of the past. My water skiing would have to be confined to ordinary sports style. The days of exhibition skiing were over. I wouldn't risk a second injury to this ankle.

At the site of the motorcycle accident in Bermuda, I had lost a considerable amount of skin and muscle tissue from the abrasive force of contact with the road. Bob Tracey had scraped the remains of my body parts from the road and had burried them under a pile of sand beside the coral wall. Just for the fun of it, the following year, I returned to Bermuda and held a memorial service at my own gravesite. I even returned the pink sand that I found inside my walking cast when it was removed in Pittsburgh.

I didn't have the guts to try the motorcycle rental again. This time I stuck to bicycles for my transportation. Now I was able to enjoy scuba diving in the crystal clear Bermudian waters and make some very pretty underwater films on the colorful coral reefs. Anytime I want to return to Bermuda, I have a legitimate excuse. Isn't it appropriate to visit one's gravesite every once in a while for a proper memorial ?

While I'm again close to the subject of scuba diving, an incident comes to mind that might be considered funny, unless you were the victim.

I'd taken the kids to a drive-in movie one evening while my wife hosted a Tupperware* party. When we returned from the show, she informed me that a member of my boat club had been calling all evening, trying to get me to do some diving for him. She was certain that he would call again and she was right. Some five minutes later, the phone rang and I answered to hear this excited exclamation, "Jezush Crish Georsh, yoush jesh gotsta shelp me. I losht my teesh in da vivver."

If you made sense out of that plea, you'll know that I had to head-out at 1:30 in the morning, with diving gear and underwater lights, to find the false teeth that Dave lost in the river. After an hour of meticulous search, the choppers gleamed in the beam of my underwater searchlight and I brought them safely to the surface. He couldn't wait. Running up to the locker room, he washed them in fresh water and some tooth paste, and popped them back into his mouth, greatly relieved and thankful for their return. I've had some strange requests to find articles that have been lost underwater, but this was one of the most unique. I get some good laughs remembering his desperate telephone calls.

While the after midnight search for the false teeth wa unusual, the aftermath of another diving job was startling.

At a marina near my boat club, a fellow and his girlfriend had gone out for an afternoon of water skiing. The man possessed a valuable "star sapphire" pinkie ring. It was set in white gold with diamonds encircling the sapphire.

Before they went water skiing, he placed the ring in his pants pocket for safekeeping. The pants were rolled up and placed in a side pocket of his runabout. When they returned from the ski trip, he was involved with tying his boat to the dock. The girlfriend, trying to be helpful, took his pants from the boat and laid them on the dock. In the process, the pants unrolled and the precious ring bounced out of the pocket, across the dock and into 25 feet of murky water.

I received an urgent call from the marina requesting that I dive to recover his ring. My air tanks were empty from a previous job, but I came to the marina anyway to check the location of the loss. The man showed me aproximately where the ring had gone into the water and explained what had happened. It was obvious that he was upset with his girlfriend and anxious about his loss. I assured him that I would refill my tanks and return as soon as possible to search for his treasure.

Coming back to the docks a couple of hours later, with my air tanks now full, I found that the couple had not waited for my return. I placed anchors and search lines along the dock and proceeded to dive and search for the ring. Two hours later, after an extremely meticulous search through the murky river water, I located the ring and brought it to the surface. I took the ring to the woman in charge of the marina office and asked her to collect my $40 fee from the man when he returned.

The following day I returned to the marina to collect my fee. To my surprise, the woman handed the ring back to me and told me to take it away, she didn't want any part of it. She informed me that the police were just there looking for the man who owned the ring. They had a warrant for his arrest. Seems that the man had been so upset about the loss of this ring that he got into a violent argument with the girlfriend. At the height of the argument, he took out a knife and stabbed her. He fled and a police manhunt was initiated for his arrest.

Flabbergasted . . . . that would about describe my reaction to this news. Now what to do about this ring ? I contacted the man's family but they didn't want anything to do with the ring. They refused to pay my $40 fee. They also refused to answer a registered letter that I sent to the house informing them of confiscation of the property if my fee wasn't paid. The ring was valuable, but it wasn't doing me any good, it wouldn't even fit my little finger. I just wanted compensated for my tedious efforts spent in finding it.

My daughter ended up with the ring. Seems that the sapphire is her birthstone and the size fit her finger. I don't consider this story humorous, but it certainly is "funny" in the other sense of that word. To the best of my knowledge, the guy never came back to town and his whereabouts are unknown. I hope he didn't consider that to be his "lucky" ring.

If any more humor comes to mind, I'll be sure to include it with the rest of the stories. Now, I'd like to move on to a new chapter. I'll call it "More Sports"

CHAPTER NINE
MORE SPORTS

Author photographs Franco Harris statue in memory of 40th Anniversary
of the Immaculate Reception event.

In the previous chapter, I told about the 1960 World Series and having a seat in the right field stands behind the play of Roberto Clemente. In further sports filming, it was my pleasure to have been associated with this fine ball player throughout another 12 years of greatness. In regular season and post season games, his spectacular catches and rifle-like throws made dramatic film footage for any game highlights. I was also privileged to be on hand for the game where Roberto made the 3000th hit of his major league career. This sent sports writers and reporters into a tizzy with stories and interviews.

My second eldest son will never forget that game either. As I mentioned earlier, I operated as a "one man band" cinematographer. I did all the filming, sound recording, etc. without assistance. On the occasion of the game where Clemente was expected to make his 3000th hit, I brought my son Jim along to help out with the extra work I knew would be required in the locker room after the game. He had the opportunity of a young boy's lifetime. I gave him my microphone and had him stand in with the rest of the media group at the after-game interview session. He held my mike up to Roberto's mouth while I recorded all his comments on sound-on film.

Not too much later, I was to again enter this same locker room and stand before locker #21 to do another Clemente film. This was New Year's Day, 1973, and the film was made with a heavy heart. Pittsburgh Pirate uniform #21 hung silently in front of that empty locker, never to be worn again. The great Roberto had been killed in a plane crash. He was aboard a plane ferrying medical supplies to victims of an earthquake in Nicaragua. He had purchased these relief items with his own money and funds that he had raised among his friends in Puerto Rico. To be certain that these supplies got to the people who needed them, he was accompanying the plane on its tragic flight. It crashed into the ocean off the coast of Puerto Rico during its takeoff. There were no survivors and Roberto's body was never found. Pittsburgh Pirate personnel and all baseball fans were in mourning.

From a wide shot of the entire locker room, my camera slowly panned over to Locker #21. Ever so slowly, I zoomed in to the uniform hanging there, never again to be worn. The zoom continued to the number on the front and finally filled the screen with a big #21. When this scene hit the air, a portrait of Roberto was superimposed over the number 21. The quiet impact of this memorial was overwhelming. No narration was necessary. The film, itself, did the job.

Just a year earlier, I had spent considerable time at the Pirate's Spring Training Camp in Fort Myers, Florida. I was producing a film entitled "How To Play Winning Baseball". This film was designed to show Little League players how to play the various baseball positions.

Many of the Pittsburgh Pirate's players were chosen to demonstrate the proper playing of their respective positions. When it came to teaching the proper play in the outfield, I wanted to use Roberto Clemente as my illustrating player.

Harry Walker was the Pirate manager at that time. He refused to permit me to use Clemente. He said that Roberto's style was "too unorthodox" to show to an aspiring young ball player. Clemente could make "basket" catches on the run and "scoop" catches that more resembled a Jai-Lai play than they did baseball. According to Walker, he did everything wrong, but had so much talent that he could get away with it. Walker insisted on demonstrating the outfield play himself.

I wish I had held my ground and insisted on using Roberto. I had no way of knowing that he would not be with us the following year. That film would have been a priceless record of his type of baseball playing. We don't always know what lies ahead or where the cards will fall.

We don't always know where the ball will fall either. Like Franco Harris' "Immaculate Reception" in the Pittsburgh Steelers-Oakland Raiders playoff game.

One thing I liked about being a correspondent for UPI Television News: They always assigned me to cover the major league sports games in the city.

That, of course, included Steeler football, and all the exciting games through the years of winning four Super Bowls.

But UPI Television News did not carry a high priority with Steeler public relations man Joe Gordon. He continuously gave me a hard time with credentials and a low priority on camera positioning for shooting the games. He catered more to the network crews.

The day of the Steelers-Raiders playoff, I didn't even get a position on the same side of the field as the other media cameras. I was relegated to a position on an isolated roof on the opposite side of the field. The customary amenities, like chili and hot dogs at half-time, were not provided in this location. This spot was for second-class correspondents.

But I think we were talking about where the ball would fall. With this point in mind, I found that the second-class location turned out to be the best spot in the stadium for coverage of the "Immaculate Reception."

For the very few of you readers who may not know about this historic event in the annals of Pittsburgh sports, I'll bring you up to date. The Steelers were loosing by less than a touchdown. The last seconds of the clock were ticking off. They had possession of the ball, but were not in very good field position. Terry Bradshaw, the quarterback, took the snap and was immediately in trouble with a blitz coming into the backfield. He scrambled, dodged, and wiggled away from a couple of almost-inevitable sacks. He changed directions several times, trying to get a pass away, desperately looking for a receiver to get open downfield. He had the fans on their feet with their hearts in their mouths. I felt the same way, but I was obligated to stick with the filming. It looked like he was going to go down a couple of times back there.

Then Terry released a "bomb," intended for receiver Frenchy Fuqua. There was a body-shattering collision as the Raider's defensive back Jack Tatum rammed full tilt into Frenchy as he defended against the pass. But the ball was not ready to fall. Striking Tatum's left shoulder pad, it ricocheted backward, toward the scattered Steeler offensive players. The ball was just about to hit the turf when, from out of nowhere, Franco Harris came running full steam in the opposite direction. He scooped down to shoelace level and, with tremendous athletic ability, snatched the ball before it touched the ground.

He continued, full speed ahead, along the sidelines and into the end zone for the game-winning touchdown.

I captured every second of this dramatic play from my vantage point atop the opposite field roof. I know I used the word pandemonium before to describe the World Series fan reaction. At the risk of being redundant, that's the only word that can accurately describe the fan reaction to Franco's amazing feat. Steeler fans hated the Raiders, and winning this play-off game was more important to many of them than winning the Super Bowl.

Then a controversy developed over the eligibility of the catch. Seems that some rule states that if the ball bounced off Fuqua, Franco couldn't advance his catch and the touchdown wouldn't count. But, if it bounced off Tatum, the touchdown was legal. All the media cameras on the other side of the field had their view of the Tatum-Fuqua collision blocked by the bodies of the players. From my point of view on the opposite side of the field it was clear that the ball had bounced off Tatum. It seems my film provided the definitive answer to the legitimacy of the catch and advancement for the winning touchdown. Second-class citizens sometimes get lucky, and this was one time I didn't mind the low priority.

I remember filming another championship game where the Pittsburgh team won what was called the "World Series of Tennis." The Pittsburgh Team Tennis franchise won the title for the year in a game played at the Civic Arena. The only trouble was, nobody came. Here we were at the top of the league, winning the championship, and they couldn't give away the tickets. The sports fans in Pittsburgh gave no support to team tennis.

Professional basketball also bombed out in this town, while the college basketball teams of Pitt and Duquesne played to sell-out crowds. The only sport besides baseball and football to get full-level fan support was Penguin Hockey. I shot a lot of hockey games for TV, some exciting, and some just routine. There was one incident worthy of noting here, since we recently mentioned about not knowing where things might land.

One of our TV sports producers wanted to do a feature about the hockey coach. He obtained special permission to allow me to shoot from a position inside the penalty box. The coach was rigged with a wireless mike and I had a big, sound-on film camera set up adjacent to the bench. The reality of that game came home to me in quite an unexpected way. The action shots were vivid and close-up. Much of the sound track was unusable as the game got tense and the language coming from either the coach or the adjacent players was not suitable for broadcast. Then I got more than I bargained for,.

My position was right at the edge of the ice, just inside the penalty box. The big camera was set up on a tripod and the huge accessory carrying case was open and sitting alongside. the action on the ice became furious and, at one point, an extremely hard body check along the boards occurred directly in front of me. The momentum of this extremely hard check propelled the opposing player over the railing immediately adjacent to my camera and his entire body plunged into my camera case.

Pulling back to a wide-angle shot when I saw the action coming my way, I was able to keep this violent action in frame and follow the activity right over the rail and into my box. Sometimes you don't know where the players will land either. That was the shot of the week.

There are other things that land in places where they're not expected to. Like race horses.

We had an annual steeplechase event at Rolling Rock in Ligonier, Pa. Every year I filmed the races for a special benefit show that aired the day following the races. We had several cinematographers covering all the various aspects of the race. There were various jumps over brush, fences, and water holes. This particular year, I was covering one of the brush jumps with a small, hand-held movie camera. As the race progressed towards me, the pack of riders jumped the obstacle just ahead of my position and one of the horses threw his rider. The horse continued to run with the pack along the inside of the track. I was unaware of this riderless horse as I set up, eye in the viewfinder and, with film whirring at slow-motion speed, panned with the leaders as they cleared the brush jump and continued down the track.

Panning from my right to my left as I followed the pack over the brush and down the track, my back was now turned to the jump. I didn't know that the riderless horse was continuing to follow the pack and was jumping the brush on the inside. As fast as I heard him scrape the brush behind me, I felt the blow as the side of his belly brushed against my right shoulder, spun me around and knocked me into a small ditch beside the track. Had I been a couple of inches farther to my right, I might have been seriously injured or even killed. You never know where the horse will land either.

How about the go-cart? One of my biggest scares, and one of my closest shaves in a near-accident situation came, of all things, from a miniature go-cart race.

We were shooting a little feature on a different kind of sport, racing miniature go-carts. I was all set up to shoot some dramatic footage from the starter's position which is located in the center of the race track. Once again, I had a hand-held movie camera. My position was cleared with all the drivers in the race. I was to stay in the starter's circle in the middle of the track and they would negotiate around my vantage point as they passed the area.

These little go-carts are very low to the ground and the driver sits low in the framework for less wind resistance and better speed. In order to get better looking action shots of these little machines, I stooped down to their level for a more dramatic effect as they passed by the low, wide-angle camera position.

Then, one of the drivers, without my knowledge or forewarning, decided to give me an extra thrill.

The previous time he passed by my position, he noticed that I was stooped down to their level. Strictly on his own he decided that next time around he was going to head straight at the camera and then, at the last second, veer sharply to his left and give me a thrilling shot.

The only trouble was, I didn't have mind-reading capabilities. Here I was, crouched down low, with my eye in the viewfinder, filming the action as the little carts came by my camera. Then, all of a sudden, I see this one vehicle coming directly at me. I thought he was going to hit me. I had no idea of how fast these little devils could swerve. I started to go to my right, still in the crouched position, just as he started to swerve in the same direction, which was to his left.

I had two seconds left to do something and I did the only thing possible. I left my crouched position and propelled myself straight up in the air with the most forceful jump I have ever made. The little cart cleared less than an inch beneath my leaping legs. The camera continued to run. but there was nothing discernable on the film, just a helter-skelter blur. I got the heck off the track and almost collapsed from the shock. There was a tremendous screaming session between me and that driver after the finish of the race. I don't think he'll ever do anything like that again. I got a wild piece of dramatic footage, but I sure wouldn't try that again for all the tea in China. Sometimes you don't know where the go-cart will land.

Since I'm on the subject of racing cars, I might as well go from the miniature sport racers to the grand daddy of them all, the Indianapolis 500. I've been assigned to cover the big race several times for various sponsors and news media. The first year I covered this classic event was as part of a team of 15 cinematographers that were producing a movie for Champion spark plugs. I was stationed in the infield to cover the second turn in the track. I remember being the only movie photographer at this position. Stationed on either side of me was a still photographer from the Indianapolis newspaper on my right and another from a sports magazine on my left.

Naturally, the exciting highlights of any high speed automobile race lie in coverage of any accidents that may occur during the course of the competition. Being a novice at filming this sport, I anxiously awaited my chance to record any such accident footage. The mighty roar of the giant race cars and the blurring speed with which they passed by my vantage point provided a certain amount of thrilling film. the repetition becomes monotonous, however, and I was looking for some better action.

Be careful what you wish for, you're liable to get it. Just as I was becoming complacent with my routine filming, one of the cars went out of control coming around the turn to my right. I was standing at the edge of the track with the other two photographers, behind the gate that permits ambulances and tow trucks to gain access to the track in an emergency. As the car spun out of control, he hit the opposite wall, almost directly across from our vantage point. As I continued to grind out the film, the car bounced off the wall in a spin and started in our direction. I remember hearing a couple of fast shutter clicks from the cameras of my fellow photographers and then I was vaguely aware that they were no longer beside me. I couldn't pay any attention to them, I was busy filming this dramatic action that was coming right towards me.

A couple of passing cars missed the spinning car and passed it on the outside. Then the car came out of his spin about one third the width of the track away from my position, facing away from me. He went sideways across the track again, hit the wall a second time, leaving parts all over the track, then bounced to a halt about a hundred yards further down the course. I stopped filming just long enough to get new crank tension on the camera spring. I noticed that I was now all alone in my position at the gate. Thinking nothing of it, I continued to film as the ambulance and tow truck went out and removed the driver and car from the track so that the race could continue. I went on filming the remainder of the race, got shots of one more, (less spectacular) accident, then returned to the pit area for some celebration shots with the winner. I was quite pleased with my shots and especially happy to learn that the only two accidents that occurred during the entire race had happened right in front of my camera. I had the only extra action covered by the entire film team.

It wasn't until that evening, at our hotel, when I saw some old films on television showing previous Indy 500 races, that I realized how foolish I had been. While watching these old films, I saw coverage of one race where a car went out of control at the same turn where I had been stationed. He hit the wall just like the car I filmed had done. Then, instead of turning away from the infield, this car hit the very gate where I had been standing and erupted into a huge ball of flame that covered the entire area.

Now I understood why the two still photographers had clicked their pictures in a hurry and had run back further into the infield. They weren't novices. They knew what could happen out there. But I guess I didn't have any choice. Cinematographers don't click and run. Movie cameras record an entire event, from start to finish, if you have the nerve to stick it out. I guess there's a fine line between bravery and foolishness.

I'm glad I didn't find out how fine that line can be. Sometimes you don't know where the big cars will land either. I just got the chills again recalling this possibility as I am writing. I can get chills writing about the next story too, but in a very different way. You'll see what I mean in the following chapter. Let's call it "Religion."

CHAPTER TEN
RELIGION

In Old Jerusalem, author shoots film from atop a minaret while producing
the Light for Many Lamps documentary.

Maybe a jump from sports to religion is a big leap, but after reminiscing on some of the occasions where I had a close call with death, remembering some of the religious films might be appropriate.

Lourdes, France; Fatima, Portugal; Medjugorje, Yugoslavia; Pittsburgh, Pennsylvania; what do they all have in common? Apparitions of a heavenly nature, that's what.

In the years just prior to World War II, Mrs. Juliana Toma lived at number 5 Wakefield Street in the South Oakland section of Pittsburgh, on property that is now part of the Penn-Lincoln Parkway, (Interstate 1-376). She was a very religious woman and prayed daily for world peace. When America became involved in the war, she prayed harder for our ultimate victory.

According to her accounts, the Blessed Virgin Mary appeared to her in her room at number 5 Wakefield Street on more than one occasion. The Virgin assured her that, with continued prayer and devotion to God, America would overcome its aggressors. Mrs. Toma says that, at first, she did not recognize the personage of the Virgin. She only saw her as a "bride," wearing a white dress with a pale blue veil. She wore a gold headband that seemed to radiate light from the shiny metal. When she realized the identity of this apparition, Mrs. Toma promised to erect a shrine on her property in honor of the Virgin Mary.

She did not count on the fact that an antagonistic and disbelieving husband would refuse permission for any such shrine. She was forced to postpone any plans for the project, even though she continued to have occasional apparitions from the Virgin in which she was assured that, eventually, a shrine would be erected.

Now let's leave Mrs. Toma and her dilemma for awhile, and meet Phillip Marrowy. Employed as a laborer in the J&L Steel Mill in the years prior to World War II, Phillip had duties that required him to take refuse and scrap to a dumping area below the hill where Mrs. Toma lived. Sometimes, when he would make these trips out to the dump, he would look up on the hillside and see a vision of a lady in white, wearing a blue veil and a gold crown. He never heard her speak, but inside his head, a voice came to him with many revelations. He subsequently enumerated these disclosures in a small book .

Phillip would tell his foreman and fellow workers about these messages he received inside his head. They thought he was hallucinating or making up stories. None of the fellow workers or his boss had ever been able to see the lady on the hillside. The only thing that kept them from being totally skeptical was the fact that many of his enumerated predictions had come true. He also told his fellow workers that the lady's voice inside his head had told him that there would be a shrine erected in her honor on the spot of the vision. They also laughed at that idea because the area was a slum section of run-down housing and overgrown dumps. Phillip, by the way, had no knowledge of Mrs. Toma's existence, nor of the parallel visitations radiating from the same area.

Fate stepped in to apparently put an end to both stories. Phillip was drafted into military service and taken away from the area for the duration of the war. Shortly after the war ended, the Commonwealth of Pennsylvania confiscated the property at number 5 Wakefield Street, condemned the house, and took the land for part of the new highway construction. Mrs. Toma was convinced that she had failed in her promise to erect a shrine to the Virgin on this location. But now, the rest of the story.

A few years later, an unexpected tax bill arrived at Mrs. Toma's new residence. The City of Pittsburgh was billing her for taxes on the property at number 5 Wakefield Street. Inquiring of the city as to why she was being taxed for property that had been confiscated by the state, Juliana was advised that the state had only taken a portion of her lot. The remaining half still belonged to her. The Virgin, she thought, had interceded in some way to save this spot for the promised shrine. But the way was not smooth. A rebellious husband still stood in her way.

In subsequent appearances of the Virgin to Mrs. Toma, she continued to request that the promise of a shrine be fulfilled. Mrs. Toma then tried to give the deed for that property, along with a donation of money for an appropriate statue, to the Catholic Diocese. Bishop Deardon was advised by his staff that the site was overgrown with seven years worth of uncut weeds, littered with rubble from torn-down houses, and generally used as a neighborhood dumping ground. He refused to consider any such spot as a suitable place for a shrine venerating the Blessed Virgin Mary. He suggested that the money be given to Mrs. Toma's pastor for the erection of a suitable statue in her parish church. She obeyed his instructions.

That night, she recalls, the Blessed Virgin appeared to her again, this time in a dream. "Juliana," she said, "My shrine is to be on the hill, whether the Bishop likes it or not. A man named Phillip will aid you. You will know Phillip by a finger missing from his hand. When you meet Phillip, you will have no more trouble from your husband." We won't hear any more about Phillip until some time later. Meanwhile Mrs. Anna Cibak, of Ambridge Pa., a Gold Star Mother who lost her son on Saipan, met Mrs. Toma at church devotions.

Learning of Mrs. Toma's apparitions and believing in them, Mrs. Cibak interceded with the husband. She asked him to sell her the property on the hill so that she could erect a memorial to her son. He wouldn't sell, but gave her permission to erect a statue on the property.

While Mrs. Cibak, Mrs. Toma, and a woman from the religious supply store traveled to the site to erect the newly purchased statue, they discussed where they might place the statue in the midst of all that rubble and overgrowth. Mrs. Toma believed that a spot would be shown to them. True to her faith, when they arrived, one area in all this mess of rubbish and debris was miraculously clear. They naturally chose this spot for the shrine and erected the statue of the Virgin Mary on this site. Soon, devout neighbors from the vicinity came and donated their labor to clear the rest of the area of all weeds and rubbish. They constructed a rustic pathway for access to the shrine.

On September 22, 1956, a beautiful statue dedicated to "Our Lady, Queen of Peace" was blessed by Mrs. Toma's pastor, Father Thomas Harnyak, in a ceremony attended by many devout people on the hillside overlooking the parkway and the steel mill.

At this point, we have to return to Phillip. He had come back to the mill after the end of the war. Sometime in 1952, he had begun to have the visions again when he took bundles of scrap metal over to railroad cars along the tracks below the hillside. Over the next four years he would again get revelations from these visions. "Like talking to the wind," he described the voice. Again, many of his fellow workers rebuked him and even thought him a bit loony. Nevertheless, many of the revelations that he wrote about began to come true. His fellow workers looked upon him with a mixture of awe and puzzlement.

Phillip was off work for a couple of weeks in September, 1956. He was not at work during the week that the statue was erected on the hillside. His first day back to work was the Sunday that the statue was dedicated. When he arrived on the job, his fellow workers were all excited. "Look! Look! On the hill Phillip, your prediction came true. They erected a shrine right where you said it would be. The statue was put there this past week."

I've used the word flabbergasted before, but that's the only word that properly describes Phillip's reaction to the sight of the shrine on the hill. He could see people gathering around the statue in some type of ceremony. He received permission from his foreman to take a short absence from work to climb the hillside and see what was going on. He never knew anything about Mrs. Cibak, Mrs. Toma, or their parallel plans and visions.

Phillip reached the site of the statue and saw that it was made of pure white stone. He came up to Mrs. Toma and said, "Missus, she wasn't all white. She wore a blue veil with gold trim." Before he could say anything more, he was astonished when Mrs. Toma asked. "Is your name Phillip?" When he replied in the affirmative, she also told him that he had a finger missing from his hand before she had an opportunity to observe his fingers.

He said his face turned red and his hair seemed to stand on end. He had never seen this woman before and she knew his name and knew about his finger defect. Father Hornyak, he said, was a witness to this amazing demonstration. He knew of Mrs. Toma's revelations from previous conversations with her. Everyone who attended the dedication was astounded at this event. When Phillip subsequently told them of the extent of his many visions and apparitions that he had experienced on this same location, the group was even more bewildered. Surely, something beyond natural phenomena had occurred here. There was something extra special about this little shrine.

There was no further interference from the husband. The neighbors and devout acquaintances of the women were impressed by all these events. They all pitched in to make the location presentable. Votive candles were purchased and kept lit in constant vigil in front of the statue. They were maintained daily, in all kinds of weather.

Devotions at the shrine increased as more and more people became aware of the unusual story that I have just related. That's where I came in. Traveling the Parkway almost daily in the time after the statue was erected, I noticed the twinkling glow of the red votive candles always shining in the night in front of this little statue. My curiosity grew each time I passed the hillside and observed the glowing candles. The persistence of these people to maintain a shrine on this desolate hillside piqued my interest. No matter what the weather -- rain, snow, or below zero temperatures, the votive candles were always lit. I decided that this merited investigation for a possible Daybreak film feature.

Piece by piece, the events that I have just related were reported to me. I arranged sound-on film interviews with Mrs. Toma and Phillip at the site of the shrine. During the course of these interviews, I was informed that there are still apparitions by the Virgin. She admonished everyone to pray for world peace in an effort to avoid a massive catastrophe to all of mankind. They said that she also promised that water would spring forth from the site of the shrine. I couldn't imagine where, on this arid hillside, any water might be found.

On my next visit to the shrine for additional filming, they showed me where a man had been digging into the ground to erect a protective fence. At one of the places where he dug to erect a fence post, a trickle of water emerged, formed a small pool and, from there, continued to flow on down the hillside. This made my hair stand out on the back of my neck.

There's something about this place that defies explanation. Miraculous cures have been attributed to this water, but they're hearsay and I have no proof of their authenticity.

Throughout subsequent years, I have watched this little shrine grow into an area of sincere devotion. Many of the faithful visit this remote site on a regular basis. The trappings around the statue have become more elaborate and the number of votive lights have greatly increased.

Each time I drive along the Parkway below the shrine,] look up and repeat the little prayer that is inscribed on the base of the statue. "Mary, Queen of Peace, pray for us."

I know my film features inspired many viewers to investigate the shrine and to become involved in the religious principles that it represents. For awhile I was inundated with telephone calls requesting information and directions to the statue. Perhaps this experience inspired me to become involved with many of the religious films I have subsequently produced. Who knows..?

I don't know if you can call this next story a religious experience, but it certainly falls into the category of "beyond the natural."

Don Riggs and I traveled to Clarion County one day to do a film feature for the Daybreak show about a fellow who was a "water witch." Jesse Aites had a special talent and gift for finding water beneath the ground. I think the accepted term for this profession is a dowser. The man could actually locate underground water by using a "divining rod". He would hold the forked branch of a tree in his two hands and it dipped downward, toward the ground, whenever he walked over a spot where water existed below the surface.

Neighbors attested to Jesse's powers. Most of the people in this rural area had used Jesse at one time or another to find water for their wells. They advised that he wouldn't take any payment for his services. He was afraid that taking money would destroy his power.

I was skeptical. Being there in the capacity of a cinematographer didn't require any belief in all these supernatural claims. I just shot the film, recording the action of the divining rod each time it dipped towards the ground whenever Jesse walked over a known source of underground water. It made me curious to see this happening right before my eyes. There must be some trick, I thought, and decided to try it myself.

Cutting a similar divining rod from the same tree, I held it in the same manner as Jesse held his stick. I walked across the same path that he walked. When I crossed the spot where his stick dipped ... nothing happened. I tried again ... no response. Then Jesse walked alongside me on my third attempt. He just lightly touched my arm with his hand. This time, when we passed over the underground water, the stick physically twisted in my hands and pointed downward. I don't mean it slipped around in my grip. I was holding that stick as tightly as was humanly possible. The stick didn't slip in my grip, it actually twisted itself against the power of my thumb pressure and pointed down to the water source.

I got the weirdest sensation and couldn't believe what was happening. When Jesse let go of my arm and I walked back across the spot ... again nothing happened. I've never experienced anything quite like that, before or since. If he touched me, the stick dipped on its own. If he didn't touch me, nothing happened. I could not make that divining stick operate on my own power. Something special was transmitted by that water witch.

Jesse professed a belief that his power was a gift from God. He would not accept payment for using his faculty to help his neighbors. He was afraid that money would negate the spiritual connection and he might loose this incredible ability to locate vital water for his friends.

There they are again, photography and water, in a most unusual situation. They keep combining to steer my destiny.

Not all of my religious type assignments were as dramatic as the water witch story. Some were routine, but provided insights into many forms of religion.

KDKA-TV used to begin every broadcast day with a feature they called "Sermonette." They closed the broadcast day with a similar feature. In order to keep ecumenical balance, the Sermonettes rotated among Protestant ministers, Catholic priests, Jewish rabbis, Orthodox clergy, and other representatives of the religions of the area.

You guessed it ... I filmed all those sermons and edited them for the shows. I was preached to by a dozen or more Catholic priests and a multitude of ministers, rabbis and other clergy. Sometimes it took re-take after re-take to get a satisfactory end result. I started to get religion coming out of my ears. I think I listened to enough sermons and preaching to last me for the rest of my life. They didn't do any harm, and I got a side benefit from all the variety of religious exposure, a mini-education in religious diversity.

It was through some of the religious filming that I made initial contact with producers of the Misterogers Neighborhood children's television program. Few people are aware that Misterogers, Fred Rogers DD, is an ordained clergyman whose ministry is dedicated to broadcasting. His children's programming subtly reflects this ministry. All his shows are wholesome and well based in the positive ethics of society. I'm proud to have been a part of the Misterogers Neighborhood production staff

For some seven or eight years, I filmed all the features that were used on the children's segments. I got quite an education too. The variety of subjects that presented themselves for features on his shows was unlimited.

On one program, a guest appearance by the famous pianist Van Cliburn was scheduled. In anticipation of this show, I traveled to Long Island City, New York, where the Steinway Piano Factory is located. There, a complete film was produced showing all the intricate steps involved in the making of a grand piano. When Van Cliburn was on the program, Mister Rogers simply walked up to his magic picture on the wall and asked it to show how pianos were made. My film then showed this interesting process, from the shaping of the wooden frame, to the insertion of the strings and keyboard.

We did many of these "How is it made" film features. I filmed and learned how all sorts of things were made. Crayons, balloons, luggage, pillows, ice cream, and popsicles were some of the more interesting topics that were covered. In the process of all this filming. I absorbed an education that money couldn't buy. Mister Rogers didn't put films and show features on the air without consultation. Two or three times a week, he conferred with a child psychologist and a pediatric specialist. They would determine if the features were properly presented and in the best interest of the children. No film got on the air without this analysis.

I remember one particular feature that I shot on a merry-go-round. I had gone out of my way to lie on my back for a special angle that dramatically portrayed the children and horses from a different point of view. The wide-angle shots made the horses seem to bound into the camera as they surged up and down while the carousel turned. I was very pleased with the results and subsequently edited a full sequence of this view into the overall film.

The film was rejected by the psychologist. I was told to do the feature over again and leave out the dramatic shots. The wide-angle close-ups of the horses' heads with their open mouths, were judged by the specialist to be too threatening to be viewed by Mister Rogers' young audience. I thought they were neat, but I lacked the perspective of the experts. I had to do the job over again without these threatening scenes.

One fringe benefit of producing films for Misterogers Neighborhood was the exposure it brought. The show was syndicated in some 300 cities throughout the country and was even broadcast in some remote places like American Samoa in the South Pacific. Being involved with such a prestigious and award-winning show carried with it some bragging rights. I remember being in New York one day, doing a film for a national corporation. The president invited me to his home for dinner after the filming.

Upon arrival at his home, I found his children in the television room watching Misterogers. I was familiar with the episode and was able to tell them to watch for a special film on the magic picture. When it came up as I had predicted, and the father saw my name credits at the end of the show, my prestige level was raised a few points with his company. Some future work came as a result of this exposure.

There was a very special job that came about through religious associations. I had the opportunity to travel to the Holy Land with the Council of Churches and produce a film entitled "Light For Many Lamps." This film centers on the three major religions of the world, Judaism, Christianity and Islam, and their intersecting focal point in Jerusalem and the surrounding holy lands.

The airline that carried the Council of Churches group to the Holy Land was T.W.A. A side arrangement was made with their public relations department to also produce a promotional film for them. It was to be called T.W.A. (That Wonderful Airplane) and it incorporated lots of flying footage intermixed with other scenes of the trip.

Because of this arrangement with the airline, I had the opportunity to fly much of the trip in the cockpit with the pilot, co-pilot, and flight engineer. There's no comparison between the view the passenger gets from a window seat and the vast panoramic view available from the cockpit.

The Alps were spectacular. We flew over these magnificent mountains on a crystal clear afternoon. Taken from the unobstructed vantage point of the front window, at an altitude of about 30 thousand feet, my aerial film of the snow-capped peaks and vast chain of mountains was priceless. Other European landmarks photographed equally well from the air as we passed over them on our way to Jerusalem, where many inspirational experiences awaited as I began filming "Light For Many Lamps".

In many ways, this movie is like a religious travel film. Although it contains many beautiful and enlightening scenes, it's not particularly outstanding, except for one thing. It is the last commercial film that is known to have been produced in Jerusalem prior to the 6 day Arab-Israeli war that significantly changed the face of that area.

I had an opportunity to see the problem from both the Arab and Israeli points of view. The ideological conflicts seemed irresolvable. But this chapter is not about war, it's about religion. I'd like to share some of my inner feelings about the Holy Land with you.

First of all, one of the most sacred places in Jerusalem for those like me, who embrace the Christian faith, is the Church of the Holy Sepulcher. This huge basilica is erected on the traditional site of the hill of Calvary, where Jesus was crucified on Good Friday. This massive church, and the area around it, proved to be the biggest disappointment of the entire trip.

The myriad sects and orders of religious congregations who jointly operate this immense facility have turned it into a hodgepodge of confusion and disorder. Candle sellers, holy oil peddlers, souvenir purveyors, hustlers, guides, and religious extremists all combine to turn the church into a carnival-like setting. This atmosphere certainly does not portray the reverence that should be afforded a shrine of this magnitude.

Furthermore, the surrounding area is filled with the cacophony of peddlers. It abounds with small, dirty shops with vendors of everything from fresh-killed meat and vegetables, to brass trinkets and soda pop. I was so disgusted with the lack of sanctity around this holy place that I included almost none of it in my final film production.

In marked contrast to the Church of the Holy Sepulcher, I found the Garden of Gethsemane an extremely reverent site. I experienced some deep emotional moments while filming here. The feelings went even deeper on Holy Thursday evening, when I returned for special vigil services at the Church Of All Nations, located in the center of the garden. I was able to climb, unobserved, over a protective fence around the garden and get away from all the tourists and visitors.

Alone in the dark amid these ancient, gnarled olive trees and massive rocks, whose antiquity truly dates back to the time of Christ, I lost all contact with the modern world. I let my mind wander and visualized scenes from 2000 years ago. This was the garden where Jesus experienced his agony before being betrayed by Judas the night before his crucifixion. If only these trees or these rocks could talk. What a story they could reveal. History took on vivid proportions in that solitary and impressive setting.

In my mind, I relived the events that occurred in this place so many years before. I recalled that Jesus had asked his disciples to stay awake and pray with him, but they had fallen asleep. I myself felt somewhat tired from a long day of travel and filming, so I had a better understanding of their human frailty.

It was difficult to imagine an angry mob invading this serene garden to arrest such a peaceful man. Some things my mind just didn't want to accept. But to keep pace with history, it was necessary to go forward, beyond Gethsemane.

Now the mood shifts from serenity to pandemonium. The next day, Good Friday, masses of people from all parts of the world flock to Jerusalem. They come to commemorate one of the holiest days of the Christian year, the day of the crucifixion of Jesus.

Along the "Via Dolorosa," the Way of the Cross, or the route taken by Jesus as he carried his cross to Calvary, Christians of all denominations gather to observe or take part in the many cross-carrying processions.

It is a deep religious experience. It's also nerve-wracking and extremely rough on anyone who tries to display any kind of common decency or manners. Pushing and shoving are the rules of the day. Swarms and swarms of people just keep converging on the area. At times it is impossible to move in any direction except to be swept along with the crowd.

Into this sea of people I plunged, camera in hand, determined to record on film the pageantry and religious fervor that permeated the activities. I was not prepared for the enormity of the throng. Initially, I was shocked by the blatant rudeness of almost everyone involved. However, once I learned the rules of behavior, I played the same game. Leaving my manners behind me, I pushed and shoved as well as or better than the rest. Finally, I maneuvered into a position where I could at least see what was going on.

Many groups were gathering at the beginning of the Via Dolorosa, wearing costumes and uniforms from ancient Roman times. They carried all kinds of props and life-sized crosses for the procession through the narrow passageways in this section of Old Jerusalem. I could see this activity as they started to assemble, but couldn't shoot any desirable film because of being jammed, elbow to elbow, with the rest of the mob.

Then I tried a little trick, and it worked. Above the street area there was a small terrace that afforded an overlook of the procession area. A number of privileged people had stationed themselves on this terrace, immune from the crushing masses below. They were not about to let anyone else interfere with their chosen location.

In my camera case, I had an old TV Photographer armband that was left over from filming the U.S. Open Golf tournament at Oakmont, Pa. sometime earlier. I placed that armband on my right arm and approached one of the young men who was guarding the terrace wall. I showed him the armband and my camera and said: "American Television". Those were the magic words. He grabbed my hand and pulled me up onto the terrace. He forced a path among the assembled dignitaries, calling out "American Television" while he maneuvered me into the best position on the overlook.

From this excellent location I obtained some spectacular shots of the pageantry below. Devout pilgrims in complete authentic costumes, and carrying life-sized crosses, processed along the Via Dolorosa in commemoration of the day of the crucifixion of Jesus. I was able to capture the entire panorama without obstruction. When these scenes were edited in conjunction with the shots taken within the crowd at ground level, the ultimate result was a feeling of actual participation in the pageant as the film was viewed.

By coincidence, the cover of Life Magazine that following week portrayed the identical shot of the Good Friday procession that I had on my movie film. It was taken from the same camera angle. The Life photographer must have been within a few feet of me, but I never saw him. I was too busy getting my own filming completed and being grateful for that old armband from the golf tournament.

Another section of Jerusalem piqued my interest when I visited there. On the site of Caiphas' palace, where Jesus was taken to be tried by the Jewish high priest, a large church now stands. It was built in memory of the apostle Peter, who had denied knowing Jesus in the palace courtyard, and then wept bitterly when he realized what he had done.

In the archeological excavation beneath the church, a dungeon had been uncovered. It is believed that Jesus was imprisoned in this dungeon from Holy Thursday night until Good Friday morning when he was sentenced to be crucified.

At the far end of this underground jail a small altar was erected in memory of the imprisonment of Jesus. It would have taken an entire truckload of movie lights to properly illuminate this vast catacomb, but I used a trick that I mentioned in a previous chapter.

(Remember the Private War of Henry Bursztynowicz?) I got some dramatic coverage of that dungeon site using that lighting technique. With the camera running, and on wide-angle lens, I moved my one portable movie light along the adjacent corridor. As the beam passed by the many columns and openings in the cells, the exaggerated shadows moved and created an eerie change as the illumination shifted towards the altar at the end of the corridor and remained on the altar for the conclusion of the scene. This resulted in a most dramatic coverage of a solemn location that deserved such a special effect. Imagination takes over while viewing this scene and the impact of Jesus' imprisonment becomes most vivid.

Perhaps this film was destined to be dramatic and impressive. Witness the cooperation of the weather. During the month of April, the majority of the days in Jerusalem, are sunny and warm, conducive to excellent photography. I had superb weather for almost all of my filming.

One exception was an unexplained storm that passed over Jerusalem on the eve of Good Friday. The rumbling, dark clouds were ominous and threatening. They gave a somber appearance to the panorama of the city. Filming this strange storm as it passed over the city set the mood for the solemn coverage of the following Good Friday events. Other than this one depressing evening, the weather was perfect. Could it be that something provided me with this one storm just to set the proper mood for the Good Friday film? Or should I merely say, "I'd rather be lucky than good" one more time?

One other impression of Jerusalem stands out in my memory: Easter Sunday morning at "The Garden Tomb." This sepulcher, hewn out of solid rock and located in a garden setting, is not the actual tomb where Jesus was laid to rest. It is similar to the biblical descriptions of Jesus' tomb, including the huge stone at the entrance. Filming this gravesite on Easter morning lent itself to some more fantasy about what really happened some 2000 years ago. I began to experience the sensations of wonder about how the great stone was rolled back on the day of the Resurrection.

After spending Holy Thursday in the Garden of Gethsemane and Good Friday along the Way of the Cross, the Holy Week grand finale was Easter morning at the Garden Tomb. The Christian portion of this film was thoroughly covered.

Once out of Jerusalem after Holy Week was ended, there were opportunities to cover other regions of the Holy Land with less crowd interference. Many of these places left lasting impressions on my memory. I'll try to share some of them with you as this chapter continues.

Bethlehem, Nazareth, Jericho, the River Jordan and the Sea of Galilee all have special references in biblical history. They were all covered on this film journey. Each was met with mixed emotions about what I thought they should be and what they actually were. I found a strange mixture of religious fervor and hustling salesmanship.

I got a chance to climb down into an archeological dig at the site of the discovery of the old walled city of Jericho. Once again my imagination had an opportunity to run wild as I descended through 5000 to 7000 years of historical levels, filming as I went. Stories of Joshua and how the walls came "tumbling down" created fantasies in my mind. I recalled old Bible stories from my youth and applied them to my current experience.

Another fascinating place was the Dead Sea. With a little check of geography, you'll find that the River Jordan flows a continuing downhill course from the Sea of Galilee until it empties into the Dead Sea at an elevation of some 1300 feet below sea level. The Dead Sea has no outlet. It eliminates the excess water by the process of evaporation. The saturation of salt and other minerals remaining dissolved and suspended in the waters of the Dead Sea is extremely high, 26 percent.

It is an unusual experience to attempt to swim through this water. It is so thick, each arm stroke feels like it is pulling through some kind of syrup. Floating on this water is another unique experience. Years ago, a scientist named Archimedes determined that an object immersed in a liquid is buoyed-up by a force equal to the weight of the liquid that it displaces. More simply put, a body immersed in the Dead Sea displaces much more water than its own weight. Floating is extremely easy. While laying on my back, I was able to raise my arms, legs and head out of the water and still remain afloat.

The one mistake that I made (two mistakes, actually) was opening my eyes underwater. the concentration of salt and minerals burned my eyes severely. I should also have controlled my urge to taste the water. It was horrible. Even with these two disappointments, I'm glad I had the experience of swimming in the Dead Sea. I'll never forget it. Photography and Water, I knew they'd get back together again before I got too much further along.

My other adventure in the Dead Sea area didn't include any water, although I soon began to wish that it had.

Author floats in Dead Sea with arms, legs and head out of the water.

Sometime in the 1950s, a shepherd boy tending his flocks in the hills surrounding the Dead Sea, followed a stray sheep into a cave. He made a discovery that was to send religious scholars into a tizzy. There, in a corner of the cave, was a sealed, ceramic earthen jar. Inside this ancient urn, a rolled-up parchment was discovered. When the ignorant shepherd boy took this jar and parchment to an antique dealer in Jerusalem, he was paid a paltry amount for this treasure. He had unknowingly upset the apple-cart of religious history. This find started an intense search throughout the entire Dead Sea area for more of these artifacts.

Other caves were discovered and other sealed jars found. Investigation revealed that these parchments were the preserved records of a tribe of people known as the Essenes. They were a remote Jewish sect who occupied the village of Quumran, along the shores of the Dead Sea. These people lived a monastic life and devoted their time to recording the religious history of their era. This dated back many years before the time of Christ. The discovery of the Dead Sea Scrolls made worldwide headlines both in religious publications and in the media of the lay world as well. They contained contradictions in the scriptures that will puzzle scholars for years to come.

Here I was at the ancient village of Quumran, filming the restoration of the site. Off in the distance, in the hills, I could see the caves that were pointed out by our guide as the location of the shepherd's discovery. I wasn't satisfied with just photographing the hills and caves from a distance, I wanted to go up to them and film, close-up, the actual site of this amazing find.

It didn't seem like too far of a walk. I set out with camera and a couple of rolls of film and started my trek across this arid dessert land. I had the idea that I'd get up to the caves in less than an hour, shoot two rolls of film and be back in plenty of time to join the tour group before they departed Quumran for other destinations.

Sometimes you have to learn things the hard way. There are erosions in the ground in this part of the world that are known as wadis. They are deep gullies and depressions in the land that have been washed out by long-gone rainstorms. These wadis were not visible as I looked across the desert towards the distant hills. However, as I walked along, I soon encountered these obstructions and found that each one delayed my progress. It was necessary to descend the steep hillside of the gully and climb up the opposite bank to continue my walk. I was eager to get to the caves and was not about to let these wadis deter me. In my eagerness, I overlooked the fact that each wadi was slowing my progress and increasing my overall exposure to the desert sun and dehydration.

I reached the caves after much delay and got some spectacular footage from within the entrance, showing the interior where the jars were found. Then, walking and changing exposures as I moved, I did a traveling camera shot from within the cave to the exitway, revealing the panorama of the desert and the Dead Sea in one continuous sequence. I was glad that I had made the effort to obtain this footage. Now the problem was getting back.

In my haste to get to the caves and shoot the film, I had not thought to provide myself with any water or liquid nourishment. I had just experienced how harsh the desert could be. Excitement had gotten me this far, now something had to get me back. Sheer determination was all that was left. I was damn thirsty and my mouth was parched and dry. I always hated hats, so I had no protection for my head. The afternoon sun was brutal and not obstructed by any clouds. I had foolishly created this situation for myself and there was no one to get me out of it. Down the hill I descended, into the desert and back in the direction of the waiting bus.

The same thing that happens to the waters of the Dead Sea was happening to the moisture remaining in my body. It was evaporating. I knew I was sweating from the heat, but my body was dry. As fast as the sweat would break forth from my body, this desert, 1300 feet below sea level, would absorb it like a giant blotter. Before I got halfway back, my energy was starting to ebb and I began to wonder if I was going to make it. As I climbed up the side of one of the remaining wadis, my eyes beheld a most welcome sight. One of the older men in the tour, concerned about my safety, had left the group and hiked out into the desert to meet me. He had the sense to bring along a can of orange soda pop.

That orange pop tasted like champagne and I don't think I was ever so glad to see anyone in my life. The renewed energy and hydration gained from the can of soda enabled me to complete the trek back without any further difficulty. An angry group of tourists greeted my return. I had caused them to be delayed in this desolate spot for hours longer than they were scheduled. Also, they were genuinely concerned for my safety and didn't need that kind of aggravation to spoil their tour. They had been indulgent in previous days with small delays in their schedule to accommodate my filming, but this had gone too far. I had to solemnly promise that I would be a good boy for the remainder of the tour and not cause them any more worry.

I managed to refrain from any further actions that would cause irritation to my traveling companions during the remainder of our stay in this half of Jerusalem. As a matter of fact, I won them over again without even realizing it. They were overcome with emotion by a departing scene that transpired as we were leaving the Mount of Olives. The story requires a little set-up for complete understanding:

The overview of Jerusalem is spectacular from the Mount of Olives. The "Dome of the Rock," an elaborate Moslem mosque, dominates the skyline, its golden dome glistening in the afternoon sun. To capture this view on film, I wanted more than just a static scene.

I found my gimmick in a Moslem Arab who drove his small donkey along the "Palm Sunday Road," giving rides to tourists. At my request, this Arab rode his donkey along the upper ridge of the mount while I filmed him. The panorama of the city below was automatically seen behind him, while the colorfully garbed Arab remained the center of attention. The man's name was Mohammed Abdul Ghannam, and he proved to be a most interesting individual. We struck up a friendship after I filmed his ride. He spoke fairly good English and we were able to engage in some lengthy conversations. I learned a great deal about the Middle-Eastern culture from our talks. He invited me to his home for dinner, and a following night, asked me to bring along some of the others from the tour. I learned more about Arab-Israeli relations from Mohammed than I did from all the propaganda that is officially thrown out by the guides and government representatives.

We talked into the wee hours of the night, discussing our various cultures and customs. He was amazed at our differences in courtship. It was almost impossible for him to fathom how a boy in America could ask a girl for a date, take her out unchaperoned, talk openly with her, dance with her and, heaven forbid, even kiss her goodnight after the date.

His culture forbade him to speak to a girl in public. He explained further: He knew when he wanted to get married. He had seen a particular girl in the marketplace shopping for groceries. He knew her name, but was prohibited from talking to her. He went to his parents and informed them of his intentions. His parents, in turn, approached the girl's parents to make arrangements for betrothal. Before these arrangements could be finalized, the girl's parents contacted all their relatives to see if any of her cousins wanted her. When no cousin claimed the right to marriage, the girl was pronounced available and wedding plans were made.

The wedding plans included payment by Mohammed to the girl's father of money, animals, or some other item of value. In return, the girl came into the marriage complete with all her clothes, dishes, and household furnishings.

He went on to tell of his wedding night which was certainly different from Western customs. His reception was held in a two-story building that had a private room adjacent to a second floor balcony. When it was time to consummate his marriage. he and the bride retired to this upper room, accompanied by the bride's mother. The mother remained in the room with a ceremonial white cloth, waiting for the act of consummation to take place.

When the bride was penetrated, and bleeding from her lost virginity occurred, the mother captured this blood on the white ceremonial cloth and went out on the balcony to display this cloth to the guests below. This was ceremonial proof that they had presented a virgin to this wedding. Their integrity was preserved. Only then did the bride and groom have the privacy of the wedding bed.

We discussed Arab-Israeli differences too. Mohammed had lost an eye in the 1948 conflict. He explained that most of the average Moslems and Jews were able to live and work together in the same villages. When the Jews had a special affair, many of their Arab neighbors were invited to their homes. The same circumstances occurred with Arab celebrations. Radicals and zealots, he explained, were at the core of the problems, not the average Jewish or Arab people. Our political and social discussions continued long into the night. In addition to being a charming host and interesting conversationalist, Mohammed also helped me with some additional filming work during the following days. It was no wonder that I had some special feelings of regret at saying farewell to this congenial man.

As our group was boarding the bus to depart for Israel, Mohammed came by on his donkey to say goodbye. It was an emotional scene. We had become such good friends in such a short time. Now, circumstances would probably part us forever. In the intensity of this emotion, I said to him, "In our country, we have a saying that if you like a man well enough, you will give him the shirt off your back." With this, I removed a sweater that I was wearing and handed it to him. He began to cry and hug me, asking why I was doing this. My only reply was to inform him that, when the wind blew coldly up on this Mount of Olives, it would give me pleasure to know that something of mine was providing him with some measure of comfort and warmth.

Mohammed tearfully released me from our embrace and walked over to his donkey that was tied up next to the bus. He cut off the brass bell that was around the donkey's neck, brought it over and handed it to me. His wish was that each time I heard the tinkling of this little bell, I would get a warm glow remembering our friendship.

The other members of our tour had witnessed this emotional departure and were crying with me as I entered the bus and waved a final salute to this interesting man. I think I was forgiven for past transgressions and the worry I had caused them back at the Dead Sea. It's a good thing I got back into their good graces, because I was going to cause them some more anxiety within the hour.

At this point in time, just before the Six Day War, Jerusalem was a divided city. Half of Jerusalem was controlled by the country of Jordan and the other half was occupied by Israel. A no-man's land lay between the two halves of the city. Passage from one side to the other was a diplomatic process involving the Mandelbaum Gate.

We were departing Jerusalem, Jordan and entering Jerusalem, Israel. Guides were processing our passports and travel documents through various customs and immigration officials at this gate.

While all this red tape was being transacted, I happened to observe that a magnificent church building over on the Israeli side had sand bags and gun emplacements in many of its windows. The site of military armament in this great church building intrigued me,

We were passing through the no-man's land between the two sides of the Mandelbaum Gate when I affixed a telephoto lens to my movie camera and proceeded to shoot some close-up shots of the gun emplacements and sand bags in the church windows. Suddenly, a loudspeaker blared out in Hebrew. An angry voice was saying something that I couldn't understand. But the guide understood only too well. He shouted, "For God's sake, George, put that camera down. They've got machine guns aimed at us and will shoot if you don't".

I didn't need any further persuasion. The camera dropped like a stone. I humbly retreated to the opposite gate with no sign of any further intention to shoot film. I'll never forget the look I got from the rest of the group. The previous day I had delayed and annoyed them. Today I had caused them real fear. I had a lot of making-up to do with this group in order to get back on their good side. I tried to behave myself and earn their forgiveness.

I almost behaved myself, but there was one other thing that I had to do while in Israel that was a little bit unorthodox. In Jerusalem, Israel there is a museum called the Shrine of the Book. Inside this unusual building, the parchment remains of the Dead Sea Scrolls are displayed. It was possible to view them, but photography is strictly prohibited. Guards maintained vigilant surveillance over the area to enforce this prohibition.

After half killing myself walking through the desert to film the caves where these Dead Sea Scrolls were discovered. I wasn't about- to let a few guards keep me from filming the genuine scrolls.

I devised a simple plan to enable me to get film of the Dead Sea Scrolls inside the Shrine of the Book. What I needed was some cooperation from some of my fellow travelers. This would not be easy. I was on their bad-boy list. Pete Couch, the tour guide, and Donna Allshouse, one of the more congenial members of the group, were willing to help with my scheme.

With my camera loaded and ready to shoot, I placed it in a TWA shoulder bag and casually walked by the guards like any other tourist. As soon as I was beyond the guard nearest to the scrolls, Pete and Donna, on pre-arranged signal, engaged in a discussion that got louder and louder and finally turned into a small argument.

The guard was distracted by the disturbance they were creating. I had just enough time to whip out the camera and quickly secure a series of wide angle and close-up shots of the parchment scrolls and the writing contained thereon. Pete and Donna concluded their fake argument as I slipped the camera back into the TWA bag and went on as if nothing had happened. None of the guards was aware that I had obtained the film. My Dead Sea Scroll sequence was complete. We kept this little episode a secret among the three of us and didn't tell any of the rest of the group about our little stunt.

After the previous problems, we didn't think they would be tolerant of any more upsetting circumstances.

There was one other thing that happened in Israel that got the group mildly disturbed. I got into an argument with a stubborn waiter in the dining room of the Tel Aviv Sheraton Hotel. I had just enjoyed a good meal, which included a meat entree. Coffee was being served following the meal. In Israel, most of the coffee they use comes from Africa. It is black, bitter, and very strong. I wanted to dilute my coffee with cream so that I could enjoy my drink.

The waiter refused to serve me cream for my coffee because I had eaten meat. When I asked him the reason, he said that it was a religious law. "So what" I replied, "I'm not Jewish, so why won't you serve me cream for this bitter coffee ?" He replied that I had to comply with their religious laws. I didn't buy that argument. I told him that I was Catholic and my religion prohibited eating meat on Fridays. However, if he was a guest in my house on Friday and wanted meat, I would serve it to him. Why wouldn't he serve me the cream that I wanted ? We had reached a stalemate. He shrugged his shoulders, pointed to the table where the cream was kept and told me to get it for myself. To everyone's shock, I got up, walked over to the table, and got the cream. They all pretended not to know me, but at least I was finally able to enjoy this bitter coffee.

Author dons appropriate garb for dinner in Arab home.

Someone later said that he probably had to break all of the dishes that I had used because of a violation of the kosher laws. I hope that was not necessary. I didn't want to cause so much trouble, just enjoy a cup of coffee. I still do not think it is proper for any person to push a facet of his religion upon anyone else. I deeply respect the Jewish religion and many of its precepts. Just don't try to force anything on me against my will.

A guide later told me that economics plays a large role in keeping things kosher in the large hotels. Wealthy Jews, who visit Israel for a religious pilgrimage, expect everything there to be like it is written in their Talmud. Any establishment that does not keep strict observance of these rules risks the loss of business. Another lesson was learned. You can't always judge a book by its cover.

One event occurred in Israel that was a highlight for me. I'm glad no one on the tour knew about it, or they would have disowned me for sure.

We traveled to the Mediterranean seaside resort city of Caesarea. This is the city where Pontius Pilate maintained his summer residence while he was governor of Judea in Biblical times. After touring and filming general scenes of this city's relics and ruins, I had a free day to do some scuba diving in the Mediterranean. Just water this time, no photography. I needed a break from all that filming work.

We were quartered in a rural villa that was several miles front the city and the seashore. I wanted to get to the sea and locate a dive shop. A happy and optimistic attitude can be contagious, I've probably spent 90 percent of my life with a smile on my face. This made a good impression on the Israeli guide and on the driver of our bus. I had made good friends with them during our tour, and now asked them how I could get a taxi for transportation to the seashore.

"You don't need any taxi," they replied. "We have the bus at our disposal." So they took a 50-passenger bus and used it for my private taxi as they transported me to Haim Stav's Dive Shop. There I made arrangements to dive into the sunken harbor of Caesarea, a section of the city that had sunk into the sea after an ancient earthquake.

The proprietor quoted me a price for the dive equipment. All of a sudden, I heard a banter of Hebrew being exchanged between my guide and the shop owner. Finally, he returned to me with a new price quote. It seems that he had originally quoted me an inflated "tourist" rate. My guide and the bus driver had jumped all over him. They explained that I was their friend and entitled to the "local" rate. They also suggested that the proprietor accompany me on a dive tour of the sunken city.

The underwater excursion was most interesting. Sections of houses and building walls still remain intact. They have been preserved throughout centuries beneath the sea. Street areas could be determined from patterns of buildings and their alignments. There were no roofs, just walls and floors remaining. It was possible to swim into the building remains and search for artifacts.

My eyes spotted the outline of a ceramic vial that was half imbedded in the ocean floor, a portion of its shape exposed above the sand. With my diver's knife, I carefully started to dig around this small vial in an effort to dislodge it from the ocean floor without damage.

It was tedious work, requiring extreme patience.

The vial was about five inches long and had a rounded bottom, a bit larger than a golf ball. This rounded base narrowed to a three-inch stem with a delicate pouring lip on the end. Painstaking care was exercised as I dug all around it. When I thought everything was clear, I gently pried underneath to extract it from the hard sand and coral. Everything came free except the little pouring lip. It disintegrated as I removed the rest of the bottle intact.

When the dive was over and we returned to the shop, the proprietor asked me what I was going to do with my little vial. Of course I wanted to keep it. It was my treasure, found and carefully extracted from the sunken city. I wanted to take it home. He informed me that I had better be careful and not let any authorities learn that I was retaining it. It seems that Israel had a law protecting all archeological finds as treasures of the State. There were stiff penalties for anyone who would try to remove these treasures from Israel.

Armed with this knowledge, I wrapped my little bottle in several layers of toilet paper and carefully secreted it in my camera case for transportation home. Had my companions learned that they were traveling with an international smuggler, they would surely have vented their wrath upon me. However, I just didn't tell anyone, and what they didn't know didn't hurt me.

With all my focus on the Holy Land stories, I passed over the fact that we made stops in Beirut, Lebanon and Damascus, Syria enroute to Jerusalem. A couple of recollections from this area prompt me to include them at this point.

At that time, the city of Beirut was enjoying peace and prosperity. I found it to be a beautiful jewel in the mid-eastern world. Panoramic views that I shot from hilltop vantage points can never be duplicated. Many of the splendid buildings, churches, and edifices of unique mid-eastern architecture have since been reduced to rubble. Bombing, shelling, and the strife of a bitter civil war have erased their existence. Even if peace is restored to the city once more, they will never be able to replace the grandeur that I was privileged to see and photograph.

Our group then traveled by bus from Beirut to Damascus, over the Lebanese mountains where Arab sheiks kept their private harems. At a halfway point along the bus route, a rest stop was made by a small village store. As the group departed from the bus, We were greeted by a young Arab boy about 12 years old. He was selling Chicklets chewing gum to the passengers and he spoke English reasonably well. While others passed him by, I was fascinated by his command of the English language and stopped to talk with him.

English, he explained, is the second language taught in all the local schools. He was mastering the language quite well. When I asked him what he wanted to do when he grew up, his reply astonished me. I still get a cold lump in my stomach each time I remember his words.

"Sir", he explained, " I would like to learn English well enough so that I can come to your country one day and study medicine. My village has no doctor and I would like to care for my neighbors who are ill." Then he added, "But first I must grow strong enough to take up a gun, kill the Jews and drive them from my land."

I couldn't believe I was hearing these bitter words of hate coming from such a young and intelligent boy. There was absolutely no doubt about his sincerity. He really meant what he was saying. I admonished him to concentrate on his noble ambition to become a doctor and not get involved in the conflict between Jew and Arab that was poisoning his young mind. I don't know if my words did any good. I can only hope they made some impression to counter all the prejudice to which he had been exposed in his village, from family, friends and neighbors. Hatred is a viscous evil.

Jews and Arabs have had their disagreements for centuries. I don't suppose the opinion of one boy will make too much difference in the overall scheme of things. Still, one never knows how a young boy's early impressions will form his later years. I hoped I had made some positive contribution to a small spark of peace in that area. These hopes continued with me as we departed the mid-east and headed for new countries.

The next chapter will cover tales of Athens and Rome.

CHAPTER ELEVEN
ATHENS AND ROME

Author throws Three Coins into Trevi Fountain to assure return to Rome.

Departing from Jerusalem and the surrounding holy land, this group was not immediately returning to the United States. They were continuing on to Greece, Italy and Portugal. A few things happened along the way that might be worthy of note.

First of all, remember the sincere friendships that I had made, in Jerusalem with Mohammed, and in Israel with Jacob and Izzy, the guide and bus driver who were so good to me. Our next stop was Athens, and this naive cinematographer was still bubbling over with the spirit of friendship. I was ripe for the picking.

The first day in Athens, I filmed some of the city highlights, including the Parthenon and the famous historical ruins of the old world. Following a successful day of movie work, I managed to take time for a short swim in the Aegean Sea before returning to downtown Athens. There were no shower facilities at the Gylfada beach where I swam, so I just dried off in the sun. I had a coating of salty, evaporated sea water on my skin as I headed for my hotel and a fresh shower.

With camera and snorkeling gear in hand I was about to cross Constitution Square. While I was waiting for the traffic light to change, a man walked up beside me and asked if I was an American. I replied, "Yes."

He went on, in an extremely friendly way, to tell me that he had been in America and loved our country. Furthermore, he suggested, he could be of assistance to me here in Athens. Knowing that I was staying at a big hotel on the square, he advised that food and drinks were very expensive at my hotel. He said that he had a friend who owned a little place across the square where the prices were more reasonable. He invited me to come with him and meet his friend.

Remembering my recent experiences with good, friendly people, I eagerly accompanied him to his friend's cafe. The initial greeting was great. Everyone seemed interested in learning about my filming in Jerusalem. I became the center of attention. His friend bought me a beer and we sat down at a little table for some more conversation while we drank. My guard was down and I expected nothing but friendship from these nice people.

A girl who had been at another table joined our small group. Then, one by one, my new friends excused themselves for other duties. I found myself alone at the table with this girl. I had a drink. She had nothing. She sheepishly asked if I would mind if she had a drink. Unsuspecting, I ordered a drink for the girl. When the waiter appeared with a bottle of champagne, lights started to go off in my head. I was being taken by the old "B" Girl trap. It had been sprung so slickly that I didn't realize my gullibility until it was too late.

The monetary shock was soon to be felt. The inflated price of this phoney champagne was 1,000 drachmas. My guard went up instinctively.

The girl, meanwhile, was doing her job well. She started to cuddle up to me in the privacy of the alcove where our table was located. In an attempt to kiss my cheek, she tasted the salt residue from the Agean Sea that remained on my skin. This seemed to turn her on. She continued licking my cheeks, my neck, and the exposed parts of my arms. She was very sensuous and I must admit that this activity was not unpleasant. However, I held my ground against her invitation to take me to her room. Furthermore, I refused to allow her to order any more of the phony champagne. She soon lost interest in me and the friendship withered away to a curt excuse for a farewell. My only problem now was to pay the 1,000 drachmas. I didn't have that kind of money with me.

The little "friendly" cafe just happened to have a bouncer whose name was Hercules. He looked like the character for which he was named. This muscleman personally accompanied me back to my hotel where I cashed some travelers checks and paid him for the champagne.

Needless to say, I was upset. I had seen "B" girls work in New York, Chicago, and even Pittsburgh. Never before had I seen such a "sting" operate under the guise of phony friendship. The hair on the back of my neck wouldn't go back down. I had to find some way to get even for this outrage.

First, I used the camera. The next day, I made a very obvious appearance outside the cafe. I made a point of being observed filming the place from every angle. The manager came out to inquire about what I was doing. I told him I was making an expose for American television to warn future tourists about the Athens trap. When I turned the camera in his direction, he covered his face and retreated back into the cafe. I knew he would tell the owner and word would get around that they were under photographic scrutiny.

My next angle was to obtain assistance from our Greek guide. It was my plan for him to contact someone at the cafe. He was to inform them that he could talk me out of my crusade to publicly expose them if only they would repay the 1,000 drachmas that they had swindled from me. I even gave him the reel of exposed film, telling him he could sell the film to them for 1,000 drachmas and I'd call it even.

He was chicken. He feared the organized clique of procurers and pimps that control the vices of downtown Athens. My plan was too bold for his participation.

I had to find some other way to get revenge on these leeches who prey on innocent and gullible visitors. One stroll around Constitution Square was enough to open my eyes to what was going on.

To find out about the way they preyed upon their victims, I spent a night cruising the square. Soon their method of operating became quite obvious. First, someone would approach you with that fake friendship routine. When that didn't work, the next step was to offer to get a girl for you. If that failed to hook you, they would offer perverted sex, drugs, or whatevei they thought might induce you to do business with them With each new contact, the phony friendship routine was always the door opener.

Once I saw how their game was played and I became familiar with the basic rules, I devised a plan of my own. I was going to beat them at their own game.

Diagonally across the main avenue from where I was staying, there was another first class hotel, the King George, a very elaborate edifice. I learned that, at check-out time, hotel quests sometimes left their room keys sticking out of the locks in the doors. It was a simple matter to walk through the upper corridors of the big hotel and locate a door with a key sticking out of the lock. It didn't take any exceptional skill to remove one of these keys without being observed. The keys at the King George were very ornamental. They had a large crown affixed to the head of the key. Somehow, one of those keys found its way into my pocket.

The remainder of the plan seemed simple enough. On the final night that we were in Athens, I fabricated a story that I thought might intrigue these smooth operators on Constitution Square. My fairy tale told of a blonde American girl who was staying with my group at the King George. According to my story, she sometimes drank too much and had run short of money. She tried to borrow from me but I did not have enough to lend her. She was desperate and said she would do anything to get out of her financial difficulties. I advised my tour guide, Pete Couch, of my plan, and he agreed to cooperate.

The final night in Athens, Pete and I walked Constitution Square with this invented story carefully rehearsed. I had the King George hotel key in my coat pocket. The plan was to sell this key to one of the pimps on the proposition that he could negotiate a working arrangement with our desperate girlfriend. Numerous prospects approached us throughout the evening, but we met with one unforeseen obstacle. The pimps weren't about to buy a pig in a poke. They wanted to see the blonde, whom we had named Donna, then they would deal. The plan seemed to be slipping away. Furthermore, Pete was just doing this for a lark. He didn't have the burning desire for revenge that I had. Finally, he became pessimistic about the whole idea and left me on my own.

I experienced no further success on the square and was about to call it quits when I decided to try an adjacent side street. Bingo! I hit pay dirt. A tall, thin man approached me with the same phony friendship routine. I should have gotten an academy award for my acting. Playing my role even better without Pete. I knew I was getting somewhere when the pimp asked if Donna would go out in a car. I told him he would have to ask her himself, I was just a messenger. When I showed him the hotel key with its attached crown, he started taking the bait.

But the game was not over. I had to make the sale. My first mistake was in only asking for 1,000 drachmas. I now got initiated into old fashioned horse trading. The man balked at this amount, reached into his pocket and brought out some money to show me that he didn't have that much cash. I knew I was going to sell the key, now the only problem was to get my asking price. We hemmed and hawed over the price for a couple of minutes and I finally agreed on 500 drachmas and sold him the key.

Now I had another problem. He wanted me to accompany him to Donna's room. My acting won another Oscar. Feigning boredom with the entire deal, and stating that I was tired and needed a drink, I suggested that I would wait in a small cafe adjacent to where we were doing our bargaining. He could go up to Donna's room meet her and make his deal in private. The guy bought my plan, paid the 500 drachmas, took the big key and headed toward the King George, while I entered the cafe where he thought I'd be waiting for them to return.

As soon as I saw him enter the front door of the King George, I beat it out the side door of that cafe and made a beeline for my own hotel. I exchanged the drachmas for U.S. dollars and went straight to my room and locked the door. I called Pete on the hotel phone and cautioned him about not going outside anymore that night. We both realized that once the guy found out he had been burned, he'd probably compare notes with some other pimps and we'd be a target for retaliation. We stayed in our rooms for the remainder of the night and prepared to leave Athens the next morning.

The tour bus that was taking our group to the port that morning was parked around the side of the hotel. I was afraid to walk out the front door, up the main street, and around the corner to the bus. Fear of being spotted by one of the pimps forced an alternate plan. Borrowing a hat from one of the other members of the tour, I found a side exit through the hotel kitchen that came out right next to the bus. As soon as I knew the bus was about to depart, I exited through this kitchen door, got directly onto the bus, and breathed a sigh of relief as the driver quickly pulled away and headed for the port.

All my companions on the tour bus noticed a distinct change in my attitude. I was happy-go-lucky again, not living under a dark cloud like the last few days. Maybe I had only gotten back 500 drachmas from that clique of vipers, but at least I had some satisfaction in knowing that I wasn't the only one who was stung.

The trip to the port of Piraeus was a welcome relief from the tensions of the big city. The cruise among the Greek Islands was a delightful departure from the metropolis. My filming continued as we docked at the island of Agina, where ruins of a great Greek temple atop this mountainous island could only be viewed by taking a donkey ride to the mountain top. This was an experience many found breathtaking and bum bumping. Filming at the top was worth the bumps, and shooting from the back of the donkey as I rode up the narrow trail, once again gave that "cinema verite" effect that Lets the viewer experience the sensation of taking part in the film.

The cruise through the Straits of Poros was very exciting. The narrow passageway appears to be too small to allow the ship to fit through the channel. All sorts of commercial activity was taking place at the shops along the waterfront within arms reach of the ship as it negotiated this tight course. It was possible to see what the people were buying at the vendors' stands along the wharf as we passed by. The scene that presented itself to my camera looked like a movie set from a time period out of the last century. The ship served as my camera dolly as we sailed by this unique location and on to more of the Greek islands.

Hydra was my favorite of all the islands that we visited. Arriving at the harbor is like sailing into a story book. It looks like something out of Homer's Iliad. A miniature fortress guards the entrance to the harbor and the view is very picturesque. That fort was the subject of at least a thousand snapshots. Everyone on the ship had a camera clicking when we came within shooting range.

Artists from all over the world have found a haven on Hydra, and it's no wonder. Picturesque scenes abound in this retreat. The downtown waterfront is ablaze with color. Pastel shaded buildings with unique architectures make perfect backgrounds for brilliantly colored fishing boats and antique sailing vessels that abound in the clear, blue water of the adjacent bay. The water of the Agean Sea is the clearest, most sparkling blue that I have ever seen. The background mountains cap off this magnificent vista. They seem to beckon the visitor to explore and stay longer. As a diver, I had to explore this crystal clear water, even though our stay on Hydra was going to be brief.

Skin diving gear was all that I had with me on this trip. There was no place on the island to rent air tanks, so my diving was confined to the waters nearer the shore. When I dove down into this clear, blue paradise, it was hard to realize that I was in water. The visibility was almost unlimited. Objects 50 feet below me seemed just beyond my reach.

I soon found out that this clarity could be deceiving. Looking below me, I saw something silver sparkling between the rocks on the ocean bottom. I had more thoughts of treasure. This appeared to be something valuable. I made a surface dive and attempted to reach bottom while holding my breath. I couldn't make it. The water was deeper than I had anticipated. Still, the temptation of that silver object glistening below was too great.

Hyperventilation is a trick that divers learn to allow themselves more time on the bottom in a deep free-dive. The procedure calls for taking several very deep breaths. It is necessary to forcefully inhale all the air your lungs can hold and then exhale with all the strength of your breathing muscles. This deep in and out breathing is repeated several times until the lungs are purged of all excess carbon dioxide and have a capacity for more oxygen-rich air. This greatly extends the amount of time that it is possible to hold one's breath before needing a new supply of air.

I knew about hyperventilation and decided to use this technique to gain additional diving time that would allow me to get deep enough to retrieve the silver object that was tantalizing me from below.

A little knowledge can be a dangerous thing. Using the ventilating procedure, I took that final deep breath and dove deep into the clear blue water towards that glistening object below. Down and down I kicked with all the force of my flippers. The clarity of the water belied its true depth. With a final kicking force, I arrived at the bottom and picked up my treasure. My chest felt like it was going to explode.

How far down was I? Can I make it back to the surface on this one breath? My body felt the pressure and my heart was pounding forcefully from the exertion of getting down that far. Looking back up to the surface, the distance was much more apparent than what was perceived when looking down. I had to get back up there pretty fast. I had the urge to inhale right now, and it was a long way up to that needed breath.

Thankfully, some instinct kept me from panicking and kicking upward with all my might. I found that, as I got closer and closer to the top, my lungs expanded again from the decrease of pressure. The remaining air increased in volume and relieved the unbearable urge to take a breath. When I finally broke through the surface, I was gasping for air and very dizzy. I nearly had a black-out before I got my treasure back to the rocky shore.

Later, I learned that hyperventilation contains a hidden danger that I was not aware of at the time of this dive. The presence of carbon dioxide in our breathing system is the factor that triggers an involuntary reflex that forces us to take another breath. Hyperventilation purges excess carbon dioxide from the lungs and temporarily inhibits that involuntary reflex. The respiratory system is momentarily unaware that it is running out of the necessary oxygen supply for the proper function of the brain. If the person continues holding his breath until the brain's supply of oxygen is exhausted, involuntary black-out can occur.

I hit the border line on this process.

Dizziness, but, thank goodness, no complete black-out. And the treasure that prompted all this effort. I almost don't want to admit what it was.

At various times, on Hydra, religious processions are held. A parade of devout parishioners ascend the cliffs overlooking the ocean for the pageantry of a candle-light ceremony. Participants in the processions carry their candles in silver, hand-held candleholders The younger members have been known to throw their expired candles into the sea, silver holder and all. That's what I risked my life for. Not pure silver, but a silverplated candleholder of no significant value. It was probably thrown into the sea by some young altar boy after the last procession. All that glitters is not .....

One treasure I did obtain on this cruise of the Greek Islands was another good friendship. God knows I needed one, after Athens.

A stewardess from Air France was vacationing in Greece and was on the ship while I was filming. She was having difficulty with her camera and, seeing that I was a professional photographer, asked me for assistance. I managed to find the cause of her camera problem and repair it so she could get the snapshots she wanted.

In the course of conversation while I was repairing her camera, I mentioned that I was heading for Rome. By coincidence, she also was traveling to Rome, but was experiencing difficulty with her arrangements. As an employee of an airline, she was traveling on a pass that was subject to lower priority than a regular passenger ticket.

Henrietta was being "bumped" off her originally scheduled flight from Athens to Rome and was being forced to take a later plane. She was concerned that the hotel in Rome would not hold her reservation beyond the regular check-in time.

When we compared hotel accommodations, we found that my hotel was only one block away from hers. I agreed to contact her hotel when I arrived in Rome, explain her delay and request that they hold her room for a late arrival. I had no further conversation with her as my attention was drawn to a "double rainbow" on the horizon, a phenomenon I had never before experienced. It was breathtaking and provided a perfect finale to my film sequence on the Greek Isles.

Upon arrival in Rome, I took care of Henrietta's hotel arrangements and then went about my business of filming in the Eternal City.

Impressions of Rome are extremely different from actually confronting the city. Externally, I found Rome to be very bland and unexciting. Dull brown colors dominate the construction materials of houses and buildings. I would have liked to have had the commission on the sale of all the dull brown roofing tiles in this city. the general overview of Rome, from a cinematographer's point of view, was boring and monotonous. That's on the outside Inside was just the opposite. I've never seen anything that could rival the exquisite interiors of Roman buildings churches, and even their houses. Artistry sculpture and outstanding interior decorations abound.

Walking the length and breadth of Rome carrying a camera a tripod, and a bag of film slung over your shoulder is an unforgettable experience. Not every building in Rome is dull and drab. As a matter of fact some of the buildings are ridiculously ornate. Along the Tiber River stands the Victor Emmanuel Memorial Building a government edifice that is jokingly known as the "Italian Wedding Cake." It is huge, chalk-white and externally decorated with every kind of sculpture and architectural curly-que that fantasy could imagine. It is also such a heavy building that surveyors report it is gradually sinking a few inches each year. It may ultimately dump itself into the Tiber.

The Castel San Angelo stands across the river at the far end of an ornate bridge. It is dull-brown, in contrast with the chalk-white of the Victor Emmanuel building. It has unusual architecture also and an interplay between the two makes for interesting filming. Colorful excursion boats ply along the Tiber, and help draw the eye to other interesting views of the city as they pass by.

Of course, everyone has seen Vatican City and St. Peter's Basilica, with all the sculptures of various popes adorning the walls of the rotunda. A photographer could spend a lifetime shooting various angles of all that art and splendor. Ordinarily, cameras are forbidden inside the Sistine Chapel, where the world-famous ceiling paintings of Michelangelo astound the eye.

I learned a little trick to circumvent the prohibition on interior filming within the famous buildings. I just purchased large post-cards of the interiors. Using special close-up lenses, I could pan up, down or across the picture card and make the film look like it was actually shot inside the chapel. When these close-ups were incorporated with regular exterior shots in the final editing of the film, the viewer is not aware of the deception. It just looks like I started outside and then went in to continue the film coverage.

The interiors of some of the museums and churches were exquisitely beautiful. The priceless works of art they contained were protected from general photographic coverage unless one paid for an expensive commercial permit. My method of using the post-cards enabled me to include these treasures in my overall film even though time and financial limitations would not permit me to photograph the objects "live" as I would have preferred.

The sculptures impressed me the most. Michelangelo's "David" captivated me. How a man can carve a piece of marble and create such a lifelike image is beyond my comprehension. Jealousy crept into my thoughts. This genius chose to capture the very instant of time before David let fly the rock from his sling and slew Goliath I longed to have the freedom to film that statue in my own way. David's eyes hold the viewer spellbound. They are set looking upward. Tracing the imaginary angle of the eyes, you can mentally measure the height of the oncoming giant Goliath. The firm set of the mouth, the clenched teeth, taught muscles and tendons in the neck, arms and legs, all convey that feeling of imminent action as the sling is poised for release. Imagination takes over. For a brief moment, as you view this masterpiece, a replay of the battle forms in your mind and you can actually feel the electricity of that moment in history.

Michelangelo was truly a genius and I feel blessed to have seen, close up, some of his master works. Someday, maybe I'll go back and get the permits necessary to film these works in my own way. I think I could employ techniques that would make them come alive for my viewers.

Rome has so much beauty and art. I could only touch on the highlights within the financial and time limits of my tour. One of these highlights was the Trevi Fountain. Everyone who comes to Rome has to see and photograph Trevi. Actually, I was quite disappointed with this famous landmark. Upon arrival in the area where the fountain is located, I found it to be cramped into narrow, close quarters in a rather unimpressive, dirty, commercial section of the city.

It took the use of a wide-angletelephoto zoom lens to make this famous fountain look good in the films. When filmed with the wide-angle setting, the area seems to be spacious and more befitting the location of this ornate edifice. Judicial use of the zoom lens then draws the eye to some of the better sculptures and avoids close-up shots of the deteriorating portions of the fountain. Naturally, I threw three coins into the fountain before leaving Rome. This is supposed to insure my return sometime in the future. Who knows?

When my filming was completed, I had some free time to just enjoy Rome. What a perfect time for Henrietta to telephone. She was delighted that I had saved her hotel reservation. She wanted to thank me for that -and for fixing her camera - by taking me to dinner at a special restaurant near the Spanish Steps.

Her invitation was accepted and we arrived at the Piccolo Mundo for what she promised would be an evening of culinary delight. What turned it into a special event was an incident that occurred between the restaurant's still photographer and me.

Several members of a wealthy Italian family were dining in an adjacent private room. the occasion was the birthday celebration of a teen-aged daughter. The restaurant photographer was trying to get a satisfactory portrait of the beautiful young girl with his Polaroid camera. The results were not favorable. Each time the little photographer would take a picture of the girl and show it to the family, their displeasure with his work was increasing. I couldn't help but notice that the girl was becoming more and more embarrassed. I felt compelled to butt my nose into his business.

I had observed one of the reasons why the girl was so self-conscious. She had nothing to do with her hands. He was simply photographing her in a standing position, with her hands at her sides. I couldn't help myself. I approached him with only the intention of suggesting that he give the girl something to do with her hands to alleviate her tension.

I made the mistake of telling him that I was a photographer from America. There went that magic phrase again "American Photographer." He began to insist that I take his camera and make a portrait of the girl. I could not refuse the invitation. She was a remarkably beautiful teen-ager. Long, black hair cascaded over her shoulders, contrasting with the expensive white gown that she was wearing. I had picked up a few tricks over my years of shooting portraits. One of them was how to overcome stark black and white contrasts by softening the lighting on the subject.

First, I instructed the waiter to ask the family to continue eating and not stare at us as they had been doing. A gentle compliment to the girl about her natural beauty put her at ease. Instead of letting her hair fall down behind her, I tactfully moved it forward to fall lightly across the shoulders of the gown. Using a small chair, I had her place one knee against the seat while leaning her elbow against the back. Taking a basket of flowers from a wall decoration, I placed it in the girl's nervous hands for a delicate pose. To solve the problem of the harsh light from the Polaroid flashbulb, I simply used a Kleenex tissue over the flash reflector to diffuse the light. The camera exposure was corrected accordingly.

Satisfied with my impromptu arrangements, I took a couple of quick shots before the family could interfere with unwanted suggestions. The family's reaction to the portrait was incredible. they were overjoyed. Words like "muta bella" and " bonissima" were flying about. Apparently this family was extremely wealthy and they were very good patrons of the restaurant. Pleasing them was most important to the proprietor and they were very well pleased.

The next thing I knew, I was receiving hand shakes and kisses on the cheek. Every kind of food and drink imaginable was being brought, complimentary, to my table. The evening turned into one big party and brought quite a satisfactory conclusion to my last evening in Rome.

One other event of interest took place as I was departing Rome. It pays for a photographer to keep his camera ready at all times. You never know what or who you may see without a moment's notice.

Walking through the Leonardo DaVinci Airport, I became aware of a commotion along a corridor leading from one of the arrival gates. I heard one airport employee mention the names Taylor and Burton. Whipping out the camera, I was able to capture a nice segment of footage depicting Liz and Richard as they arrived in Rome, just having completed a movie in Mexico and looking for a needed vacation. A little diversion from an otherwise uneventful departure.

Well, not a totally uneventful departure. I had some travel mix-ups between Pete Couch and myself that merit a mention. Let's make that another chapter and call it "Spain and Portugal"

CHAPTER TWELVE
SPAIN AND PORTUGAL

Seacoast of Estoril, Portugal.

As travel agent in charge of our group, Pete Couch was concerned because of a threatened strike situation with the TWA pilots. He wanted to fly with our group from Rome to Lisbon to make sure that we were not stranded by the upcoming airline pilots' strike.

He had a problem. He had used up his available free pass time on TWA. His free passage to Lisbon was arranged via two other airlines: Iberia Airlines to Madrid and Portuguese Air to Lisbon. He asked me to do him an incredible favor. I had a valid ticket, made out in my name, direct from Rome to Lisbon. He had travel agent passes, made out in his name, from Rome to Madrid and from Madrid to Lisbon. He requested that I switch tickets with him and assume his identity while flying the above routes.

I had to travel through three countries with his name on the tickets and my name, photograph, and identification on my passport and other documents. I didn't like the idea, but he was in a jam, so I switched tickets.

Pete and the travel group left Rome several hours before my departure. I had to keep reminding myself never to show my passport at the same time I presented my tickets. Everything went OK leaving Rome and arriving in Madrid. The hang-up came in Spain when flights were changed and I had an unexpected layover. Not wanting to be cooped up in the international travel section of the airport for several more hours, I left the safety of the passenger lounge and departed for a tour of Madrid. This forced me to clear Spanish customs and immigration authorities on departure and on return.

The only close call that I had was returning to board Portuguese Air for Lisbon. I had properly shown my passport, but the security people were not letting anyone past the gate unless they displayed their airline ticket. I had anticipated this possibility and had practiced showing my ticket with my thumb casually blocking the name. It worked. No confrontation with the customs, immigration, or security people. I could breathe easier now, but my heart didn't stop racing until several minutes after we were airborne. I felt like an international spy.

The flight to Portugal was pleasant and uneventful, except for the landing. Portuguese Airlines flew the French Caravelle jets. I was certain that they hired ex-basketball players for pilots. We actually dribbled down the runway, bouncing up and down off the surface several times before settling down for a final landing. A little added thrill to an otherwise uneventful flight.

Now I'm all alone at the arrival gate in Lisbon. Pete, who was supposed to meet my flight, is not there. The delay and other mix-ups confused him. He didn't come out to the airport to meet me as had been prearranged. I had the problem of getting from the airport to my downtown hotel, which was quite a few miles away. The cost of a taxi was prohibitive and my financial resources were down to a minimum. I asked about bus transportation. Better than I had expected, a public bus line ran by the airport road, just outside the terminal driveway. I was advised of the proper route number and within 15 minutes I was aboard the bus and on my way into downtown Lisbon.

It was my good fortune to share a seat on the bus with a young college girl. She was a senior at a Lisbon university and a student of the English language. She was thrilled to have an American companion for the bus ride into town. I gave her an opportunity to practice her English language skills. As we drove through the historical section of Lisbon, she happily pointed out many of the points of interest. I was getting a guided tour and lecture as we passed by all the important landmarks. I even took some pictures through the bus window as she pointed out some particularly important sites.

Our arrival in downtown Lisbon coincided with the dinner hour. I politely asked this young lady if she would be my guest for dinner at the hotel. Graciously, she accepted my invitation and I escorted her into the dining room where Pete and the rest of my group were already dining. Pete's eyes almost popped out of his head. The rest of the group were equally astonished. He had been extremely worried about me and had told the rest of the group what he had done about exchanging airline tickets. When I didn't show up on the expected flight from Madrid, they all began to assume the worst possible scenario. They imagined me in some Spanish jail, awaiting charges on immigration violations or some other difficulty. Really, they were all worried about me. They were also frustrated at not having any means of communication between countries in order to determine my whereabouts.

Then I show up with this beautiful young girl on my arm, walking into the dining room as though nothing had happened. Remember, I had been a source of considerable aggravation to them in Jerusalem and Israel. This time I had them amazed. My young companion was so charming, she really captivated them. Her knowledge of Lisbon and her command of English held their interest and took the focus away from my mischievousness.

Once everything settled down, I was able to get back to my filming work without further concern. Lisbon contained some picturesque vistas and at the Castle of St. George, atop the mountain overlooking Lisbon Harbor, I had my first encounter with white peafowl. I had never seen a pure white peacock before and I spent half the day following these birds around, waiting for the opportunity to film one of the males in full feather spread. When one of them finally did fan his gorgeous feathers into a full arch, the resulting film was worth the wait.

Bullfighting in Lisbon, as in all of Portugal, is quite different from the type of exhibition found in Spain and Mexico. In Portugal, they do not kill the bull. Rather, once the bull is fully antagonized by peccadores, mounted on beautiful horses and displaying extraordinary skill, the moment of the final charge is unique.

Nine young men, clad in fancy dress regalia, stand in line, single file, in front of the bull and blocking his line of charge. The lead-man haughtily taunts the bull until he begins to charge their line. At this moment, the young men in the line do a quick backstep to absorb the shock of contact with the bull. When the bull's head plows into the line, the lead-man grabs for the horns. Man number two and man number three separate and go for the bull's neck. The remainder of the men in line also separate to either side of the bull and put pressure against his body. The final man in line has the job of grabbing onto the bull's tail and holding on for dear life. This tail-holder controls the bull's leverage. The object of all this is to bring the bull to a complete standstill. The group is working against a stopwatch to immobilize the bull in less time than their competitors in other matches.

Slow-motion footage of this action proved extremely thrilling, especially when one group of men didn't get the proper initial hold. The charging bull went through them like a bowling ball knocking over tenpins. These guys literally take their life in their own hands. There were bruises and bloody cuts abounding when their bull was declared the winner of the contest. I think this is a much better sport than when the bull is killed. The Portuguese should be congratulated on their civility.

A few miles up the coast from Lisbon is the city of Estoril, the center of the section known as the Portuguese Riviera. It is a picturesque little town with a casino, historic buildings, and a fabulous beach resort area that naturally attracted me.

Following a brief filming session to cover the highlights of the area, I devoted my time to appreciating the magnificent beach and satisfying my natural attraction to the water.

The water of the North Atlantic was chilly this early in the season. The sun was bright and the air was warm, but staying in the water for any prolonged period of time was only for the adventurous and the sturdy. Ten minutes at a time was my limit in this cold water. Only one other person was hearty enough to join me in this brisk swim. My swimming companion was a dark-skinned man, obviously a visitor from another part of the world, like me.

When I had enough of the cold water, I started to exit to the beach. The dark-skinned man also finished his swim and exited at the same time. As we came out of the water, he asked if I was an American. When I replied that I was, he started to tell me that he knew someone in America. Having been burned by phony friendship in Athens, my guard was up against any approach. I'm glad I didn't totally discourage him, because the conversation had an unusual twist and a surprise ending.

OK, the man knew someone in America. Big deal! His home was in Morocco and the man that he knew had been a soldier in World War II. The American had been billeted with this man in his home in Casablanca. He went on to tell me that his acquaintance was from Pennsylvania. I lost some of my aloofness and my attention picked up. When he further remembered that the man was from Pittsburgh, my guard went down and I was anxious to continue with the conversation. To keep a long story from getting any longer, I'll get to the point. When we were through comparing notes, the man who had been billeted with this Moroccan during World War II was my dentist's son. Small world! On the Portuguese Riviera, I meet a man from Morocco and the only American he knows is the son of my dentist. I thought that was worth telling. We never know who we will meet, anywhere in the world.

Returning to Lisbon for the final day of the trip, I had the opportunity to film on the mountain across the harbor from St. George's Castle. There, in majestic splendor, stands a huge statue of Jesus, with his arms outstretched across the sea. It is the exact replica and twin of the statue of "Christ of the Andes" that overlooks Rio De Janiero from its mountain top. Fabricated by the same sculptor, it faces the other Portuguese-speaking country, Brazil, far across the ocean. I felt like the statue was looking homeward. For me, that was a good omen. We were departing that evening and returning to Pittsburgh for the completion of a most interesting and adventurous odyssey.

I had covered ten other countries of the world on this trip. As interesting and magnificent as some of their cities were, Pittsburgh looked better. My home town outshone all of these foreign capitals.

I liked it back in Pittsburgh so much, I think I'll devote another chapter to some more of the things that went on in the Golden Triangle.

CHAPTER THIRTEEN
THE GOLDEN TRIANGLE

Returning to Pittsburgh, the first order of business, after family reunions, was to get the Holy Land feature technically produced. Once Light for Many Lamps was edited, narrated, and put into production, the prints were distributed by the public relations department of Blue Cross as a public service project. They have entertained and enlightened many civic and church organizations through these succeeding years.

With the agony of editing and technical production now finished, it was time to get back into the mainstream of news and public affairs filming in the Pittsburgh area once more. I covered many routine assignments, but a few perhaps worthy of mention in this chapter.

These stories are all "flashbacks," so the exact order of their appearance in this book is not necessarily of prime chronological importance. For instance, I was just remembering an incident that occurred at the Boy Scout Jamboree when the Pittsburgh district was the host for scouts from around the entire country.

Through some previous associations with scouting, I was chosen to be the official TV photographer for the Jamboree. I was responsible for filming the activities of scouts from various other cities and shipping that film to their local TV stations for coverage in their home area.

Scouts came from every state of the union, as well as the Virgin Islands and Puerto Rico. It was the scouts from Puerto Rico who impressed me with their devotion to their hero, Roberto Clemente. When I mentioned that I knew him and had filmed many of the highlights of his career, they swarmed all over me. They were eager for any scrap of information that I could provide about this man that they worshiped. They would not admit that he was dead. Their faith in this man was so strong that they assured me he had survived the plane crash into the ocean. They believed he had the strength to swim ashore and save himself. He just had amnesia, they had convinced themselves, and soon he would reappear to once again become Puerto Rico's champion athlete.

Such was the mystique that our Pittsburgh Pirate star had woven into the hearts of Puerto Ricans everywhere. The faith and optimism of these boy scouts was evidence of the general feeling of the entire country. Their belief that he would somehow reappear had a strange effect on my feelings. All the memory of that lonesome locker room came flooding back from that sorrowful New Years Day. I didn't have the heart to throw cold water on these boys' dreams, so I kept my feelings to myself and let them continue with their hope.

I read a little quote somewhere that stated, "Nothing dies that is remembered." With that thought in mind, 1 am convinced that Roberto will be alive a long, long time, both in his native home of Puerto Rico and his baseball home in Pittsburgh. The memory did not drown with him that fateful New Years Eve.

The memory of another drowning victim remains in my mind throughout all these years. Her tragic death prompted me to produce a feature film on water safety and the proper use of life belts and jackets. Water and photography continue to merge into my career with forces that shape my actions.

A nine year old girl was playing with her six year old brother along the banks of the Allegheny River in the Penn Hills section of the riverfront. She was wading in chest deep water when she somehow wandered to a spot that was over her head. She struggled in the deep water and was going under. her brother tried to push a board out to her, but he was too late. She couldn't grab it in time to save herself. The water closed over her head and she disappeared from site.

Emergency calls came in to the Penn Hills police and fire rescue. Since this is a volunteer fire department, whistles sounded to call the firemen. I was in my boat, with diving gear aboard, when I heard these urgent calls. Learning from my police radio that a child was lost in the river, just about a mile from my location, I immediately drove the boat to the site of the accident and began a diving search for the child.

A few minutes later, a diver from the fire department joined me and we made a search pattern of the river bottom around the area where the girl was last seen. In another 15 minutes, we located her frail, lifeless body on the bottom and brought her back to shore. Such a delicate little child to be so quickly robbed of life. I shared the grief with her parents and all involved with the rescue work.

Once my feeling of grief subsided, I felt a sensation of outrage take its place. I was angry in the knowledge that a two-dollar ski belt around her waist would have saved her life. The family lived along the riverfront. Somehow they should have known about the safety devices available to "waterproof" their child. I was determined to do something about increasing that knowledge and awareness of water safety. Water and photography again: I was going to use television to get that message across.

Arrangements were made for one of the local TV personalities to do a film feature with the water safety officer of the Pennsylvania Fish Commission. This feature covered all aspects of flotation devices and life saving aids. In addition to doing the filming, I arranged for my three sons to go into the water and actually demonstrate each type of belt, vest and flotation cushion, to point out their advantages or disadvantages.

A half-hour program was produced for airing on television. I had satisfied some of my anger over that child's drowning. Maybe her death wasn't completely in vain if she inspired this film. Perhaps it will alert many others to avoid a similar tragedy.

The United States Coast Guard was also impressed by this film. Later that year, I was called to a meeting of the waterways safety committee where I was presented with an award for doing the most that year to promote water safety. It would be hanging on my wall today except it carries the signature of Richard M. Nixon. I never liked Nixon enough to put anything on my wall with his name on it.

Several years later, I had the misfortune to discover the body of another drowned person. This time it was a man in his 40s, who knew better but ignored safety rules. He took his new boat for a test drive without any life jackets aboard. When the boat had an accident and sank, he was unable to swim to the shore because of the cold water. He disappeared from sight as his terrified family watched from the riverbank.

Police and volunteer firemen dragged the river for days with no sign of his body. His wife kept a constant vigil, continuously urging them to spend more and more time in the search, all to no avail.

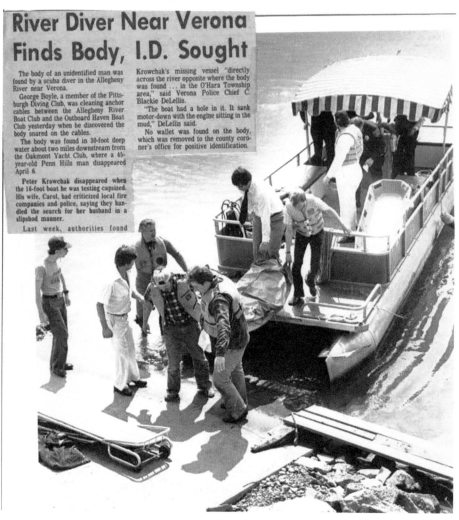

River Diver Near Verona Finds Body, I.D. Sought

The body of an unidentified man was found by a scuba diver in the Allegheny River near Verona.

George Boyle, a member of the Pittsburgh Diving Club, was cleaning anchor cables between the Allegheny River Boat Club and the Outboard Haven Boat Club yesterday when he discovered the body snared on the cables.

The body was found in 30-foot deep water about two miles downstream from the Oakmont Yacht Club, where a 45-year-old Penn Hills man disappeared April 6.

Peter Krowchak disappeared when the 16-foot boat he was testing capsized. His wife, Carol, had criticized local fire companies and police, saying they handled the search for her husband in a slipshod manner.

Last week, authorities found Krowchak's missing vessel "directly across the river opposite where the body was found . . . in the O'Hara Township area," said Verona Police Chief C. Blackie DeLellis.

"The boat had a hole in it. It sank motor-down with the engine sitting in the mud," DeLellis said.

No wallet was found on the body, which was removed to the county coroner's office for positive identification.

Author (left foreground in diving gear) directs recovery of the body of a drowned man that he located on bottom of river.

One day, almost three weeks after his drowning, I was painting my houseboat in the parking lot of my boat club. Suddenly, a woman came running through the lot and dashed to the riverbank. She had binoculars in her hands and was frantically scanning the river to observe a floating object that was drifting by in the current.

The object turned out to be a log. The woman turned out to be the wife of the drowned man. She was still keeping vigil at the waterfront. When I spoke with her. she told me about the boating accident. She had the life jackets in the trunk of their car, but her husband had been in such a hurry to test-drive the boat that he ignored her admonition to go back and get them. Little did I know that just three days later, I would become much more deeply involved in this story.

Outboard Haven Marina just three doors away from my boat club provided dockage each year for more than 100 boaters. These docks were stabilized against the drift of the current by 18 steel cables that were attached to huge concrete anchors imbedded in the river bottom upstream from the docks. Each autumn, when the docks were taken in for the winter, these cables were detached and dropped in the water. Each Spring, I would put on my scuba gear and locate the cables, attach each one to a line that extended down from a surface float, and then workers in a small boat would pull them up and attach them back onto the docks.

Starting nearest to shore and working my way outward towards the middle of the river, I had 14 of these cables located and brought to the surface. Number 15 was located next and I continued underwater along the length of the cable, freeing it from the river bottom and accumulated debris. The water was murky, dull-brown in color and visibility was limited. As I neared the end of the cable, suddenly I saw a face.

For a second or two it didn't dawn on me what I had discovered. In the dark water, 25 feet below the surface, the face looked like it belonged to a department store mannequin or a display dummy. Then I got a close-up view of the ear. Human ears are unique in design. No mannequin can compare with their delicate structure. The conversation with the wife just three days earlier became vividly clear. I had found her husband, just lying there on the river bottom, reclining on his back and looking upward as though he were in his coffin.

A cold chill went through my body with the startled realization of what I had found. I carefully examined the body. He was not caught on anything and not entangled in any way. He was just lying there with no means of stabilization. The abdomen was bloated and gave the appearance of being buoyant enough to allow the body to drift further down current if disturbed in any way. This location was more than a mile downstream from where the accident had occurred. He had gotten this far in three weeks.

Now that I had found him, I didn't want to risk the possibility of having him drift away while I surfaced for help. I had a 35 foot line attached to a float on the surface. My end was attached by metal hook to the cable. Carefully, I detached the snap hook from the cable, delicately passed it through the man's belt and then reattached it to the cable. Satisfied that the body was secured, I ascended the line to the flotation buoy and called over the work boat. "You'll never guess what I've got on the bottom of this line." They were astonished when I informed them of my gruesome find. (Actually, they were flabbergasted, but I've used that word too many times already)

Police, coroner and fire rescue units were all notified. I directed the rescue divers in the recovery of the body. For at least two weeks after the discovery of this body, every time I tried to go to sleep at night, that murky face would appear and disturb my peace of mind. I don't envy the divers who regularly search for bodies in the course of their duties. I never want to have another experience like that.

To get away from the topic of death that filled the last two stories, maybe I can relate an opportunity that I had to save someone's life.

Dan Mallinger, a local television personality, also operated an advertising business. One of his clients manufactured a new type of Christmas-tree holder. Dan was promoting this invention by way of a television commercial.

Early in November, Dan used his own house as a studio and erected a large Christmas tree in his living room. In order to provide enough lighting for the television filming, Dan used photoflood bulbs in metal reflectors. These were the kind with spring clamps that allow themselves to be attached to any suitable object in the room. He used several of these clamp-on lights to provide the necessary illumination of the room.

Because of the large amount of electricity (amperage) drawn by each light, extension lines were run from other parts of the house so as not to overload any one electrical circuit.

My filming went smoothly, with Dan's lovely wife Marlene acting the role of demonstrator for the commercial. Once the filming was over, Dan began to dismantle his lights while I dismantled my camera.

The next scene is indelibly inscribed in my mind. Dan walked by my tripod, carrying one of his lights in his left hand. With his right hand, he reached over and grabbed one of his other lights. All hell broke loose. His body began to undulate and shake uncontrollably. An eerie, pulsating scream bellowed from his mouth. He fell backwards onto the living room couch, still screaming and shaking. He couldn't let go of the lights. It was obvious that he was being electrocuted. My first instinct was to immediately run to his aid. Then I remembered something that had happened a year earlier at my boat club. This memory probably saved both of our lives.

The incident that I remembered was a tragedy at our boat docks. A teen-aged son of a member, and another young man, were about to go for a canoe ride. The boy placed the canoe into the water and then lowered himself into the water, using a support pole for the electric lights on the docks as a brace. His hands were still in contact with this light pole as he entered the water. Unknown to him, there was some kind of a short-circuit from a wire loosened by a storm the previous night.

When his body hit the water, he completed an electrical ground for the stray electricity that was flowing through the light pole. He reacted in the same way that Dan was now reacting as the electrical current flowed through his body. His companion, reacting like I was about to do, came to attempt to rescue him. He made the mistake of coming into contact with the boy's body and now the electricity was shocking him also and he couldn't release his grip on the first boy. A double electrocution was in progress. Fortunately for the companion, another boater had the sense to use a wooden paddle to pry his body from the first boy.

He was badly shocked, but he survived. The member's son was not so fortunate. By the time he was pried loose from the light pole with the wooden paddle, too much electricity had penetrated his body. He could not be revived.

This tragedy instantly flashed through my mind as Dan lay writhing on the couch. Instead of rushing to his aid, coming in contact with his body, and creating a double tragedy, I started grabbing at the many electrical extension lines that were coming from every part of the house. These lines were spread out like an octopus and were running in every direction. I didn't know which one was the culprit. I just pulled with all my might at every one of them, ripping them out of their distant wall sockets. One of them was the guilty line. As soon as it was removed from the source of power, Dan's awful screams ceased and he went limp on the couch. His terrified wife had simultaneously run out from the kitchen to come to his aid. She touched his body without realizing the electrical danger. Without that memory of the previous tragedy at the boat club, there may have been three bodies discovered in his living room that November afternoon.

I don't suppose it's much comfort to the parents and family of that teen-aged boy, but the memory of their tragic experience, and the lesson learned from it, helped prevent the loss of three other lives, one of them my own.

At least the Mallinger story had a happy ending. Dan suffered no serious effects from his electrical shock. I pulled the wires away from the wall outlets before the current had enough time to do any damage to his system. He is now the business agent for all of the radio and television personalities in the Pittsburgh area.

Since I'm talking about saving lives, there's one other guy that I have to include in this life-saving business, my fellow photographer and good friend, Les Banos. It's a good thing that I saved his life, because he has had more adventure stories occur in his lifetime than I could put into two books like this.

How did I save Les' life? Very simple, I kept him from falling out of the open door of an airplane. We had removed the door of my friend Rudy Nuzzo's Piper Cherokee in order to obtain clear, unobstructed aerial photography of the Pittsburgh Pirate training camp at Bradenton, Florida. At the time of this adventure, Les was the official photographer for the Pirates. He wanted some aerial views of the training camp and the four baseball fields that made up the McKechnie Park complex.

To accommodate his needs, we removed the side door of the airplane and took off for the filming. In order for Les to obtain an oblique angle for his filming through the open left side of the plane, Rudy put the plane into a sharp left turn, banking the plane with the left wing pointing towards the ground. As Les turned to his left and leaned forward to get his pictures, I noticed that his safety seat-belt had become unbuckled. There was nothing to prevent him from falling out the open door to his death.

Instinctively, my left hand grabbed for his trousers. I was able to get a grip on his regular belt and a portion of his pants. I held on for dear life until the plane pulled out of the turn and he could refasten his safety belt. Just a simple little grab, but if I don't catch him and hold on, he goes right out the door, a sky diver with no parachute. If he wants to thank me, he can stop procrastinating and write a book of his own. This man's life and adventures would make what you're reading in this book seem like just an appetizer before the main course.

To give you an idea of what I'm talking about: Les was born in Hungary in the years prior to World War II. When Hitler and his Gestapo began taking over all of Europe, Les volunteered to serve with the allied OSS (secret service). They were able to substitute Les' identity for that of a German national youth who had been living in Hungary. What happened to the real German, Les will have to tell you.

Assuming the identity of the German youth, Les was able to join the German armed forces and work within the army as an undercover agent for the allies. Because of his education and training, he was selected for the elite SS Corps. He worked directly within the German forces that were occupying Hungary all during the war.

Soon he attained a high rank within the SS and was responsible for issuing all sorts of travel permits and official papers. Through his inside efforts, many false papers were issued. Allied flyers who had been shot down over German controlled territory, but rescued by Hungarian partisans, were able to escape and return to their bases by using these false papers.

Les and his family and friends in the underground was also responsible for saving the lives of hundreds of Hungarian Jews who were otherwise destined for slave labor or death camps. Some were issued false papers. Others were saved by hiding them behind a false wall in the basement of his aunt's business establishment.

Every day, for more than the six year duration of the war, his life was in constant danger as he walked the tightrope between German officer, Hungarian patriot, and Allied counterspy.

I hope this short summary in my book will inspire Les to document the many stories, adventures, and tales of human drama that were at the core of his existence throughout those awful war years. He can conclude with a happy ending, because he survived, made his way to America, and ultimately ended up in Pittsburgh as a fellow TV news cameraman.

IF THEY CATCH YOU
YOU WILL DIE

The story of a young Hungarian who infiltrated the SS as a spy
Whose mission consisted of saving the innocent lives of the persecuted
and serving the Allied Intelligence

By Les Banos

Les Banos finally did write that long-overdue book entitled "If They Catch You You Will Die".

Another routine news story did not have a happy ending. As far as I am concerned, it will not have a complete ending until something is done about proper lighting of river barges at night. I intend to devote some of my future time to this project.

Take a minute and look at them some night, plying along any navigable waterway. "Black Death" I call them. Barges stretching out hundreds of feet in front of the pushing towboat, with vast sections that are unlit. The only illumination on most of them comes from red and green lanterns on the right and left front corners of the lead barge, and a flashing yellow light in the center. The remainder of the front barge and all the barges in between (as many as five deep) have no lights whatsoever.

The newsfilm story I covered, that aroused my anger with this condition involved a man who had just purchased a new boat and was showing it off to a girlfriend and her child. I'm not excusing the man's actions in the accident that followed. He obviously made a great mistake. His mistake, however, was compounded by the failure of the barge company to provide side lights to the string of barges that he hit broadside.

With his girlfriend and her child in his new boat, he set out for a ride across the river. He was unaware, as he left his dock, that a string of barges was passing by at the same time. The lead barge had passed by the dock and the tow boat was four barge lengths behind. With no side illumination on these rusty-brown hulks, the man apparently did not realize that there was a dark wall of steel between his dock and the opposite side of the river. Everything must have looked like blank, open water as he slammed into the side of one of the barges, killing all aboard.

It is my considered opinion, after lengthy study of river conditions at night, that a tragedy such as this could be prevented. Nighttime barge traffic should be required to display periodic amber lights along their sides, outlining their size and shape. These lights would not have to be of any high intensity and could be shielded to prevent interference with the captain's night vision. I compared the barges with tractor-trailer traffic at night along our highways. Some of these trucks have amber lights outlining their entire trailers and are easily identified for their size and shape. Other trucks, with only the minimum lighting required by law, leave doubts as to their identity until the approaching driver is much closer.

I'm still trying to determine the proper medium for carrying my message about lighting these barges properly at night. A television documentary was my original plan. However, I'm not sure how to show on television what you cannot see after twilight with the naked eye. In 30 years of boating, I've been angered by this lack of sufficient lighting many times. In conversations with other boaters, they all share my indignation and concern. We're just not sure how to get past the government red-tape that regulates these barge companies.

Someday a proper solution will come to me. I assure you readers that I will put my energy and talents towards alleviating this potential threat to boating safety that nightly plies our waters in the form of "Black Death."

For now, let's get away from such ominous subjects and turn to a lighter vein. How about teaching blind children to ski? That's right, down a snow-covered hill with two boards strapped to their feet.

The Western Pennsylvania School for Blind Children had some very unique and very brave pupils. Some of their adventures are worthy of mention here. Their trip to the Laurel Mountain Ski Resort was a highlight of their winter semester. Ski instructors spent the entire day with these blind kids, teaching them to safely negotiate the slopes with a little assistance from a friendly instructor.

I got a tremendous good feeling from filming this feature. The courage and spirit of these blind children was complemented by the dedication and patience of the ski instructors as they devoted the entire day to teaching these children to master the ski slopes and enjoy the delights experienced by their sighted peers.

To begin the training, two ski instructors would hold a bamboo pole horizontally between them. The blind child would hold onto the pole while they made a short descent. As they proceeded down the hill, the child was taught how to brace ankles, turn legs, bend knees etc. When the boy or girl mastered these basic instructions, the bamboo pole was removed. Now the instructor stayed beside the child, calling out directions as they skied together down the hill.

Before the day was over, all of the children who had ventured into this activity were skiing, unaided except for verbal calls, down the intermediate slope. It made for a great, human interest film feature. This "Blind Children Skiing" film was produced as public relations feature for the School for Blind Children. When it was edited and completed, I personally delivered it to the Public Affairs Directors of all the local TV stations. Coincidence plays a strange role in our plans at times.

The very day I delivered the ski film to Channel 11 TV, the public affairs director was facing a big dilemma.He had just completed the major filming of a documentary concerning the colorful manager of the Pittsburgh Pirates, Danny Murtaugh. Thousands of feet of film had been shot and a scheduled air date for the show was less than 30 days away. He had full sponsor involvement and commitments to be honored.

His problem was that he had just been forced to dismiss his cinematographer and editor due to some personal problems. He was impressed by the Blind Kids Skiing feature and asked me if I could handle the editing and production of his documentary.Well, he had some equipment in his editing lab that I had never seen before, but you know I never let anything like that stop me before. I told him I could manage all his production facilities and he hired me or the spot.

I cut my production teeth on "The Whistling Irishman," as the Danny Murtaugh documentary was called. I learned multiple sound mixing, dubbing, re-recording, and all the laboratory preparations necessary to get a full-length documentary on the air. There were also many engineering values within TV station operations that had to be learned. I mastered all of them and began an interesting new career in television documentary production.

Perhaps these endeavors should be covered in a new chapter called... Documentaries.

CHAPTER FOURTEEN
DOCUMENTARIES

Western Penitentiary, Pittsburgh PA

TV documentaries are not all fun and games. Public service films touch on all aspects of human needs and problems. I spent the next couple of years involved in producing films that were principally aimed at improving conditions in the viewing community.

Drug problems, juvenile delinquency, vandalism, law enforcement, prostitution, child abuse, abortion and many other subjects of serious importance to public service, all got their share of focus and attention. Each month, a documentary about some specific community concern was produced and aired.

The bright spot in all these monthly documentaries was that twice a year we departed from the serious problems and produced a sports special. One of these was the "Tale of Two Terrys." This feature compared the two competing Pittsburgh Steeler quarterbacks, Terry Bradshaw and Terry Hanratty. Lots of good football footage and some interesting sports interviews made this show come to life. The show won an award that year, but what was more important to me was the break from the serious work and the chance to have a month of fun filming.

Then it was six more months of alcoholism, poverty, homelessness, education problems and other heavy subjects until the next sports special. This one featured the Steeler's number one draft choice, Franco Harris. More good football footage and trips to Penn State and Philadelphia to bring his high school and college careers into focus. When we traveled to Philadelphia to interview Franco's high school coach, 1 managed to wrap up that interview in the morning hours so I could promote a detour to Atlantic City for an afternoon of body surfing in the Atlantic Ocean before returning to Pittsburgh. Never let your work interfere with your fun, I kept reminding myself.

Then it was back to serious work once again. And I mean really serious. The next topic was so intense, it required two half-hour shows to completely cover the subject. It was entitled, "Pick a Number from One to Life." It documented life within the walls of Western Penitentiary. My involvement with this filming even involved being locked up in the cell block with the rest of the population and becoming a prisoner to show a "cinema-verite" view of penitentiary life.

Producer Donna Tabor and I had considerable involvement with many of the prison activities and projects prior to the ultimate filming within the cell block. Weeks of gaining inmate confidence and cooperation were spent preparatory to the final, in-cell production work.

This was an entirely new atmosphere for me. Some things went well and others were kind of scary. I remember the day I was supposed to begin my lock-up time. There was some mix-up of information between the deputy warden and the sergeant in charge of the cell block.

One of the inmates had written a poem about his cell. This poem was to be included in the overall narration of the documentary. Film footage of a cell was needed to portray the things he talked about in his poem. At this time, I was only supposed to go into a cell and shoot enough footage to cover visually the words of the poem. I was not supposed to be permanently locked up until later in the day.

The sergeant didn't get this final detail quite clear. When he took me to the cell for the poem-filming scenes, he put me inside and locked the cell door. He left the area, thinking that I was scheduled to stay there until the next un-lock time.

Let me tell you, words cannot describe the feeling that comes over a person when those prison cell doors roll closed and you're actually locked in for good. I couldn't believe the change that came over my personality. I started to feel like a caged animal. An instinctive panic set in, deep inside me.

I forgot about the poem. I was trapped and didn't like it. This was not according to the plan. I didn't want to create a fuss and jeopardize the success of my filming. A low profile was important. Nevertheless, I didn't like being locked up in this prison cell when I wasn't supposed to be there. I started checking every possible angle for a means of escape. That's right, "escape" burned itself into my mind. How did the doors work? How strong was the steel? Might it be possible to use the metal leg from the bed to jam the closing mechanism on the cell door? All these thoughts and many more came racing to the forefront of my conscious mind. I was amazed at the animal instincts that arose from within me. It was an experience I'll never forget. One thing for certain, you never want to be in a situation where you face a jail door closing on your freedom. It's terrifying.

Finally, I regained my composure and resigned myself to the circumstances. I filmed the necessary sequence to cover the inmate's poem requirements. When this was finished, I had nothing to do but wait and wait and wait some more, contemplating this environment with a new respect.

Perhaps it was better that I spent all this time locked up. The other inmates started taking me for granted. When un-lock time finally came, I walked out of my cell along with all the others. The only difference was a camera, attached to my shoulder recording a cinema-verite coverage of this cell block activity as we all marched, single file, down the winding stairs and through the prison yard to the mess hall for our meal.

The camera continued through the line in the mess hall, recording the food service and eating procedures. At this point, I almost got into some difficulty.

Most of the inmates had been cooperative. They realized that we were producing a film that might somehow help improve their overall conditions and gain them some additional educational or social benefits. When I came through the mess line with camera still running, I selected a seat and placed my food down alongside one of the inmates. I made a bad choice.

I should have noticed that there was something unusual about the fact that there were too many vacant seats at this particular table and only one man was occupying it. Innocently, I sat down there with the camera still running and began to remove the food from my tray.

The hostility from this one inmate was vehement and bordering on violent. I made an effort to talk to the man in order to explain what I was doing.

This too, was a mistake. He was about to attack me when two other inmates intervened, ushered me quickly away from his table and got the situation calmed down, somewhat.

Then they explained my predicament. I had chosen to sit with the most hated inmate in the prison. This guy had killed a cop. Then he kidnapped a mother and child and subsequently killed them. He disposed of their bodies and no one has been able to find them to this day. Everyone avoided him and to speak to him meant certain trouble. I almost learned the hard way.

The remainder of the documentary went smoothly, by comparison. As I mentioned earlier, the show was so intense that it took two half-hour documentary time slots to cover the scope of the work. The show won the "Golden Quill" award for the year. It was also selected in consideration for nominations for a TV "Emmy." This made me and producer Donna Tabor very proud of our accomplishment.

Just when we felt we were making a significant contribution to the community with these monthly documentaries on community affairs and social problems, the station lost its sponsorship due to some technicality that was totally unrelated to our work. Instead of putting the sales department to work vigorously to obtain new sponsors, the management chose to dissolve the documentary production unit. Donna was relegated to some mundane public service writing duties. I was transferred to the news department. I considered this a step backwards, now that I had graduated to much more challenging production work.

Nevertheless, I put myself 100 percent into the newsfilming and vigorously pursued this work again. One fast-breaking story involving a police shoot-out on the North Side proved to be a little more than I could handle.

An escapee from a local jail had been found, barricaded in the basement of an old building on the North Side. He was heavily armed and refused to give himself up, although surrounded by squadrons of police.

I heard about all this activity on my police monitor in the car. I was driving home from a drive-in movie with my children in the automobile. We had just seen Clint Eastwood in "The Good, The Bad and The Ugly". There had been lots of shooting in the movie. Now Dad is heading for the real thing. Parking the car a block away from the police lines so the kids would be safe, I took the camera and portable light and proceeded to cover the story.

After filming general scenes of the police presence in the area, I concentrated on the drama that was unfolding as a police lieutenant crawled on his stomach up to the cellar door. He was able to stay out of the line of fire by laying beside a small concrete wall at the top of the basement steps. It was possible to communicate with the escapee by shouting down the outside stairwell. He was attempting to negotiate a peaceful end to this stand-off.

His communications broke down, however, and the escapee began shooting wildly through the barricaded door. The surrounding police returned the fire and also used tear gas from several directions. The lieutenant was pinned down on his stomach beside the stairwell.

The barrage of tear gas was somewhat excessive and everyone in the area was suffering from the effects of this noxious gas, myself included. When the rounds of shooting died down, everyone thought the lieutenant would crawl back from the doorway. He just lay there, not moving. We all thought he was shot.

Two paramedics rushed to his aid, grabbing him by his ankles and dragging him across the lawn towards the safety of an adjacent wall. In order to get good newsfilm of this activity, I had to leave the safety of the wall. At this point, the man inside began shooting again and we could hear bullets whizzing overhead. Running for cover, I stumbled in the dark over some broken concrete in the yard, and I started to fall. My first instinct was to protect the camera. Cushioning it in my arms, I let my knee take the brunt of the fall. Naturally, the knee hit a chunk of broken concrete which made shredded wheat out of my knee cartilage.

Injured knee, eyes streaming tears from the gas, and nose and throat burning from the irritation, I still felt the finale of the story warranted hanging-in until the escapee was captured. Thank goodness it was only a few minutes longer. The man couldn't withstand the effects of the tear gas and surrendered meekly.

Good news for the lieutenant also. He was not shot. Just overcome by the tear gas. He had to keep his head down for protection, out of the line of fire. The heavy tear gas drifted across the lawn and overcame him before he could crawl away from the stairwell.

My kids, in the meantime, had been sitting in the car, just a block away, listening to the police radio. They heard the calls for reinforcements and reports of the shooting. They could hear the actual sounds of the exchanges of gunfire. We had just seen a wild, shoot-em-up movie at the drive-in. Their imaginations were working overtime and they were scared and concerned for my welfare.

When they saw me limping back to the car, they thought I had been shot. The youngest, especially, was horrified. I quickly explained that I had just mashed my knee and had to go to the hospital to get medical attention both for the knee and to flush my eyes of the irritating tear gas. First, however, I had to get the film to the lab. I had a scoop on this story. No other photographers were on the scene at this late hour. I wanted to be sure it got on the air for the first morning news show. We hit the air with an "exclusive."

That's the way I covered news stories. Full attention to getting the best newsfilm possible and scooping the competition at every turn. I remember spending a Thanksgiving holiday accompanying a police manhunt in search of a fugitive who had shot a security guard during an attempt to rob a drug company. My reporter, Wayne Van Dyne, and I had talked the State Police into taking us airborne in their helicopter for exclusive coverage of the search activities. When we looked down and saw a newscar from a competitive TV station back at the command post, we asked the pilot to let us down in an adjacent field so the competition wouldn't know we had obtained aerial coverage that they didn't have.

Landing in the field may have foiled the competition, but we also had ourselves in a bit of a predicament. A rain-swollen creek lay in our path and blocked our way back to my car. It was necessary to take off shoes and socks, roll up pantlegs as far as they would go, and wade through this frigid water to get back to the action again.

From the helicopter, I had observed and filmed an unusual concentration of police activity along one particular wooded area. I wanted to get back to that area as soon as possible because my instincts told me they were on to something there. As soon as I got my shoes back onto my numb feet, I drove to the above mentioned section just in time to see the police bringing the suspect out of the wooded area. With camera continuously operating, I ran to the scene just in time to catch them bringing him to the police car. The film continued as they frisked him, placed him in handcuffs and took him away to be booked.

One minute later and I would have missed this dramatic action footage. This story was the lead film in a package that won another Golden Quill award for newsfilming that year. A little bit of extra effort paid off in the resulting award-winning film.

Then I found out the hard way that I was putting out all this extra effort to no particular avail. Do you think management gave a damn? I soon found out they didn't.

Just a week after I had won three major awards for newsfilms and features that I had produced for that station, something most unpleasant happened. My newscar was burglarized and a station-owned camera was stolen. Because I hadn't locked the camera in the trunk, as they would have liked me to do, they ignored all the extraordinary efforts I had made on their behalf in the past and just told me I was fired.

That's right, "You're fired" was the thanks I got for all my hard work and dedication. Was I going to take this lying down? Hell no!

Through legal channels I forced an arbitration hearing on my case. It was quite an experience. You know from previous chapters how much I treasured friendships. This was no exception. I learned not to trust people that I thought were my friends. Especially middle management people who are fighting their way up the corporate ladder. They don't care if they have to step on people on their way up.

At the arbitration hearing, a battery of station management personnel and two attorneys sat on one side of the table to represent the company. On my side of the table was myself and an 80-year-old union representative who was suffering a stomachache and not functioning very well. The station's attorneys had prepared their case against me in a 13-page volume, bound in a plastic cover, very neat and orderly. They were smugly confident that they had this case all wrapped up and I wouldn't stand a chance against all of them at this hearing.

They made a gross underestimation. First of all, when I opened up this 13-page book they had prepared about me, I couldn't believe my eyes. It was filled with false information, exaggerations, and some downright lies. I couldn't believe that people (who I thought were my friends) could do something like this. I don't get angry often, but this book really set me off. My anger didn't show in any outward manner. Inside, I massed an enormous amount of determination that they would not get away with this travesty .A hearing that was anticipated by the company attorneys to be cut-and-dried did not conform to their expectations. They had allotted half an hour to this arbitration procedure.

I turned it into a tooth-and-nail battle that lasted all day and into the evening hours. The two attorneys had to call their offices and cancel other appointments for the day. I was taking their case apart, word for word, sentence by sentence and leaving nothing to chance.

My previous experiences in court, both as a witness and the time I tried my own case, helped me in this hearing. I called in witnesses to refute some of their allegations and gave detailed explanations in my own testimony to discredit and refute other parts of their infamous book.

The arbitrator's decision took an awful long time in being handed down, but when it finally came, it was worth the wait. I had won the case. The station management was ordered to reinstate me and put me back to work as a news cameraman. I had cleared the smear they had tried to put on my name and had vindicated myself. As a matter of fact, some of the arbitrator's remarks were somewhat embarrassing to management who had been unable to stand up to my testimony and cross-examination.

I had won my job back, but I didn't want it. In the interval of time, while waiting for the arbitrator's decision, I went to work for a competing station doing more desirable work for more money. I was doing film production for a children's program that was extremely interesting. I didn't want to go back to newsfilming anymore.

It would have been nice had I been able to retrieve my lost wages from Channel 11. Seems I won the war but lost the peace. In my intense concentration on refuting the false allegations against me, I neglected to make a formal request at the hearing for back pay. The old union representative wasn't any help either. He neglected to advise me of this necessity and I ultimately lost my request for back pay.

Money isn't everything. I had cleared my name. Now I was working on a new project, with people that I liked That ought to be covered in a more upbeat chapter. Let's call it "More TV Stuff."

CHAPTER FIFTEEN
MORE TV STUFF

Author flies in WWI vintage fighter plane to make aviation films.

"Someplace Special" was the name of my new show. It had the capacity to go anywhere and do anything that might be of interest to children of grade school age. The hostess of the show, Cindy Kennedy, was a delightful, pixie-like little lady. A bundle of energy with enthusiasm bursting in every direction. Working with her was fun and we got involved with all kinds of stories. We did films similar to the Misterogers format, but geared to an older child.

Every so often, we would need kids to play a role in one of our feature stories. I had a built in-supply with my own children. There were ages to suit almost every need. We used my youngest son, Tom, when he was about 8 years old. Tom carried us aboard the inaugural] flight of United Airlines Boeing 747 Jumbo Jet service from Pittsburgh to the West Coast. Using Tom as an actor, we showed our young viewing audience what it was like for an unescorted youth to travel across the country under the supervision of airlines personnel. This experience was definitely a highlight for my 8-year old son

For a Halloween special, we traveled to West Virginia, where an authentic castle nestled in the hills outside Berkeley Springs was the setting for a spooky, ghost-story telling feature. Once again, my children helped out by being models for the film. They had a ball, running in and out of the castle rooms and corridors dressed in ghostly Halloween costumes and playing their haunting roles. We really put ourselves into these features.

Kids wrote letters to the show asking to see things that pertained to their interests. We covered these letters in our feature section. One young viewer wanted to know what happens to a letter once it is mailed. We followed a letter from the time it was placed in the corner mailbox until it was delivered to the addressee. I filmed all the activities of the Post Office in this feature and learned a considerable amount about the details that go into the handling of our mail.

Another of our viewers, a girl of grade school age, informed us of her fantasy. She had always wanted to play football for the Pittsburgh Steelers. We made her wish come true, on film. Several of the Steeler players volunteered to participate in a game with her after their regular practice session. I think I had as much fun as she did while I was shooting the film.

"How do they make candy bars?" questioned another young viewer. That set us off on a project to film all the operations of the.D. L. Clark Candy Company, makers of the famous Clark Bar. Each time I filmed one of these features, I learned as much or more than the kids. I didn't know they made their own peanut butter for the candy bar centers. The melted chocolate that covers the bar is flash frozen just before wrapping. I never would have thought of that. This job was very educational, but, more than that, it was fun.

Another enjoyable feature was filmed at the Vimco Spaghetti factory where we covered all types of spaghetti, fettuccini, and noodles being manufactured by incredible machines. The pasta making resembled a ritual dance with noodles and lengths of spaghetti swaying to unheard music. We edited the finished film to a musical score and had a fascinating feature.

And there was always the Zoo. Kids (and adults too) never tire of interesting animals and their unusual and unpredictable activities. The aviary also made an excellent location for filming features on exotic birds. Nature lovers have no shortage of places to observe unusual flora and fauna in the Pittsburgh area. They all make for great film features. Each time the script called for children to be actors in the feature, I would call upon my kids to fill the role. They always did an excellent job and made me proud.

Concurrent with the Someplace Special features, I had an opportunity to do more free-lance work. Aviation was a principal feature in many of my filmings. Through the years of working on the Daybreak show with Don Riggs, we had many occasions to put together short features about people who were building small, experimental aircraft in their homes. Little by little, these short features accumulated into a formidable stockpile. A full-length feature began to take shape.

WORLD-TRAVELING PHOTOGRAPHER'S HIGHLIGHTS

In addition to the home-built aircraft, there were also pilots who restored antique aircraft of World War One vintage. Some of these planes were put back into their original condition and kept looking like new. These adventurous flyers would take to the air in these antique planes for special occasions. We made many film features about their flying activities. I got to fly in some of the darndest pieces of flying machinery that could be imagined.

For instance, we made a trip to Center Hall, Pennsylvania where an old farmer had a WW I vintage, French LaRhone flying machine. This aircraft has an engine that rotates with the propeller. That's right, the whole engine turns around with the spinning of the prop. It requires a special, fine grade of oil to lubricate its bearings and rotating machinery. Castor Oil... Yeah, the fishy smelling stuff we used to hate when we were forced to take it as a tonic when we were kids. .

The only way we could get the owner to fly the LaRhone was to bring up a large jug of caster oil for lubrication. Once he got the oil in the engine, he was able to start that big old noisy bird. It was an experience to see the entire engine rotating inside the cowling. He flew the plane all around his farm land, making several low passes over my camera position for dramatic effect. The damn thing sprayed caster oil all over the area underneath its path. He managed to douse me with the smelly stuff before the filming was completed. Such a price I had to pay for my art. I smelled like fish oil for several days.

Flying in two-seated World War I fighter aircraft was more of a thrill. In order to get good close-up footage of the pilot's face, I got to fly in the forward cockpit. Now I know why the old time aviators wore those leather caps with the chin straps and why they needed the goggles.

That big propeller is right up there in the open, directly in front of you. The wind blast from that giant fan is like being in a hurricane when you fly in the front cockpit. The small plexiglass windscreen is only minor protection from the icy blast of the propeller wash.

Aerobatics in these old planes was another thrill that I won't soon forget. Turning upside down in an open cockpit, trying to hold on to a 16mm movie camera and shoot film while praying that the safety belt is not as antique as the plane, is quite an experience.

Getting back to the guys who built their own experimental aircraft, they were a breed apart. One fellow in Wexford first built himself a barn so he would have a place to build his airplane. Another family in Crafton hadn't seen the surface of their dining room table for several years. It was constantly being used to lay out blueprints of fabricate fuselage and wing strut parts.

One man in West View had been working on his homebuilt for more than seven years. All the various pieces were hanging in his garage and basement, carefully marked and catalogued. The family had no idea of the size or shape of the plane. They just had a basement and garage full of pieces. Since everything was complete except the final assembly, I boldly suggested that they carry everything out into the back yard and put the pieces together. I wanted to film something that looked like an airplane.

At first I thought the man's wife was going to kill me for making such a rash suggestion. The amount of work involved was enormous. However, once they started to carry parts out into the yard, they began getting excited about seeing the plane take its shape. Neighbors joined in to help carry the pieces out into the yard. I obtained a vantage point from their second-floor window. Using a wide-angle lens to encompass the entire back yard, I did a fast-motion montage as the pieces came together. The "time-lapse" photography effect quickly showed the formation of the final shape of the plane.

Well, you should have seen that once reluctant wife. She joined with her husband, the entire family and several neighbors as they jumped up and down like a bunch of kids. After seven years of work, this was the first actual view of what their airplane was going to look like. they were ecstatic, and so was I, as I shared their joy in seeing the results of their labor take shape. A year or so later, I was also able to film the inaugural flight of this experimental plane for another part of the overall show.

One week-end each year, the Experimental Aircraft Association holds its annual "fly-in" . All these restorers of antique planes and builders of homemade experimental's assemble to show off their handiwork, fly their planes, and generally enjoy their interest in this special branch of aviation.

This fly-in provided the icing on the cake for obtaining enough additional aerial footage to put together a full length aviation feature. Don entitled the show "By The Seat Of Your Pants" as a tribute to old time flyers. These first aviators didn't have sophisticated instruments. They flew their planes literally by the feeling they got in the seat of their pants when the aircraft changed position.

The feature was a big success. It won many special awards and acclamations from the flying fraternity. It began making the rounds of every meeting of a flying club in the surrounding area. Don had to make extra prints as out-of-state requests came in to show the film to their groups too.

It was so popular that a sequel was called for. There was enough left-over footage from the homebuilt features that judicious editing produced a second full-length feature entitled, "How Did You Get It Out Of The Basement?" I think the title is self-explanatory. But, in case your imagination is not giving you the entire picture, there is more than one case of a builder of homemade aircraft that misjudged his measurements and actually had to tear away a portion of the basement wall in order to get the finished plane outside. A cute piece of cartoon animation depicts this activity for the opening of the film.

These two aviation features continue to please audiences to this day. The time-worn prints are still in demand for groups and clubs. I had a great time shooting this film-- Just another example of "Never Let Your Work Interfere With Your Fun".

Another flying film that I did -- with the Air National Guard -- interfered with my fun a little bit, but it was my own dumb fault. For a TV promotion, I was cleared to fly with the Air Guard on a training mission. I was to film some features to promote recruitment including special air-to-air filming of maneuvers and acrobatics.

Assigned to a T-33 Jet Trainer, I got my preliminary instructions on various emergency procedures, including how to blow the canopy and eject from a disabled plane in an emergency. The major that gave my briefing made everything seem so real that I imagined myself ejecting from the plane and parachuting to the ground after the seat was blown away and the chute opened automatically.

The actual flight was not so dramatic and probably would have been quite routine except for an eating error that I made prior to the flight.

We flew to the airfield at Syracuse, New York. I made all the preliminary shots throughout the morning with no extraordinary happenings and no problems. Everyone was extremely cooperative and the filming went great.

Then it was lunch time. The mess hall contained rows of large tables that were set up for the onslaught of hungry pilots, mechanics, and grounds crew. Generously spaced on each table were large bowls of fresh peanut butter, ample amounts of butter and stacks of fresh baked bread. The aroma of this fresh bread was tempting. I couldn't resist partaking of a slice, liberally spread with soft butter and plenty of that good-tasting peanut butter.

When I was a little kid, a special reward for doing a chore around the house was an extra piece of peanut butter bread. I felt like a kid again. The first piece was so good, I helped myself to a second one, and maybe even a third, I honestly don't remember.

What I do remember was that an hour later, I was sharing the cockpit of that T-33 jet trainer with the major who had been my instructor. We were flying a mission back to Pittsburgh and had some F-85 fighter jets in our squadron.

Once we were airborne, I was getting great shots through the clear canopy. The F-85s on our wingtip would peel out and roll up over my canopy and then go into a steep dive on the other side. My pilot followed suit while I kept the hand-held camera running.

The forces of gravity have a strange effect on the human body. I was able to hold the camera up to my eye as we rolled over to follow the F-85s and I could still keep shooting while we followed the jet into the steep dive. When it was time to pull out of the dive, however, that was another story. I don't know how many "G-forces" we were pulling as we came out of that dive traveling at speeds in excess of 500 miles per hour. I only know that the weight of my arms and the weight of the camera being held by them increased manyfold.

The camera just pulled down from my eye and forced itself into my lap. All my strength was insufficient to get it back up to my eye again until we completed the arc of the dive and started climbing again. It was a thrill that no amusement park ride could provide. I was enjoying this experience immensely until I became acutely aware of the peanut butter. If only I had eaten a sensible lunch, there wouldn't have been any problem.

The aerobatics and G-forces that I was experiencing while trying to keep the camera up to my eye began to have their effect on my stomach. The peanut butter taste was backed up into my throat and combined to create a nausea like I had never known before. I wanted to be sick in the worst way, but pride was taking over my emotions. Stubbornly, I fought the urge to be violently ill. I wasn't going to let that major see me throw-up in his plane.

The taste of the peanut butter backing up in my throat was horrible. Somehow, I managed to set my will against being sick and continued shooting film until we landed at Greater Pittsburgh Air Base. As soon as we were on the ground, the major lifted the canopy and I got a blast of cool, fresh air that sustained me until we taxied to the hanger and I could exit the plane. I managed to hold onto my lunch and the airsickness subsided as soon as I touched solid ground. The only ill effect that I had was that I couldn't even look at a jar of peanut butter for at least a year after that occasion.

The films turned out great and I'm glad my eating indiscretions didn't affect their outcome. I guess I interfered with my own fun on this one.

I'm in the mood to recall another film feature that not only didn't interfere with my fun, it actually added immensely to my enjoyment while I was shooting it.

The American Wind Symphony Orchestra is a unique group of young musicians. They were brought together by a very special conductor, Robert Austin Budreau. In addition to being the director and conductor of the orchestra, Budreau is also captain of an extraordinary showboat vessel that becomes a music hall on water and the sound stage for the orchestra's performances.

This special showboat has hydraulic lifters that raise the entire center of the vessel and convert it into a massive band shell and sound stage. Concerts are held in this unusual setting for all who flock to the waterfront to see this strange boat and hear the expert musical performances of the orchestra.

Not only did this special vessel ply the waters of Pittsburgh's three rivers, giving concerts at many cities, large and small, along the waterways, the boat was constructed with the capacity to sail larger bodies of water. Its scope and area of coverage could be expanded to distant waterfront cities and towns.

I had done some television features covering this fine orchestra, and the conductor was pleased with my work. I was chosen to accompany them on a Canadian tour, through the Great Lakes and into Kingston, Ontario. The experience was exhilarating as once again photography and water came together in a most pleasant fashion.

Traveling through the Great Lakes and the Welland Canal System is a boater's dream, especially in the Summer months. This 190-foot vessel named "Point-Counterpoint II, took the lake chop and light waves like a real cruiser. After concerts in other cities along the way, The ultimate destination was Kingston, Ontario. the town turned out in force to see and hear this special treat. The waterfront was a sea of heads for the main concert, which provided my key footage for the overall film feature,

In addition to concerts from the waterside, the members of the orchestra also give special concerts in the community. This is their way of saying thanks for the support that is given to these fine young musicians by the hosting cities. A concert in a house of worship is generally scheduled whenever possible.

In Kingston, the house of worship was the Anglican Cathedral, a magnificent structure worthy of gracing any major metropolis. I set up in advance for this concert. My lighting, microphone placement, and main camera position located in the cathedral balcony, I had an overview of both the orchestra site at the altar as well as the ability to pan to the audience of parishioners in the pews.

All the pieces in the program were well received with polite silence following the completion of each number. Then, for a finale, the conductor chose to play "The Battle Hymn of the Republic." The music that these young musicians put forth on this number was soul inspiring. They literally filled the cathedral with the fervor of their rendition. It sounded so full and vibrant that my emotions actually got the best of me. It was so beautiful that I couldn't stop the tears from welling up in my eyes. I was having difficulty focusing on the close-up shots of the various musicians because my eyes were blurred with tears.

When the cymbal-crashing, drum-rolling finale thundered through the halls of this great church in a final crescendo, the otherwise reserved congregation was overwhelmed. Cathedral or no cathedral, they spontaneously applauded this inspiring performance. Their applause carried over to the clergy, who found themselves clapping vigorously with an enthusiasm not usually seen within the cathedral sanctuary. These kids were just plain great and deserved every moment of this acclamation.

Other concerts at hospitals, old folks homes, and special back-yard performances for patrons and sponsors made up the rest of the concert tour activities. This provided me with enough footage to produce three features.

But one promotional film was all that was needed. The task of editing all this footage into a condensed form that would tell the story of this wonderful orchestra was not going to be easy. One thing I learned about editing, it's like diamond cutting, a lot of good material has to be cut out in order for the finished product to sparkle at its finest.

With editing and technical production complete, the finished film began to do a public relations and marketing job for the orchestra. Conductor Boudreau had even greater plans for his young musicians and their special showboat. Plans were being made to do a tour of the Caribbean and Central America the following year. Advance emissaries would need this film re-done in the Spanish language in order to show it in the Latin-American countries.

I loved the challenge. I never worked in a foreign language before. I had to get my script translated into Spanish, re-recorded by a Spanish speaking narrator, and finally, I had to re-edit the sound track to match the corresponding scenes in the film. Normally, I hate editing. It's tedious and boring and requires spending a large amount of time confined to a small area. Intense concentration is required to do a good job.

This Spanish re-editing was different. It was such a delightful challenge that I didn't mind the long hours and the tedium of the work. It was an education. I especially got a kick out of matching Spanish words with scenes where I already knew the narration in English. "Never let your work interfere with your fun." My little sign remained above the editing table and the motto held true for this production.

The Spanish version of the film was used extensively in Latin America and helped considerably in promoting a successful tour for the orchestra. They traveled to Puerto Rico, some Caribbean islands, and several countries in Central America. In each port-of-call, my film had educated the patrons and sponsors with advance knowledge of the orchestra's functions. Because of this, they were greeted by enthusiastic and prepared supporters and that made everything go much more smoothly on this long journey.

Even greater plans have progressed for the orchestra. They changed their name to American Waterways Wind Orchestra and conducted a much more extensive tour in subsequent years. My film had to be re-edited into two more foreign languages, French and German, to go in advance of their tour to Europe, Scandinavia, and Russia. This Pittsburgh-based organization has certainly shown the world the quality of performance that we produce in the Golden Triangle. I'm happy that my film contributed so much to their success. Are you ready for some big game hunting?

Another film feature involving elk, big-horn sheep, and trophy-size deer merits some mention here. Somehow my name came to the attention of a big game hunter who wanted to make a film of his expeditions into the southwest to hunt the above-mentioned animals. The hunter interviewed me and questioned me at length about my physical condition and stamina. He wanted to know if I could keep up with him in the wilderness and stay abreast of his activities enough to obtain the necessary hunting films. I assured him that I was in excellent physical condition. With weekly swimming, scuba diving, water skiing, and other sports activity, I felt that I could keep up with him in the mountains and forests. Furthermore, I got considerable exercise just lugging around all my photographic equipment on every job. He accepted my assurances and we were off to New Mexico.

There's a lot of United States between Pittsburgh and New Mexico. I had the opportunity to film much of it as we traveled cross-country in a camper truck loaded with photographic equipment and hunting gear.

Many areas of the country are quite impressive.

The Mississippi River at St. Louis, with the giant arch dominating the skyline at the western side of a huge bridge, was a majestic site. Photographing this view at sunset was an inspiration. Welcome to the West, it seemed to signal. I also learned an interesting story about the erection of the giant arch.

When the construction crews were ready to join the two sections of this arch at its apex, they found that the side that got more sunlight than the other had expanded from the heat. There was a considerable amount of difference in the heights of the two sides to be joined. To solve this expansion problem, the contractor needed the help of the St. Louis Fire Department, and all the fire hoses they could muster. The trick was to spray water on the heated half of the arch and cool it enough that junction could be made at the top when the heat expansion was reduced.

That must have been quite a sight, all those fire hoses cooling the sunny side of the arch. According to the story, the trick worked. They were able to join the final beams at the top and complete one of the most unusual structures in the world. I bet it's one of the most photographed pieces of architecture as well. I certainly did not spare the film when I had it in my sights.

Continuing west, the scenery varies from endless fields of agricultural growth to breathtaking mountain ranges. Once we were in New Mexico, Albuquerque proved to be an interesting city with its thrilling cable-car ride up the side of the mountain. It seems like you can see half the world from the gondola that rises to the Sandia Crest, some 10,678 feet above sea level. Everything seemed very modern in Albuquerque.

Santa Fe was just the opposite. Once the camper slowly made its way up the steep mountains to reach the state capitol, it seemed we entered a city that looked more like "old" Mexico. Pastel adobe buildings abound. I got the feeling that I was going back in time, to the days of the old west. The Mission of San Miguel of Santa Fe has kept its authentic appearance from the 1800s. Much of the surrounding area looked the same. These were great places to visit and shoot incidental film footage, but they were not the principal reason we had traveled some 2000 miles.

Our first destination was a "rancho" somewhere between Roswell and Carlsbad, in the dry, dusty, desert-like southern portion of the state, not too far from the Mexican border. Here, the big game hunter was to stalk and shoot a trophy class "oudad," the big-horned sheep. We were going to be assisted by Mexican "wet-back" ranch hands who were quartered in a line shack several miles out in the desert from the main ranch.

These Mexican ranch hands are a story in themselves. They were men who had been caught illegally crossing the border from Mexico into the United States. They were under orders of deportation. By some convenience, the immigration authorities were considerably backlogged in their paperwork. It sometimes took many months before these men's cases could be heard. In the meantime, they had a choice of rotting away in some jail or detention camp, or "volunteering" to work for a local rancher, at ridiculously low wages, until their hearing came due.

Well, I'm sorry to say, I did my job extremely well. I set up a filming position with camera mounted securely on a tripod and a large zoom lens attached to accommodate both wide-angle and close-up shots. The Mexicans herded a beautiful specimen of big-horned sheep to the ridge just above the hunter. They backed-off so that they and their horses would not be seen in the background.

A better game-hunting sequence has probably not been seen in any of the innumerable hunting films that proliferate on the sportsmen's scene. With the zoom lens on wide-angle, I have the hunter in the foreground, looking like he is stalking his prey. In the background of this same wide-angle shot, this magnificent, big-horn sheep comes running over the ridge, directly into view and into the sights of the hunter's rifle.

I'll give the hunter credit for one thing. He was an excellent marksman. With one clean shot through the heart, he dropped that animal like a stone. The ram never knew what hit him. When the gun fired, I zoomed in to a close-up as he fell. He tried to lift his head for one brief instant and then died in the next. That one choice of camera position covered the entire scene. Even when the animal fell, his body turned in the direction of the camera to display those trophy-sized horns. I didn't like this work, but I was making superb hunting pictures. Once we finished with shots from every angle of the big game hunter displaying his trophy, this part of the film was completed and it was time to get out of this dusty, dry desert and back to some kind of civilization.

Before we left the line shack, I had an opportunity to play hero for the Mexican ranch hands. A huge, hairy tarantula spider had invaded the camp. The ranch hands were terrified of this creature. I had a pair of hunting boots on my feet and I simply used them to step on the big spider and eliminate the problem. They thought I was very brave. They timidly approached the dead spider asking, "Es muerte? Es muerte?", wanting to be perfectly sure he was dead before they would come back into the camp. When I assured them that he was indeed dead, they thanked me and sent me back to civilization with their blessings.

It had taken several days out on that line camp to complete the filming and finally line up that kill shot. We had stayed with the Mexicans in their camp all that time. Since they are technically prisoners, no beer or alcoholic beverages were permitted in the camp. Now we were returning to the main ranch and a new experience awaited me tequila. I never had any experience with this liquor and didn't want to appear ignorant when the rancher offered this drink. The trick goes like this: You put salt on the back of your hand, suck on a fresh lime, drink a shot of tequila, lick the salt from your hand and then suck some more lime.

I followed everyone else's example, and tried my first shot of tequila. I've never had anything so foul-tasting in my mouth. I wanted to spit it out, but pride prevented me from doing so. I tactfully retreated to a pitcher of Margaritas which seemed pretty good in comparison to the raw tequila. I think the others were laughing at me behind my back, but they'll never get me to drink that stuff again.

New Mexico, from South to North, is a land of extremes From the barren and arid desert in the South, we traveled to the Northwestern corner of the state and entered the Jicarilla Apache Indian reservation. This is a land of beautiful mountains and forests that looked like heaven after spending several days in that desolate desert.

The Apache Indians have large herds of mule deer that graze on their reservation. They obtain a substantial] amount of income for their tribe by selling hunting permits to the white man. The odds of shooting a trophy buck are pretty good with one of these permits. Naturally, the big game hunter had purchased a permit and was off to shoot another trophy.

We almost didn't make it. Our sleeping quarters were in the camper attachment on the back of the pick-up truck. This camper had an extension over the cab of the truck that provided space for one double bed. The kitchen dinette folded down and converted into another double bed. My sleeping quarters were in the dinette conversion. The hunter chose the over-cab bed for himself. The night before the hunt began, we retired early and left instructions for our Indian guide to wake us at 7 a.m.

In contrast to the hot desert land of the southern part of the state, we were up on the Continental Divide, several thousand feet above sea level. The air was thin and cold. A penetrating chill filled the camper and the hunter lit the propane stove and left one of the burners going throughout the night while we slept.

Our guide was keeping "Indian time." His idea of 7 a.m. turned out to be more like 8:30 when he finally banged on the door of the camper to wake us. The hunter was a habitual chain-smoker. He kept a pack of cigarettes beside his bed so he could light up as soon as he awoke. This morning, his matches would not light. While still laying on his bunk in the upper level, he had tried to strike a match, but it just died out as soon as it was struck.

The hunter tried to raise his head and I saw him flop back down again in a dizzy stupor. We hadn't been drinking, but he was acting like he was drunk.

Then I noticed that I was also lightheaded and felt funny. Then it came to me. The burner on the propane stove had been on all night. It had consumed almost all of the oxygen inside our camper. The hunter was having the worst effect from this because his bunk was in the over-cab position, up high in the room. He wasn't drunk, just passing out from lack of oxygen. That's why the matches wouldn't stay lit too. There was nothing to feed them.

Slowly, I rolled onto the floor, afraid that I might also pass out before I could get some fresh air into the camper. I got the door open without any trouble and advised the Indian of our predicament. He helped me outside and then used a blanket to fan some fresh air into the camper. As soon as some fresh air got back into our quarters from this forced ventilation, w got enough oxygen and everything was all right. The hunter blamed the Indian guide for not coming to wake us on time. Actually, I thanked my lucky stars that he came when he did. He could have been another hour later and it would have been too late to save us.

We soon forgot our little brush with danger and set out to get the film shot on the hunt for a trophy mule deer. The mountains and forest were picturesque and the scenery was spectacular. Clear, crisp weather provided excellent conditions for great photography. We saw lots of deer, but none good enough to satisfy the requirements for a trophy shot. Several days were spent climbing up and down the mountains until he finally got the deer he wanted.

The deer he ultimately shot was a true trophy buck. Although I hated to see it killed, once again his marksmanship was superb. He put the animal out of its misery instantly with a perfect shot. Again, the film was wrapped up with the usual posing shots and we were off to hunt another trophy animal, the mighty bull elk.

Before we left the Apache reservation, a curious event occurred. The famous archery champion Fred Baer paid a visit to the reservation. He was purchasing a permit to hunt deer with a bow and arrow. What was so unusual about his visit was the demonstration he gave to the natives on the use of archery equipment. I shot a priceless little piece of film depicting a "white man" showing Apache Indians how to be proficient with a bow and arrow. The demonstration that he put on was extraordinary. His marksmanship was uncanny. Those Indians just stood there with their mouths hanging open, amazed at his skill.

Now the final hunt was begun for the massive trophy elk. We left the Apaches and headed for an area north of Chama where the altitude rose to over 10,000 feet above sea level. This is really thin air. As a matter of fact, if I remember correctly from my aviation filming, some of the lesser powered aircraft, like the Piper Cub, can't even take off at this altitude. It's above their maximum ceilings.

Elk thrive at this altitude and the guide for this area knew just where they congregated. He had a four-wheel-drive truck and took me over logging roads where I obtained excellent footage of herds of elk grazing and foraging. I also got a few telephoto close-ups of some pretty big bulls intermingled with the forest trees. With these establishing shots completed, it's time to go hunting.

Talk about cheating, this hunt took the cake. The hunter paid the guide to drive his truck along the logging roads of the upper mountain ridge. He rode in the back, ready to shoot if a big bull elk was spotted. He even devised a signal whereby he would slap on the cab of the truck if he spotted a trophy elk. The first day, he got an excellent shot of a really big bull, but the animal ran off down the other side of the mountain, leaving no signs of being wounded.

A search of the area where the shot was fired revealed that the bullet had struck an intervening tree branch and had exploded against the branch, never hitting the elk. The hunter had been using hollow-point bullets. The reason he gave for using this type of ammunition was that when a hollow-point bullet hits a vital organ, it explodes and immediately destroys the entire organ, causing instant death. That explained his quick kills on the big-horn sheep and the mule deer. This type of bullet was not going to work up here in elk country due to the thick, intervening shrubbery and branches.

The next day, he switched to steel-pointed bullets and we went back up to the top of the ridge, an estimated elevation of 11,000 feet. Once again he rode in the bed of the pick-up while the guide drove slowly through the area where the elk were known to congregate. I kept the camera ready at the side window of the truck. My heart was not in this filming, but I decided that he was going to do it this way no matter what I said, so I just wanted to get it over with.

We saw him at the same time. I started filming as the rifle went off. The mighty bull elk shuddered from the shock of the bullet but he did not fall. He had been heading in the same direction as the truck. The hunter anticipated that he would continue in this same direction and was leading the elk with his scope for a second shot when the elk fooled him. Instead of continuing in a forward path, the elk bolted in the opposite direction and headed the other way. He was out of sight, down the other side of the mountain, before a second shot could be fired.

We stopped the truck and went over to the area where the first shot had been fired. He had definitely hit this one. A puddle of blood was on the ground. As we followed the tracks of the runaway elk, more blood was seen as the trail progressed.

We started out together, the guide, the hunter, and me with the camera. The trail led down a mountain ravine and then up a small rise, over another ridge, and down another ravine. As long as the trail led downhill, we stayed together. When the trail led back up another grade, the guide and I were outdistancing the hunter and leaving him farther and farther behind.

We must have tracked that trail of hoofprints and blood for about three miles before the guide and I finally found the expired elk at the top of another ridge. The steel tip bullet had apparently gone straight through his chest without destroying a vital organ. This powerful animal had enough stamina left in his system to run another three miles up and down ravines before finally succumbing to the effects of the bullet wound.

This definitely was not my idea of sportsmanship, but I kept my mouth shut and did my job, filming picturesque trophy type close-ups as the guide held the head of the big elk in an advantageous pose. But where was the hunter? I needed him in the final shots for the conclusion of the film.

We waited and waited for him to catch up. Finally, I back-tracked along the trail of blood. About a mile back, I found the hunter at the foot of a ravine, sitting on a log, red faced and out of breath. Of all things, he was lighting up another cigarette, even though he was exhausted and could hardly catch his breath in this thin air.

My only thought at the moment was, "Well, I'll be damned. He interviewed me to see if I could keep up with him. Ha Ha!" He was too pooped to make it the rest of the way up to the elk. Later, we got a jeep and dragged the animal to a location near the road.

I was able to get tne hunter in a final series or tropny shots at this closer location and complete the film.

For me, the story didn't end up on the mountain. I had to return to Pittsburgh, process and edit the film, and try to make it look authentic and sportsmanlike. This I accomplished. The final blow came when the finished print was delivered and the hunter didn't have the money to pay for it. Reluctantly, I took a promissory note from him to cover what was still owed on the production of his big game hunting film. I should have kicked myself in the pants right then and there. He took off with the film, deserted the area, and left me with a worthless promissory note. That note had enough rubber to bounce all the way back to New Mexico.

One lesson this experience did teach me: I never took on another job without getting paid in advance. The next story will show how that paid off, but good.

A group of adventurers had been researching the activities of German submarines that operated off the New England coast during World War II. They had some detailed information about one particular sub that had been sunk somewhere off Block Island, RI. From all their studies, they learned that this was an experimental submarine and the Germans reportedly had been using mercury as a ballast fluid. A large quantity of mercury would have been necessary to operate the system. That mercury was extremely valuable and represented a sunken treasure worthy of location and salvage.

They had a group of investors involved with them in this project and they approached me with the proposition of making a movie of their expedition. They wanted documentary coverage, including underwater filming of the submarine when it was found. They wanted me to come along with them for a piece of the action, instead of cash payment.

As I stated earlier, I had learned a very expensive lesson from the New Mexico film. I was not about to be burned by any Rhode Island adventure. The only way I would take on this project, I told them, was if all my fees and expenses were paid in advance.

There was considerable resistance to my demands, but the day before the expedition was to leave for Moutauk Point, I received a call to come and pick up my money and airplane tickets. I joined the expedition, paid in full.

We arrived at the marina on Montauk Point on Friday evening and loaded a mass of diving and electronic equipment aboard a chartered 65 foot Chris-Craft cruiser. We were ready for an early departure on Saturday morning. This was to be a two-day, week end charter for the purpose of locating the submarine.

Early Saturday, I loaded my underwater photographic equipment aboard and began filming all the activities on the boat as an impressive array of electronic gear was put into position. A specialist from Massachusetts Institute of Technology had come aboard to operate this sophisticated gear. One of the large pieces of electronic equipment was a magnetometer. This instrument was reported to be capable of measuring objects on the floor of the ocean and determining their character. I shot a lot of footage as this device was set up.

The expedition set out with "Loran" and other direction finding devices put in use to locate and pin-point our target on the ocean bottom. I was enjoying a perfect sailing day, moderate water conditions, and ideal weather for my filming. Everything that they were doing was recorded on film for the documentary. All the electronic instruments were filmed as they performed their tasks.

We sailed around Block Island and approached the proper latitude and longitude coordinates as determined by Loran positioning and the chart data. The magnetometer was placed into service and a series of parallel passes were started to electronically map the ocean's bottom. This was all interesting and I thoroughly enjoyed shooting roll after roll of film of this activity. We spent the entire Saturday making parallel runs without finding our target. At dusk, the search was terminated. We returned to port with plans to start out again early Sunday morning and complete the mapping of the search area.

Very early Sunday morning we returned to the boat only to find an extremely angry captain. It seems the electronic expert from M.I.T. had brought along a lady friend who ignored the warning sign that was posted in the marine toilet. She tried to dispose of a sanitary napkin in this delicate plumbing fixture. The result was a burn-out of the toilet's pumping motor.

The captain was understandably angry. Worse than that, he was not able to replace the motor since no supply house was open on Sunday. He refused to take his 65 foot boat out into the ocean swells without this pumping motor. He said he would be in danger of scuttling his vessel should high seas force water into the intake and he hadn't the pump motor to expel it.

The charter was canceled. A frantic search of the marina failed to find any other suitable boat that was available for charter on such short notice. The expedition was out of business and everyone lost his investment. Everyone but me, of course, thanks to the lesson I learned in New Mexico. I was the only member of the expedition who was going home financially secure.

The investors would not stake the group to any more money for exploration and the entire project was scrubbed, thanks to one sanitary napkin.

Some other searches for lost treasure were more productive. Let's make that another chapter.

CHAPTER SIXTEEN
TREASURES

Top: Author, with self-made underwater camera, shooting scenes in the Bahamas for sunken Spanish treasure film.

Bottom: Author, in Scuba gear on the ocean bottom in the Bahamas, displays some of the Spanish "pieces of eight" coins.

Dozens and dozens of stories have been written about treasure salvage procedures in the Bahamas and along the Florida coast. Some of these operations have really hit it big with fabulous finds of sunken gold, silver, jewels, and priceless artifacts.

What the success stories don't usually cover is all the years of struggle, disappointment, and smaller finds of minimal value that provided only small encouragement to those who continue in this rigorous work.

Financing for treasure salvaging in the earlier years came from speculative investors. They took a big chance risking their funds on such a long-odds venture. One of these investors was from the Pittsburgh area. He was more fortunate than some of the others. The expedition in which he invested located one of the sunken Spanish ships. They had excavated a fair amount of sunken valuables from this lode.

He had the option of being paid off in cash, or taking his share of the expedition's findings in gold, silver, and artifacts. He chose the latter and set forth to make the best use of his portion of the treasure. His idea was to make a movie about how the treasure was found and then display his portion of the loot as he showed the film. He planned to earn a living by charging an admission fee for this display.

It was my good fortune to be chosen to produce the movie. My slogan regarding work and fun was perfect for this job. Our base of operations was Nassau, Bahamas. The vessel used for all the filming was a 100 foot yacht. The boat also served as our living quarters unless we chose to use the apartment also available in downtown Nassau.

Paradise Island was our home port and paradise was a good identifying word for this entire production. I had the time the facilities, the money, and the best weather anyone could ask for to do the filming. There was crystal clear water for underwater filming and picturesque islands for background scenery and support locations. This job was like being paid for a vacation. I almost cried when I had to return to Pittsburgh for the real work portion of the production, the editing.

We had cheated a little bit for the underwater filming. Picking a good location, amid picturesque coral reefs, we re-buried the coins and artifacts. They were found and recovered again for the benefit of the movie camera. I didn't feel bad about staging these scenes. All we were doing was recreating the original finding, not making up anything that had not already been done.

We also searched island beaches with metal detectors and filmed "findings" of washed-up "pieces-of-eight." These were the ancient Spanish equivalent to our silver dollar. Through beach searches and underwater explorations and findings, an interesting and exciting story was produced. It was edited into a movie that made a good promotion for his treasure display.

The last I heard of this investor, he had a display trailer for his treasure and was traveling throughout the Midwest, setting up at shopping centers, sports shows, regattas, and fairgrounds to show my movie and display his treasure. Apparently he is making a good living at this endeavor. I'm glad I had a chance to contribute to his success. A couple of the pieces-of-eight that he gave me are among my most treasured keepsakes.

Sometimes salvage diving doesn't have the rewarding results just described. Such was the case of the "Tropic Rover."

"The largest sailing catamaran in the world" is how she was advertised. The Tropic Rover, 152 feet of awesome grandeur, half the length of a football field, inspired onlookers with her massive sails and sleek lines. Her twin catamaran hulls were so large that runabouts pulling water skiers would run between them, pulling their skiers right under the center of the ship for an added thrill.

The Rover was primarily used for day cruises. She departed Nassau for sightseeing around the New Providence Islands on almost a daily basis. That's what she was doing when the storm hit.

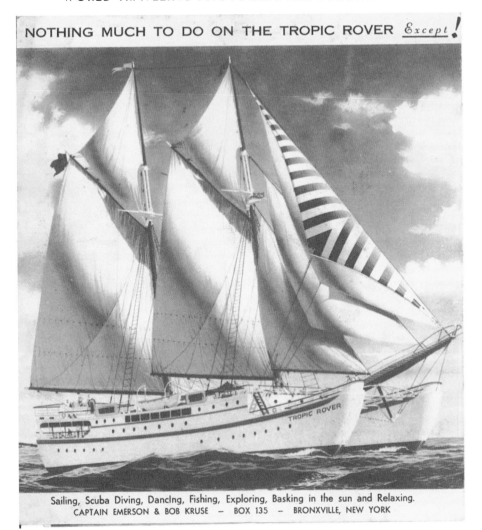

NOTHING MUCH TO DO ON THE TROPIC ROVER *Except!*

Sailing, Scuba Diving, Dancing, Fishing, Exploring, Basking in the sun and Relaxing.
CAPTAIN EMERSON & BOB KRUSE — BOX 135 — BRONXVILLE, NEW YORK

A "Nor'easter," the old mariners called it. A sudden, violent storm of almost hurricane proportions, blowing in from the Northeast with a fury that caught the big sailing ship in its clutches.

The captain was aware of the approaching storm and was headed back to port. Ordinarily, he would sail directly on a course that would take him along the inside of Paradise Island, directly to his dock. However, a new bridge had just been completed linking Paradise Island with downtown Nassau. The huge masts of the Tropic Rover were too tall to fit under this new bridge.

It was necessary for the captain to sail around Paradise Island and approach his dock from the opposite direction. This took considerably more time and gave the storm a chance to catch up with the ship. Fate was definitely not on the side of the Rover this stormy day. Just as the captain approached the narrow channel entrance to the harbor, he was forced to come about, change course, and make way for an out-going ocean liner that was already in the channel and headed out to sea.

The Nor'easter was about to claim another victim. As the crew reversed the huge mainsail for the change in direction, a massive gust of wind hit the sail full blast and ripped it from top to bottom with a thundering roar that survivors said sounded like a bomb had exploded.

The bow of the Tropic Rover is about to smash into the rocks of the breakwall as an alert crewman snaps this shot in the howling storm that dashed the ship to its death.

Loss of the mainsail severely affected the maneuverability of the ship. Auxiliary diesel engines were started immediately. These engines were no match for the fury of the storm. Powerful winds and massive waves were

The side of the Tropic Rover as its dingy is about to be smashed into the rocks of the breakwall while storm size waves continue to pound the ship to pieces against the rocks.

pounding the Rover and forcing it in a direction the captain did not want to go.

A distress call was put out and a tugboat was dispatched to lend assistance. Things looked better when the tugboat arrived and managed to get a large towing line shot over to the Rover. The line was attached to forward cleats and everything appeared to be ready for them to be towed into the harbor. Then, for some unknown reason, one of the crew members of the tug threw some surplus tow line into the water from the afterdeck just as the tug-boat was backing into position to begin the tow.

The excess line fouled the propeller of one of the tugboat's two engines. It wrapped itself around the shaft so tightly that the engine stalled. In the fury of this storm, one engine was not enough for the tugboat to maneuver. They had to cut loose and limp back to port to save themselves.

The Tropic Rover was in a serious emergency situation. They had a full complement of passengers and crew aboard, including a very elderly lady and a woman who was pregnant.

Two forward anchors were dropped in an attempt to ride out the storm at the mouth of the harbor. The anchors were unable to hold against the force of the huge waves that lifted and dropped the ship with each oncoming crest. Both auxiliary engines were employed, full throttle forward, but they too proved ineffective against the power of the raging sea. All that the anchors and engines could do was to prolong the inevitable. The storm was persisting in blowing the ship in the direction of a huge pile of rocks, an artificial breakwall that had been erected to protect the main island against just such a storm.

They had gained a little time, that was all. But time was essential in this emergency. The tug-boat captain found that with his one engine, he could navigate in the relative safety of the calmer waters behind the breakwall. He maneuvered into position in the lee waters behind the big pile of rocks and waited until the storm blew the Rover to the other side.

A line was shot over to the Rover's galley deck. Instructions were given to make a chute, or safety slide, from the remains of the mainsail. It was pulled from the galley deck to the other side of the rock pile and secured by the tug-boat crew. As the storm began pounding the stern of the Rover into the rocks, passengers were escorted to the galley deck. One by one, they slid down that huge slide to the safety of the waiting tug-boat crew.

Elderly lady, pregnant woman, children, remaining passengers and crew, all slid down the mainsail chute to safety. All hands were rescued as the waves continued to pound the Tropic Rover to smithereens against the huge rocks. The only serious injury to a person occurred the following day, after the storm, when one of the crew walked out on the breakwall in an attempt to salvage some of his gear. He lost his footing on a slippery rock, fell and broke his leg.

One hundred and ninety thousand dollars worth of sailing vessel was pounded to death upon those rocks.

The following week, I was asked to dive on the wreck in an attempt to salvage anything that could be recovered from the ocean bottom. I brought all my diving gear to Nassau and began the salvage attempt.

I might as well have stayed at home. It was unbelievable down there. The fury of the ocean is endless and unrelenting. There was nothing left but a pile of twisted, shattered rubble, strewn all over the bottom and among the rocks.

The ship had carried two 16-foot Boston Whaler runabouts, each with a 35 horsepower outboard motor. They were smashed beyond recognition. Huge metal bulkhead doors, which had once separated compartments on the lower decks, were twisted like pieces of children's licorice candy. A Moessler security safe was aboard for storage of valuables. All I found was the heavy door of this safe, ripped from its sturdy hinges by the force of the waves. Plumbing pipes and electrical conduit were twisted and strewn in every direction. The hundred and ninety thousand dollar ship had been reduced to a hundred and ninety dollars worth of scrap metal, nothing more. It was unbelievable. My respect for the power of the ocean grew immensely after this experience. My respect for the creatures that live in the ocean grew also.

The Rover had used large truck tires as bumpers along her sides when she was at dock. I found one of these tires laying on top of a pile of rubble, about 25 feet underwater, where the ocean floor met the breakwall. I tried to see what was underneath the tire and started moving it out of the way. Mistake!! A moray eel had decided to make his home inside the tire. I hadn't noticed him until it was too late. He disliked my disturbance of his home, uncurled, and struck out at my leg.

Fortunately, my muscles were taut from the strain of moving the large tire. He only made a slight, skin-piercing bite as I retreated in shocked surprise. There were many other piles of debris to examine; I abandoned this one as the eel claimed "squatters rights." The bite was not serious and I continued with my futile underwater search with greater caution and a renewed sense of respect for these unpredictable underwater creatures.

The salvage dive on the Tropic Rover put me in touch with some interesting people who inhabited the Nassau Yacht Haven Marina. One of them was another salvage diver who lived on his boat at the marina and went out daily in search of wrecked ships.

He had just found an ancient wreck. It was so old that the cargo was thoroughly encrusted with coral rock overgrowth. This coral was very hard, and digging the cargo away from its encasement was extremely difficult. We got into a conversation at the marina and he told me that he wanted to dynamite the reef in order to get at the cargo. He had no experience with explosives and didn't know how to go about this job.

Author blowing up the lock and dam on the Monongahela River.

Fortunately for him, I had experience with explosives. I had just spent two months setting dynamite charges underwater to blow up an obsolete lock and dam on the Monongahela River at Rice's

Landing near Pittsburgh. Hearing this, he wanted to strike up a partnership with me for this one salvage job. He then informed me that the cargo he had located consisted of a large pile of ingot bricks that were encased in this coral rock.

He had one of the ingots aboard his boat and he showed it to me. It was a mystery. The metal was soft and pliable. It wasn't silver; we were fairly certain of that. Nor was it lead; that possibility was eliminated too. The only other metal he could conceivably think would be valuable enough to transport on an ancient Spanish ship was platinum.

Neither of us knew what platinum looked like in its raw state. The only thing that we did know was that it was extremely valuable. Of course I got stars in my eyes (or were they dollar signs?). The idea of a partnership on a platinum find was unbelievable. A sample of the ingot was cut away and taken to a laboratory in Nassau for evaluation.

That was the longest afternoon I ever spent. We sat at the Pilot House in Nassau Yacht Haven, waiting for the telephone to ring with the lab report.

Imagine your feelings right now, if someone told you that you had won the lottery or just inherited a sizable fortune. Visions of wealth are intoxicating and the fantasies they provoke are indescribable. I wish I could re-live that afternoon again with all its wonderful daydreams. Re-live it, that is, up until the phone rang.

The call came in the late afternoon. The call pleased my partner very much. The lab informed him that his ingot consisted of 90 percent pure tin. My bubble just burst and reality bounced back into existence. Pure tin was a good find for him. He was in the salvage business. This reef full of tin ingots would provide him with a good income once he was able to blast them out of the coral rocks. But I couldn't give up a photographic business and spend the time necessary to salvage that pile of ingots for the amount of money I could get from the sale of the tin. It just wasn't practical. I did agree to show him how to handle explosives.

As a parting gesture, I accompanied him to a construction supply company to advise him on the purchase of the necessary dynamite and blasting caps.

My final moments with him were unforgettable. He drove a Volkswagen Beetle. Together we took his car to the supply company where I showed him the proper type of dynamite and blasting caps to purchase. He decided to take the explosives right then and there. We loaded the cases of dynamite into the front trunk section of his Beetle. It was a beastly hot day and I noticed that the dynamite was old stock. Some of the sticks had little beads of sweat oozing from their covers. That meant that they were unstable.

"Little beads of sweat" oozing from dynamite are nitroglycerine. They are subject to exploding under conditions of jarring or shock. I cautioned my partner to be extremely careful on our return trip to the marina because any sudden blow to the nitro could blast us into kingdom come. On the way back, I carefully took the blasting caps in my lap and nursed them like a newborn baby.

He didn't pay much attention to my warnings. He drove that little VW like he always did, with reckless abandon. A couple of times he hit bumps in the road and that car bounced like a carnival ride. I held my breath and prayed that nothing would let go. Well, they say God protects fools and drunks. He wasn't drunk, but he surely was foolish, so I guess he qualified for divine protection. We made it safely to the marina, unloaded the dynamite and, after a few final instructions, I ended the short partnership and said goodbye. That's the closest I'll ever come to being wealthy, but I don't care. I have riches that money can't buy, and I wouldn't trade them for any fortune. Still, it made a good dream while it lasted.

Some of the greatest riches I possess don't relate to monetary wealth. They come from knowing that my films have in some way been responsible for the betterment of my fellowman.

Over the years, I've had occasion to produce public service films for most of the United Way agencies. Central Blood Bank, Goodwill, the Red Cross, the Salvation Army, and many other similar organizations have benefited from films that I produced for them.

The TV stations where I worked produced telethons for local charities. Children's Hospital was a particularly notable recipient of funds raised in these broadcasts. I'll never forget my first assignment to shoot film at the hospital for use in the fund-raising telethon.

The director assigned me the task of going to the hospital and showing these children and their infirmities. He specifically instructed me to show close-ups of braces, crippled limbs, and anything that would tear at the hearts of the viewers and provoke them to make generous contributions. these instruction were given to me the evening before I was to go to the hospital for the filming.

That was a dreadful night for me. I couldn't sleep. I didn't want to take this assignment. The thought of deliberately focusing my camera on the infirmities of these unfortunate children upset me terribly. I knew I had a responsibility to the station and the program to do my best. I reluctantly left the next morning to do my job.

There was a surprise in store for me at the hospital. These children had such courage and spirit that they captivated me. It wasn't necessary to focus on their infirmities, they were obvious and came through automatically. Their optimism and positive attitude overcame the disabilities. What I thought would be a film filled with pity turned into a show filled with hope. For the next 18 years, each return visit to the hospital for telethon filming was fortified by the spirit of these courageous young patients.

The same attitude was prevalent at Camp Variety the Variety Club's summer camp for crippled children. The director of their telethon wanted me to concentrate on the kids' disabilities so viewers would be more willing to contribute to the cause.

Once again, the director was wrong. It was not necessary to concentrate on wheelchairs, braces, and hand crutches. They were part of the overall picture and could not be overlooked. What came through, over all the items of disability and handicap, was the shining spirit of these kids. They took their infirmity in stride and made the most of the facilities of that camp.

A baseball game may have been unorthodox because bases were rounded in a wheelchair, but the spirit and competition was as keen as it is in any professional sports team. The kids in the swimming pool also had a marvelous time, braces and withered limbs notwithstanding. I came away from that camp with an uplifted spirit and my film reflected this spirit also. There were other fringe benefits from producing films for the Variety Club telethons.

Variety, as you may already know, is the "Heart of Show Business." Most of the professional performers and entertainers are members of Variety and support their charities. Any time a performer came to town, I would film a portion of their show and then go backstage after the performance for special sound-on vignettes of each star making a pitch for support of Variety's charitable activities.

Over the years, I was able to see almost every notable show and performance that came to town, as well as meet all the stars during the backstage filming sessions. My camera put me in touch with a lot of interesting people. I'm grateful for that exposure as well as the entertainment I enjoyed while filming all their shows. Variety has always been my favorite charity. The time and efforts I have devoted to their cause have been some of my most worthwhile hours. In my opinion, this is life's real treasure. It can't be measured in dollars and cents.

Dollars and cents were needed to make the telethons successful, however. I know that a lot of money was raised through these shows and I'm blessed to have had some part in their success. I also feel fortunate that my filming talents have been beneficial to the Western Pennsylvania School for Blind Children and the Rehabilitation Institute of Pittsburgh, for whom I have made lengthy public relations movies to promote support for their great work. I have no way of knowing just how much benefit has been derived from these films, only that their directors are pleased with the support that they get after showing the movies.

One institution, however, stands out in my mind in a very special way. It's the Allegheny Valley School for Exceptional Children. The late Bob Prince, whom most people remember as the colorful broadcaster for the Pittsburgh Pirates, was a member of the board of directors of this special school. Bob didn't have any budget or money for making a film. He was just a really good friend and had a way of persuasion that was unique.

He talked me into making a film about the activities at the school. He then arranged for this film to be shown in a downtown motion picture theater in conjunction with the premier showing of the movie "My Fair Lady." This benefit premier was a black tie formal affair. The proceeds, of course, went to support Allegheny Valley School.

I had to rent a tuxedo to attend the affair and see my own film projected on the full-sized movie screen. It was quite a night. Champagne reception, ladies in formal gowns with jewels, fur coats, and tuxedo-clad escorts in full array. Then it was time for the show.

Exceptional children, perhaps you know, are "God's Angels Unaware." The folks who devote their time to the care of these special little people mostly qualify for election to sainthood. The patience and love they bestow daily to these multiply-handicapped boys and girls became quite evident as the film progressed. The story needed no narration. Just the tinkling background music supplied by Johnny Costa on a "celeste" piano, while Daybreak's Marcy Lynn sang a very special tune, "Hush, hush, whisper, who dares, Christopher Robbin is saying his prayers." I don't believe there was a dry eye in the theater, especially not mine. This little film served its purpose well.

Following the emotional success of the My Fair Lady premier, Don Riggs decided to run the film on his Daybreak television program the following day. By a marvelous coincidence, as the film feature was airing on TV that morning, a certain woman was getting dressed to go to work. She stopped her dressing routine as she was captivated by the faces of these children and the obvious tender loving care they were receiving at the school. This woman was the treasurer of the employee charitable contribution fund for one of the major communication companies in the area. She was entrusted with a sizable amount of money and was looking for a suitable charity that would benefit significantly from their donation. Allegheny Valley School, as presented on the television feature, seemed to fit the bill and be a good place to channel their employee contribution funds.

She contacted the director of the school that morning and, to keep a long story from getting too much longer, arrangements were made to channel enough money to significantly contribute to the building of a badly needed new wing for the school. This greatly broadened their ability to care for these exceptional children. One of my most prized possessions is a letter from Bob Prince, thanking me for my part in making this needed addition to the school become a reality. That's the kind of treasure I was referring to that money can't buy. Doing something that results in helping those less fortunate. It became my creed and, with your indulgence, I'd like to end this chapter with a short poem that I've written to express it more clearly.

<u>MY CREED</u>

I'll pass through this life

Just like all of the others

And I know all the rest

Are my sisters and brothers

And if I can help

Some of them on my way

Then my time here on earth

Will have been worth my stay

I hope some can say

When my time has drawn nigh

That their lives were made better

Because I passed by

..... by George

CHAPTER SEVENTEEN
POTPOURRI

Julio Colosanti is rescued from entrapment in an excavation cave-in just 15 mins before a TV news deadline. Author (left background with press camera) is just putting protective slide back into film holder prior to a mad dash back to the TV station and record setting scoop on the evening news.

There were spin-offs from the charitable work that I mentioned in the previous chapter. Well-paying spin-offs too, including some special medical photography. Quoting the Bible is not my talent, but there are some lines in there about "Whatsoever you do for my least brethren ..." and "Cast your bread upon the water and it will come back one hundredfold." This seemed to hold true in my case. Some of the medical people, who were associated with the charities that I had helped, had need of technical and instructional film production. What was better, they had budgets that would pay for the service. The charity work had fringe benefits that were financially rewarding.

One of the most intricate medical films involved the first transplant operation of ovary tissue from a donor patient to a recipient at Magee-Women's Hospital. Three operating teams were necessary to complete this procedure. The first team was involved with removing the proper amount of ovary tissue from the donor. The second team had the responsibility of enclosing the ovary tissue into envelope packets that were made from the corneas of human eyes.

Eye cornea tissue is unique. It is just porous enough to allow nutrients to pass through while being fine enough to strain out antibodies that are carried in the bloodstream. These antibodies have the special function of attacking and destroying any foreign matter introduced into the body and its organs.

The purpose of enclosing the ovary tissue in eye cornea envelopes was based on the theory that, once the packet was implanted into the abdomen of the recipient woman by team number 3, the antibodies could only attack the outside of the envelope. The ovary tissue inside would receive a supply of nutrients from the recipient's own body through the porous walls of the cornea tissue. By the time the antibodies were able to destroy the envelope, the ovary tissue inside would have become vascular with the patient's own blood supply and not be attacked.

Filming teams number 1 and number 2 was not particularly difficult because the pertinent activity took place in full view. Team number 3 presented a special problem. My angle of view was blocked by the chief surgeon, who had to work directly over the implant area. It was necessary to improvise in a hurry.

Finding a tall stool in the back of the operating room, I placed it alongside the chief surgeon. With his permission I climbed atop the stool. Prom this precarious perch, with delicate balance, I shot over his shoulder from directly beside his head. I'm glad that scuba diving and swimming taught me to hold my breath for long periods of time. Each time I shot a sequence of film from this position, I held my breath until the activity below me was completed.

One thing further blocked my view of this delicate procedure — the surgeon's left hand. I took a bold risk and cautiously whispered in his ear while he operated. I told him that if he wanted the film to clearly show the intricacy of his work, he would have to keep his left hand from blocking the camera's view.

To my relief, he was not disturbed by my interruption and cooperated by moving his hand out of the way enough for the camera to clearly record his handiwork.

The results were worth the risk I took. When the film was completed, I screened the finished product with the surgeons in the hospital's large auditorium. As the film progressed, the chief surgeon paid me the finest compliment I have ever received. "I've seen a lot of medical films," he remarked, "but these are the best I've ever watched." Every intricacy of the suturing technique was clearly visible and would make an excellent instructional demonstration. His praise was worth almost as much as the excellent pay I received for the production.

In addition, I felt I had made a significant contribution to the medical education of the residents and interns who would learn from observing these films. It's important to know that you've made some contributions to the betterment of mankind. We can't all be Jonas Salk and lay claim to preventing polio, or be a Christian Barnard or Thomas Starzl and replace a human heart or liver. They all have support teams, however, and every little bit helps. I'm happy that I had my chance for that little bit of help.

Speaking of a little bit of help, the guy in this next story got a whole lot of help, and he surely needed it.

Julio Colosanti was a laborer, working for a company that was excavating a sewer tunnel on the South Side of Pittsburgh. He suffered the misfortune of being trapped in a cave-in of that tunnel. He needed all kinds of help. He was pinned and partly crushed by the material from the cave-in. Fellow workers and rescue teams spent the entire day in exhausting efforts to extricate him. Julio, meanwhile, was conscious throughout all this ordeal and even helped direct his own rescue.

The cave-in occurred in the morning and I had newsfilm coverage of all the rescue activities on the noon news, but no coverage of Julio himself. He was down inside the tunnel, trapped and hurt, and his courageous ordeal was out of camera range. All through the afternoon a vigil was kept as rescue work progressed at an exasperatingly slow pace. They had to be careful not to cause any further collapse or Julio might be killed.

Deadline time was approaching for our 7 p.m. news show. These were the days before videotape. The news stories were recorded on 16mm motion picture film. This film required a lengthy processing procedure before it was ready to be put on the air.

At 6 p.m., the night-shift cameraman came to relieve me at the cave-in site. The rescuers were optimistic now. They almost had him free. Just a little more careful digging. Some of the close-quarters digging, they advised, was being done by Julio himself. It was so confined down there that they couldn't get by him to do that work. They'd soon have him out, but we wouldn't have time to get back to the station and get the movie film developed in time for the 7 o'clock show.

Then an idea came to mind. If we can't have the movie film in time, why not lead-off the show with a still photo of the rescued man? I had my Speed Graphic (old reliable) in the car, film holders loaded with black & white film. the TV Station has a darkroom and a technician who works for the promotion department. Hope he hasn't gone home yet.

One quick phone call revealed that the darkroom man was still there. He promised to have chemicals and an enlarger ready for a super-rush job. Carl Ide, the news anchor, was advised that, if they got the man out in time, he would have a rescue picture to lead off his show.

At 6:45 PM, a jubilant and thankful Julio Colosanti was lifted out of the cave-in excavation by triumphant rescue workers. He was smiling and waving to the throng of reporters and photographers.

As the rescued man was carried directly in front of me, I banged out one quick flash photo and ran immediately to my car. Driving as fast as I could make that car travel, I raced across the bridge to the downtown section and straight to the KDKA-TV Studios. Not worrying about the illegal parking, I rushed the film to the darkroom where the chemicals were ready and waiting for it to be developed.

As soon as the negative was cleared in the hypo solution, it was placed "wet" into the pre-focused enlarger. An 11 by 14 print was being exposed on the enlarging paper as Carl Ide rapped on the darkroom door on his way up to the studio to go on the air. He was worried about having the picture ready in time for the opening of the news show.

I assured him that I would have it ready in time. I was already in the process of watching the miracle of photography take place one more time. On this plain white sheet of enlarging paper in the developing tray, the image of a smiling and waving Julio Colosanti was intensifying before my eyes. As soon as the picture reached the necessary density, I slammed it into the fixing solution for 10 seconds to stabilize it. Grabbing a stack of paper towels, I took the dripping wet picture from the darkroom and raced up the steps to the news studio, blotting it as I ran.

With only seconds to go, I slapped the damp picture onto an easel in front of a pre-set live TV camera. The studio cameraman focused the live camera on the photograph and the director immediately opened the show with a shot of a triumphant rescue that had occurred just 15 minutes earlier, all the way across the river on the South Side. We scooped everybody with that shot.

Later that evening, I stopped in at the Press Club for a drink. One of the Post Gazette photographers, Paul Slantis, was at the bar and bragging to everyone that he had made the "bulldog" edition of his morning paper with his photograph of the rescue.

Well, I was entitled to some bragging rights on this story. I informed him that I had led-off the 7 p.m. news on TV with my picture of the rescued man. Instead of congratulations, I got severely rebuked and called a liar. "That's impossible," Paul insisted." The guy didn't get lifted out until 6:45. You couldn't possibly have done what you claim." The only person who saved me from his further vilification was the bartender at the club. He had seen the TV news at 7 o'clock and verified that the lead-off story started with my photo of Julio.

Slantis had to back down and apologize. Then we had a good laugh. When we looked at his picture of the rescued man, on the opposite side of the excavation trench, shooting the same picture from the reverse angle, there I was in the background of his photo, making my shot. When I examined my picture more closely, I had him in my background as well. As I remember, the next round of drinks was on Paul's tab. It's fun when things go right.

Other times, things can take a strange turn and trouble is right around the corner. Like the day of President Kennedy's funeral.

I mentioned earlier in this book of my strong feelings for our late President Kennedy. I was greatly impressed when I met him as a senator, and even more impressed when covering his presidential visit to Pittsburgh. Needless to say, the news of his assassination hit me like a ton of bricks. I was involved in film coverage of Pittsburgh's reaction to his death from the time of the shooting to the day of his funeral.

Special requests came out from the White House for every city in the country to pay special respect at the time of the funeral. All traffic was to stop, bells were to toll and special church services were requested. My assignment was to cover the downtown area and film the city's response to these requests.

I was standing at one of the main downtown intersections waiting to film the stopped traffic. No one was stopping and I was frustrated with the motorists lack of compliance with this well-publicized request. The driver of an 18-wheeler saw me with the camera and a frustrated look on my face. He asked what was the matter. When I informed him that traffic was supposed to stop for a while out of respect for the time of the President's funeral, he said, "Don't worry, pal, I'll stop them." He turned his massive truck sideways in the intersection and stopped everything. I got excellent shots of a complete traffic stand-still.

Next, I needed shots of bells tolling in a church steeple. To get a close-up shot of one particular set of church bells, it was necessary to go to one of the upper floors of the Bell Telephone building to a window that was level with the belfry.

Just as I was about to enter the building, a motorcycle policeman drove up to the curb and spoke to me. "Isn't it a shame," he sadly revealed to me. "The President's father just passed away." I was heartbroken with this news as I sadly entered the telephone building. The elevator dispatcher and one of the operators were engaged in conversation about the same topic. They also had just learned that the President's father had just died, right at the time of his funeral. We expressed our mutual sorrow at this tragedy and I continued to an upper floor and made my film coverage of the tolling church bells.

Following completion of the bell ringing scene, I departed the upper floors of the building via another elevator. The operator of this elevator was crying at the news of the death of the President's father. Several other passengers were also obviously upset. Filled with emotion at this news, I walked another block to my next assignment, Trinity Cathedral, where a memorial service was being conducted by the same Bishop whose mother I had rescued from the fire at the Episcopal Home for Ladies.

On my way into the crowded cathedral, I mentioned the news I had just heard to one of the ushers at the doorway. I then made my way up to the front of the sacristy where I started filming Bishop Pardue's eulogy and the reaction of the congregation. Just then, the usher with whom I had spoken came walking up the main aisle with a note in his hand. He interrupted the Bishop's sermon to hand him the note.

A gasp went over the crowded cathedral as Bishop Pardue informed everyone of the death of the President's father. Then he interrupted his regular sermon to offer prayers for both father and son on this sad occasion. That's another time I had difficulty in focusing the camera because of tears in my eyes.

Departing the cathedral a little before the service ended, I stationed myself atop a pair of steps across the street for a good vantage point from which to film the exit of the crowd from the cathedral. As I waited for their exit, my big boss, Harold Lund, vice president of Westinghouse Broadcasting Company and general manager of KDKA Radio and Television, came walking by my position. He stopped to speak with me on his way to the Variety Club for lunch. Of course I informed him of the tragic death of President Kennedy's father. He was most concerned and upset. He left without further conversation and I filmed the exodus of the congregation from the cathedral.

As soon as I finished filming the cathedral crowd, I got to a telephone and called my assignment editor. I wanted to know if there were any further assignments to shoot before taking the film to the processing lab. I remarked to him how sorry I was to hear about the President's father.

"Don't tell me you've heard that phony rumor too, " he exclaimed. "There's no truth to it. It's all a hoax."

Oh My God ! ! I'd just been responsible for Bishop Pardue proclaiming this misinformation to about 2000 pious mourners. They had prayed together for both father and son. Now these people would fan out and, having heard it directly from their Bishop, would no doubt tell the story to everyone they contacted.

Worse than this,I had told Mr. Lund. He was on his way to the Variety Club and would probably relate my false rumor to many important members and guests. They would certainly believe the vice president and general manager of the number one radio and TV station in the city. I had to stop him at once.

Telephoning the Variety Club, I learned that he had just arrived and was hanging up his coat. "Get him to the phone quick," I hollered. The excitement in my voice got prompt action. I was able to redeem myself with the boss by explaining the way I got the story from the cop and from the elevator dispatcher and operators.

Fortunately for me, he hadn't had an opportunity to talk with anybody yet. My false information did him no damage. I never told him or anyone else at the station about the events at the cathedral. If they read this, it'll be the first that they find out. Needless to say, I felt terrible that day and needed something to go right to make amends.

Things weren't about to go right just yet. Sometimes it never rains but what it pours.

My next assignment was a free-lance film in Florida.] took advantage of a chance to fly south with my friend Rudy Nuzzo in his Piper Cherokee. Yeah, the same plane that Les almost fell from before I grabbed his belt.

We departed Pittsburgh in the morning with reasonably good weather. The plane headed south under visual flight rules. Everything was fine until we were about 40 miles North of Charlotte, North Carolina. Bad weather started setting in below us as well as dark clouds moving in from above. Visual flight conditions were deteriorating and it was time to file an instrument flight plan and go under the guidance of air traffic control.

Before we could accomplish this, all hell broke loose. The auto-pilot instrument went haywire, spinning wildly in the dashboard of the plane. The other navigational instruments also ceased to function and power was lost to everything but the radio, which had back-up battery power. At the same time, clouds below were merging with clouds above and we were loosing our layer of visibility.

With all electronic navigational aids gone, Rudy was reduced to flying like the old time aviators. All he had to rely on was the needle ball level and the air speed indicator. We raised Charlotte tower on the radio and were advised that the ceiling was 4,000 feet. We could come down through the lower cloud level and break out well above ground level with a reasonable margin of safety.

What they didn't mention was the fact that they were having freezing rain conditions throughout the area.

When we broke through the lower cloud layer, the freezing rain hit our windshield and instantly coated it with a layer of ice that looked like the frosted glass in a bathroom window.

In all my years of aviation filming, I've never gotten into a plane with a pilot I didn't trust. This was no exception. Even in these severe conditions, I had complete faith in Rudy's ability as a pilot. He wasn't about to fail me.

One thing a pilot has to learn early, if he wants to survive: Swallow your pride. When you have an emergency, don't be afraid to let the people on the ground know that you are in trouble. We radioed Charlotte tower and advised them of our predicament. A voice came back in a Southern drawl and asked if we would like them to turn on their landing lights. It was 11 o'clock in the morning but we told them, "We'll take everything that you've got."

Not only did they turn on all the field and runway lights, they also activated the strobe-light approach.

Thank God they did that. Rudy's side of the windshield was completely blanked-out by the ice. The plane's defrosters were ineffective in clearing a path of vision. I had a little bit of engine heat escaping through a cowling below my side of the windshield. A defroster vent was picking up enough of this heat to defrost an area about the size of a silver dollar in front of me.

Through this tiny hole, I was able to spot the strobe lights leading to the runway approach. I was able to guide Rudy in the proper direction to the airport. We were only going to have one shot at this approach. In addition to icing-up the windshield, the freezing rain was also starting to form ice on the wings. Pretty soon the plane would not be able to stay in the air.

When we were about a mile away from the runway, Rudy made a 90-degree turn to the right. This allowed him a brief view of the strobe lights through a small open vent in his side window. If you're trying to picture this; he's in the left seat and I'm beside him in the right. The plane is now flying perpendicular to the runway for a minute. Rudy is getting a visual bearing and holding a mental image of our position.

Now he turns 90 degrees to the left, parallel with the runway, but with the flashing strobe lights and the runway to the left of the plane's approach path. As we reach the outer limits of the airport grounds, he starts to slip the plane sideways to the left. Now it's up to me. He can no longer see the runway or the lights. He has nothing but bathroom-glass frosted ice in front of him and might as well be blind. Through all of this, he has been flying without the aid of instruments, mostly by the seat of his pants.

My job is to put us over the runway by looking out my right side-vent and checking the color of the lights as we drift to the left, towards the landing path. The infield is covered with blue lights and the runway has all white lights marking its course. So I call out, "There's a blue light, another blue one, another blue one. A WHITE ONE!I ANOTHER WHITE ONE! ANOTHER WHITE ! "

On my cues, Rudy descended until the wheels touched concrete. He brought the plane to taxi speed along that runway as someone from the tower called on the radio with instructions to taxi to the general aviation area. We advised them that they would have to guide us there because we couldn't see anything out of our windows. A supervisor's voice came on the air with this unforgettable comment in his southern drawl, "Hey y'all, that was a pretty good landing for someone who can't see to taxi." To which we replied, "Thanks, but we never want to do it again."

When we stopped, I opened the door, but couldn't get out on the wing because it was a solid sheet of ice. We knew we'd had one chance to get that plane down and thanked our lucky stars that we didn't panic. The electronic devices were repaired and we were able to continue with our flight the following day. I was delayed in getting to my free-lance job, but when I related this story to my client, he was willing to excuse the delay and told me " I oughta write a book".

They say that bad things usually come in threes. Then I owe you one more unpleasant happening before I close this chapter. I guess almost having all my family films destroyed by an arsonist's fire should be classified as a bad thing.

A friend let me use a room on the second floor of his house for an editing lab. I had a project under way to put together all of the old films of my entire family. These old films went back to movies of my mother and father's wedding. They included my own wedding films and pictures of my children throughout all their lives and developmental stages. I was also editing all the out-take footage I was able to salvage from all the old TV shows where I had used my kids as actors.

I had segments of my oldest son, George III, when I used him in a scene to open the "How to Play Winning Baseball" feature for the Pittsburgh Pirates. My daughter Rosemary allowed me to completely bandage her for a role in a film about fire prevention. I had silent film, sound-on film, black & white and color film of all my family's activities, exotic trips, first communions, confirmations, graduations, weddings and anything else you could think of for a man to photograph and record on family films. There were boating and swimming scenes, my hilarious first attempts at ski-jumping and barefoot skiing. I also had coverage of my wife and older daughters Barbara and Patti's first water-skiing achievements, and my other son, Jimmy, on his first surfboard ride. There was roll after roll of family events too numerous to mention.

I had just completed two weeks of steady editing and splicing. All the films were put together and stored in ten large, one-hour rolls. These rolls were tight-wound on cores, placed in zip-lock plastic bags, and put into metal cans for storage in my friend's second floor room. I made plans to get the entire family together for an upcoming holiday and have a big screening of all the old films we hadn't seen for many years. Some of the films they had never seen.

Then some madman set fire to my friend's house and wrecked havoc with everything inside. All his furniture, appliances and belongings on the first floor were completely destroyed. The fire burned through the floor on the second level and some of my cans of film actually fell through the floor and into the rubble of his destroyed apartment below. Others remained precariously perched at the edge of the burned out hole, ready to fall through at the least disturbance. The exterior of the cans was badly scorched.

I arrived on the scene unaware that the house had been burned. As soon as I saw the extent of the destruction, my heart sank. My stomach was churning and I actually went into a mild case of shock. A lifetime of film records were in those cans. I didn't dare think of how I'd feel if I couldn't salvage some of it.

I found some of the cans in the first floor smoldering rubble. The silver metal cans were burned black. Inside, the plastic zip-lock bag that had been protecting the film was melted from the heat and adhering to the tight-wound film. Water from the fire hoses had gotten into the cans. All the film was wet and in danger of sticking together.

The remaining cans were still on the second floor, scorched from the heat and about to fall through the burned-out section of the floor. Against the admonitions of the fire marshall, I got an ironing board that hadn't burned and placed it across the weakened floor. I crawled out on the ironing board, reached the cans and handed them, one by one, back to my friend. The floor rafters held and I didn't fall through. That was the least of my worries. All I could think about was saving these precious films.

The cans were taken to Les Banos' motion picture lab where a super effort was made to salvage every foot of this mistreated film. Hour after hour, I hand-wound all that footage across a table set up with portable hair dryers blowing warm air onto both sides of the film. I had to dry it properly before it warped.

Every foot of film was carefully cleaned by hand. The melted plastic bags were stripped away from the tight-wound film edges by carefully slicing and scraping with a hand-held razor blade. Some of the film was so badly moistened that it was necessary to re-process it through inert chemicals and dry it again.

It took a tremendous amount of work to salvage all the footage but every frame was saved and suitable for projection again. When the family got together on the holiday, I didn't spoil the enjoyment of all their favorite films by telling them about the fire. that arsonist creep had made things tough enough for me. He wasn't going to spoil my family's enjoyment too.

In an earlier chapter, I mentioned how valuable pictures can be to family memories. Nothing brought this fact home to me more powerfully as almost loosing everything in a stupid fire. I'm having everything transferred to video tape for protection now. I'll even make a protection copy of that videotape and keep it in a safe location, away from the original films.

Maybe, dear reader, you ought to do the same. Take measures to protect your precious picture and film memories. If something happens to them, they cannot be replaced. At least put your negatives in a safe place, away from your pictures. That way, only one element is subjected to any disaster. I wouldn't want anyone else to suffer the deep feeling of potential loss that struck me when I first discovered that awful fire.

Now that's three bad things in a row in this chapter. I think I'll end it right here before anything else bad is remembered.

Let's completely change the subject and make the next chapter about South American Adventure.

CHAPTER EIGHTEEN
AMAZONAS

Top: Native children in Letecia, Colombia S.A. test the strength of the author as they use his arms for gymnasium bars during a holiday respite from shooting the documentary "Amazonas".

Bottom: Amazon natives retrieve exotic fish from the river traps as members of the Aquafari supervise. The author (center with movie camera) shoots footage for Amazonas documentary.

The Pittsburgh Zoo is one of the finest in the country. Over the years, I have shot more film features there than I can remember. One of the special features that I did was a series of 13 half hour shows entitled "What's New at the Zoo." The director and president of the zoological society liked the films that I made at the zoo. When they had vast plans for an "Aquafari" into the Amazon jungles of Brazil, Colombia, and Peru, they asked me to come along on the expedition and produce a documentary film.

The reason they were mounting this expedition centered around the opening of a new, multimillion-dollar aquarium, "Aquazoo," which was nearing completion. They wanted to have something special for the dedication ceremonies. The purpose of the aquafari was to bring back exotic specimens of tropical fish and marine life to highlight the grand opening of the Aquazoo. The principal focus and center of attention for the aquafari was the rare freshwater pink porpoise that is found only in the upper tributaries of the Amazon.

In addition to being a working expedition, the aguafari was scheduled to be a media event from its very beginning. WTAE-TV Channel 4 was sponsoring the documentary film. They sent director Bob Horvath along with me for assistance. The Pittsburgh Post Gazette sent their reporterassociate editor John Golightly to file daily stories about the progress of the expedition. The zoo also had their public relations representative Lee Nestor along on the trip. Nestor was a qualified writer and still-photographer.

he Carnegie Institute and Museum also participated in this venture. They sent Neil Richmond, curator of reptiles, to assist with the collection of alligators, lizards, and snakes. The curator of the new aquarium,Bill Flynn, was in charge of the selection of rare fish. Supervising the expedition was the president of the zoological society, Ed Magee, who brought along his wife Kate. Rounding off the expedition was the architect of the new aquarium building, Larry Wolfe, who was also a member of the Explorer's Club of Pittsburgh and a well-rounded traveler and explorer.

We were given a big media send-off at Greater Pittsburgh Airport where we boarded a DC-3 for the first leg of our journey which took us as far as Florida. There we picked up the president of Paramount Aquariums, Fred Cochu, and he transported us the rest of the way to South America in his C-46 cargo plane.

For purposes of media attention, the C-46 was painted with the name of the Pittsburgh Zoo and the aquafari sponsors, WTAE-TV and the Pittsburgh Post Gazette. It was named "El Orgullo de Leticia," which translates to "The Pride of Leticia." That's the name of the town in South America where we would be headquartered. I simply nicknamed it "The Flying Quonset Hut." That drafty old plane was our home for another 36 hours of noisy, grinding flight.

We had one delightful interruption, the island of Curacao. A jewel in the South Atlantic just off the coast of Venezuela, it was as far as we could fly on that first day. We were scheduled for an overnight stay in Curacao and I would get a chance to mix water with photography again and keep my little pattern on its natural course.

The tropical waters around this island are crystal clear and the coral reefs are abundant with all types of colorful marine life. I took this opportunity to take my mask, snorkel, and flippers to the beach and get in some underwater exploration of my own. Bill Flynn, the aquarium curator, accompanied me. He had only a face mask, no snorkel or flippers.

We swam out a few hundred yards from shore to where the depth was about 15 feet. Beautiful coral reefs and ledges rose from the white sand bottom to about 8 or 10 feet below us. This was comfortable skin-diving depth for Flynn to negotiate without flippers. We proceeded to surface-dive down to explore, and marvel at the beauty that was below us. The clarity of the water was extraordinary. We had almost unlimited visibility to enjoy all the exotic, colorful fish and marine life that populated this living reef.

With the flippers, I was able to get down more easily and stay a little deeper than Bill could do comfortably with only his mask. Kicking with your bare feet takes more exertion and tires you out sooner. Flynn was spending more time on the surface while I continued to dive again and again into this marine wonderland that I was privileged to visit only as long as I could hold my breath.

One particular reef was undercut below its surface, somewhat like an open-faced cave. I saw some good-sized fish in that cave on one of my dives. I returned to the surface took a couple of deep breaths and dove back down again for a better look at these big fellows.

As I swam under the ledge of the reef into the underwater cave, I heard a muffled cry of alarm come from the surface. Immediately concerned for Bill's safety, I exited the cave and swam upward to join him at the surface. "What's the matter?" I asked. "Are you in trouble?" "Not me," he replied. "You're the one who was in trouble. Didn't you see that big shark?"

I didn't see any sharks at all, and didn't know what he was talking about. Then he explained: As he watched my last dive from his position on the surface of the water, a huge shark had come from the opposite side of the reef and had made a pass at me just as I was entering the cave. I never saw the big fellow who was taking more than just a look at me.

We needed no further encouragement to retreat immediately from that area before we aroused his further curiosity. Without scuba gear, swimmers on the surface are an easy prey for a hungry shark. I hated to leave that beautiful paradise, but a devil had invaded and it was time to head back to the shore.

Bob Horvath had accompanied Flynn and me to the beach. He was not a proficient swimmer or diver so he waited on the beach for our return. When we got back to the beach, he related an interesting incident that had occurred just off-shore while we were out diving.

The water was very shallow where we entered from the beach, partly sandy and partly scattered with small coral rocks. Around these rocks were colonies of migrating sea urchins. For the benefit of those not familiar with underwater marine life, a sea urchin is a round creature, varying in diameter from about the size of a golf ball to about the size of a baseball. Protruding from their spherical bodies , in all upward directions, are dozens of thin, needle-sharp spines. I call them the "ocean's pincushion" or "porcupines of the sea".

Flynn and I had seen the proliferation of these urchins and had been very careful to avoid contact with their sharp little spines. Horvath had heard us cautioning each other about them as we went out.

While we were out on the reef, three sailors from the Royal Dutch Navy came to the beach for a swim. As they were about to enter the water, Horvath tried to warn them about the sea urchins. They laughed at him and treated him like a "greenhorn" who didn't know what he was talking about. With cynical disregard for his warnings, they ran off into the shallow water to enjoy their swim.

Their enjoyment was short-lived. One of them, the leader, got about 20 yards offshore and, while running, stepped directly onto one of these spiny creatures. Dozens of needles pierced his foot and he pitched forward in agony, only to land with both hands on top of two more urchins. They pierced both his hands with many more needles. The sailors left immediately to get medical attention for the leader, never once looking at Horvath or acknowledging his warning. In spite of the sailor's painful injuries, we had to laugh at how arrogance can sometimes be its own punishment.

It was time to depart Curacao and the last reasonable comfort we would enjoy for three long, difficult weeks. The Amazon was still hours away. We were apprehensive about this unfamiliar world that we were about to invade.

As the flight path of the plane crossed the Equator, it was necessary for those of us who had never crossed this mythical border to be initiated into King Neptune's Court. this involved a "baptism" or rather a dousing with water, and some other indignities that accompanied the ceremony. Certificates were then issued to each of us, raising our status from "pollywogs" to true world travelers. A little levity in an otherwise boring flight.

But the flight wasn't boring for long. Soon we were over the Amazon jungle. It is difficult to imagine anything so vast and unpopulated. We flew for hours over nothing but masses of dense vegetation. I think you could drop the entire state of Texas into this huge jungle and no one would ever find Texas again.

Captain Dave Brown, our pilot, removed the window from the cockpit to facilitate clear filming for my movie camera. He then dropped the plane to tree-top level so that I could get some dramatic footage of the jungle. The only trouble was that he didn't tell anyone else what he was going to do. When he banked the plane at a steep angle to put my open window at a good position for shooting the film, everyone else thought we were about to crash into the jungle. I had no idea he would make such a drastic maneuver, so I didn't think to warn the others about the impending change in altitude. They couldn't argue with the pilot, so they vented their fear and anger on me. OK, after what I had done to the people on the Holy Land trip, this was nothing new. I was prepared to take the heat, but the incident was quickly forgotten. We were approaching our destination.

We were over Leticia, a little river town at the intersection of the borders of Colombia, Brazil and Peru. It's situated on the Amazon some 2700 miles upstream from the mouth of the river. Captain Brown circled the town so that I could get some good aerial footage of our new headquarters. The rest of the expedition members were now used to the oblique angle of the plane and didn't bother me anymore with their complaints. They were busy taking snap shots out the side windows of the plane and were much more understanding.

From the air, the town resembled Verona, Pennsylvania. Once on the ground, we knew we were in South America. The cultural differences were evident. We were about to experience a new way of life. We thought we were ready for the challenge.

The expedition was headquartered in two stucco houses, located on a dirt road that turned into a quagmire when it rained. We had electricity as long as the town generator functioned. Well water, pumped from a cistern, supplied washing and toilet functions. None of us dared drink any of the water for fear of dysentery. I did use the water for mixing my film-developing chemicals and rinsing the developed films. I had made the mistake of volunteering to process the pictures taken by the Post Gazette editorreporter. This chore added greatly to my misery in the succeeding weeks.

Being near the equator, the temperature in this region stayed in the 100-degree range throughout our entire tour. Sometimes, in the middle of the day, the temperature would rise to 115 degrees. The humidity in the jungle area is always very high. Taking care of my motion picture film and cleaning algae growth from my cameras was a full-time task. I had to keep the film stored in insulated coolers and carry any spare rolls in an insulated shoulder-bag. Heat and humidity are two of the worst enemies of any photographic film. They don't do the cameras any good either.

Volunteering to do the Post Gazette's film developing seemed like a piece of cake back in Pittsburgh when I offered to assist them. Now, with the heat humidity and primitive water supply (sometimes with thick masses of gooey, green algae plopping out with the water) I had bitten off more than I wanted to chew.

Where was that young boy who was so fascinated with the magic of photography? Conditions like this can take away the magic in a hurry. I had to unroll spools of film, inside light-tight black canvas bags, with sweat pouring from my hands. If my sweat gets on the film, it makes it sticky and difficult to load into the developing tank. It was next to impossible to keep my sweat from getting onto the film; it was just dripping from my hands like a slow leaking faucet because of this intense heat. A job that I could do in 10 minutes under normal conditions was now taking the best part of an hour, and a most uncomfortable hour at that.

Temperature control of the processing solutions was another problem. I had to make concentrated solutions and then dilute the developer with ice cubes to bring the temperature to where the film could be developed without reticulation, or losing its emulsion from the heat. This worked OK while we were in the semi-civilized surroundings of Leticia. Once we took the expedition into the jungles, it was another story.

Developing film from muddy river water, in an elevated thatched hut, in the middle of the Amazon jungle, and getting it dry with a minimum number of insects sticking to its emulsion is a "fait accompli." Nevertheless, John Golightly sent home continuing reports of our expedition, accompanied by picture negatives that, in spite of imbedded insects, enabled the Post Gazette to carry a daily series, graphically depicting our adventures and the progress of the aquafari.

The progress of the aquafari was mixed. On one hand.the accumulation of smaller fish and marine creatures was going nicely. Fred Cochu and his agent had contacts with Indians and other natives all up and down the Amazon and its tributaries. They had put out advanced word that zoological people were coming to the area with interests in obtaining all types of rare species of fish and marine life. The Indians and natives kept the creatures and fish that they caught in pens along the river. They waited for our caravan of boats to arrive and inspect their specimens.

That caravan of boats was unique. Long, wooden boats with thatched roof covers, propelled by some South American version of an outboard motor. Two boats carried expedition members and their immediate supply needs. The other boats contained large, water-tight crates for containment of whatever fish would be selected for the long trip back to Pittsburgh.

Bill Flynn had the final word in the selection of the specimens. As new curator of the aquarium, he knew what species and types would attract visitors to the aquazoo. He also knew what species would be valuable for trading with other aquariums in the United States, once we returned. If Flynn said OK, we took the fish. If he said no, we moved on to the next collector.

At one of the collector's traps, Flynn was pleased to find an arapiema, one of the oldest species of fish in existence today. The fish was extremely rare and valuable. The only problem was that the native fish collector was not sophisticated enough to know that we couldn't use a fish that had been caught by harpooning. This magnificent fish had a harpoon wound in its side and would obviously die unless we could do something to save it.

First, we put the injured fish in a water-tight crate that had been filled with medicated water. After the medication from the water had an opportunity to seep into the harpoon wound, the fish was wrapped in a wet towel and carried over to a makeshift operating table. One of the native fishermen prepared to suture the wound with a needle and thread. Antiseptic was applied and the wound cleansed with cotton swabs. Then it was treated with merthiolate and neatly sutured.

As I filmed this procedure, I thought it was something like the medical documentaries I had produced back in the hospitals in Pittsburgh. But this was taking place in the middle of the Amazon jungle, hundreds of miles from nowhere. There was also irony in the fact that the fish was receiving better treatment than most of these natives could expect. Once this rare fish was preserved for the Aquazoo, our caravan proceeded along to other sources.

In addition to collecting from the natives, we also had nets of our own. Countless hours were spent in casting and pulling-in these large nets. Many small fish were captured by the aquafari in this manner, but the principal target of all these efforts was the elusive pink porpoise. Timing of the expedition was planned for our arrival in the Upper Amazon region at the end of the rainy season, but the high water was remaining a little bit longer this year. This frustrated our netting efforts. The porpoises could get below the nets because of the unusually high water.

The Amazon is an amazing river. Natives here tell that from rainy season to dry season the water level along the banks drops as much as 100 feet. Even where we were operating, 2700 miles upstream of the Amazon's gaping mouth, the river is still extremely wide.

"How wide is it?" you ask. Well, when we first arrived, I looked across a huge expanse of water and was impressed by the distance to the other side. Then one of the local people advised me that I was not looking at the opposite bank. What I saw was an island. There was that much more river on the other side of the island before you could see the opposite bank. That's a mighty wide river.

In just the three weeks that we were here, the water dropped so much that, in the final week, I was walking in places where I had photographed people in boats just two weeks earlier. At high-water time the river is so swift that the force of the flowing water undercuts the river banks. Huge sections of land break away from the shore and are carried downstream by the swift currents. They look like "floating islands" as they pass by. Small trees and bushes still stand erect as the river takes a piece of land from its upper banks and carries it to the delta below.

Since the water was too high to capture the pink porpoises in our nets, concentration focused on other creatures from the jungle. The expedition moved over into Brazil where a visit was paid to a Tecuna Indian tribe. Their primitive way of life provided an element of variety and cultural contrast for my film. The jungle provides them with all the essentials for basic existence. Modern civilization has only begun to make small inroads into their daily living habits.

The Tecunas told us of a large anaconda that they had seen in a swamp area not far from their village. Bill Flynn wanted the big snake, so we set off into the jungle to locate it. I was in for a thrilling piece of footage as Flynn, Larry Wolfe, and two of Cochu's agents prodded the huge constrictor out of a tree with sticks. Grabbing him by the tail, they dragged him through the swamp and onto a grassy area. He was wrestled into a burlap bag, his first step in a long journey back to Pittsburgh. When we got back to camp, I wanted close-up shots of the snake. It took six strong men to hold him for a portrait.

Other jungle creatures were collected and trapped as well. Going out at night in smaller boats, the guides would locate the South American cayman alligators along the banks of the tributaries. Shining a flashlight into their gleaming red eyes tranquilizes them. They remain still long enough for another man to slip a noose over their snout and pull it tight enough so that they can't open their mouths and make use of their vicious teeth. But that's only half of the job. They can do a lot of damage with their slashing tail. The captors have to know just where and how to grab them without getting "tail-lashed." The guides that we had were fantastic jungle men. They knew how to handle themselves in all these situations and provided me with excellent subjects for my filming.

One of these guides, Francisco, was so adapted to the jungle I believed that if he stood in one place for more than a couple of minutes, his bare feet would grow roots. Imagine my consternation one night when Francisco and I were traveling in a small boat with two other guides, hacking our way through flooded jungle overgrowth with machetes. We had been making our way through this watery jungle for a considerable amount of time when he turned to the other guide and let out a cry of "Aye yi aye yi aye" and indicated that we were lost. For the next couple of hours, I just placed my trust in those guys and prayed.

Finally, we broke through to a small tributary and they were able to trace it back to their destination. I never let them know how scared I actually was. Its no fun to be lost in the jungle at night and have your imagination turn into your worst enemy. You wouldn't believe the creepy thoughts that can run through your mind when you're not able to see what's out there in the dark, in a strange and mysterious jungle where every sound recalls some youthful terror remembered from an old Tarzan movie.

After that scare, I was due for a little fun and enjoyment. A companion of one of the guides in Leticia had a small boat with a motor powerful enough to pull a water skier. The guides talked him into taking me for a ski ride.

That's one water-ski ride I'll never forget. They had an old pair of water-skis with a double binding on one of them, for slalom skiing. They had never seen anyone go on one ski before and I provided them with a good show. It was too dangerous to ski on the Amazon with the high water, swift current, and floating debris. We took the boat into one of the "black water" tributaries where the calmer water was ideal for slalom skiing.

The only trouble was, there was not enough open water. This tributary had patches of open water that were connected by channels where jungle vines overgrew the waterway, making a tunnel of vines and vegetation. The boat driver just zoomed through these tunnels with the engine wide open. I had to crouch down to half my height to keep from becoming entangled in the vines and branches. I never knew what was coming next, but I figured, "If the boat can make it, so can I." The trick was to stay low and hold on for all the thrills. A most enjoyable break in an otherwise miserable trip. Thank goodness for the water; the photography end of this Job was no fun.

Another part of this trip was no fun either, and I got an unexpected water break that I didn't want.

Our caravan of boats traveled to some very remote tributaries. We would stay three or four days at a time at primitive locations in the jungle. One of these locations we nicknamed "Doanverry" Brazil. It was nothing more than a thatched-roof hut built on stilts about 15 feet above ground to allow for high water in the rainy season. The native who owned this hut permitted the members of the aquafari to sling their hammocks inside his hut. This provided some degree of shelter for the night.

There were no sanitary facilities, so daily toilet necessities required a trip into the jungle weeds. Because there was a woman member of the aquafari, the trips into the weeds were a bit more remote. This is where contact with the troublesome South American "chigger" became a source of extreme annoyance to many of us. We had been inoculated against tropical diseases, but there was no repellent that seemed to work against infestation from this microscopically small red spider. It was so tiny it could crawl into a hair follicle. There, it would deposit eggs inside a pore and secrete a protective liquid that caused a histamine reaction and eruptions on the skin that were worse than any mosquito bite.

Most of the members of the expedition experienced some difficulty from these chigger eruptions. A couple of us, myself in particular, were extremely unfortunate. They counted about 250 of these irritations all over my body. Those darn spiders worked their way to the most intimate parts. They seemed to concentrate on areas where clothing was tight. Belt lines, crotch area, buttocks, ankle areas where socks were tight etc.. As if life wasn't miserable enough with all the heat and humidity, the jungle added this irritation to complicate matters even further.

Well, I was miserable enough and didn't want to add to my exposure. The next day, instead of retreating into the jungle weeds for my daily toilet necessities, I borrowed a little dug-out canoe from one of the Indians. I paddled to an area

out of sight of the hut for my daily routine. Paddling back, I found that since I was considerably heavier than the little Indian who owned the canoe, It was riding much lower in the river. Water was starting to flow in over the gunwales with each paddle stroke. Before I could get back to the hut, the canoe filled up with water and sank.

To sink a canoe in a Pennsylvania river on a blistery hot day would be a delight. Down here, it was a different story. In the same area where my boat was sinking, just the previous afternoon, an Indian fisherman had been catching piranha. These flesh-eating fish with razor-sharp teeth have been known to attack an animal in the water and strip it to a skeleton in a manner of minutes. The knowledge of this danger instantly came to mind as the boat was sinking. I swam as hard as I could, dragging his water-filled canoe back to the shore as quickly as possible. Visions of old jungle movies and piranha attacks terrorized me into using all my strength to get back fast.

The terror I had originally experienced was miraculously replaced by a deep feeling of physical relief. The immersion in the water took away the exasperating annoyance of the chigger bites. Once I retrieved the Indian's canoe, I got a little braver about being in the water. I was willing to risk attack by the piranha for some more relief from the irritating itch of the chigger bites.

Taking the air mattress from the bottom of my sleeping bag, I stripped down to my undershorts and risked floating on the air mattress in the water near the dock. Believe me, I stayed close to the dock because every once in a while a curious little piranha would make a quick hit at the side of my body, and I would make just as quick an exit to the safety of the dock. After a minute or so, I would regain my nerve and go back out on the mattress again until another piranha tried to take a bite of my hide. I repeated this floating and retreating action for an hour or more and found that the relief from the itching was worth the risk of the bites.

While the chigger is a very tiny spider and proved most annoying, we also encountered the very opposite. One evening, inside this thatched-roof hut, several of us were enjoying a steaming hot cup of fresh brewed coffee. (Not the South American kind, this was Nescafe' brought from the USA in a jar). Bill Flynn always drank from an oversized enamel coffee mug. He was sitting on an overturned barrel with his big mug of hot coffee resting on his knee. Suddenly, we all heard a "kerplop" and saw a splash in his mug. The biggest spider that I have ever seen had fallen from the thatched-roof of the hut and had landed dead center in Bill's hot coffee. The steaming hot coffee killed the spider instantly as we looked on in startled surprise. The body of the spider filled the oversized mug while the legs hung down in every direction along the sides.

As curator of the aquarium, Bill was used to many kinds of creatures in the course of his daily work. However, I think he felt a bit like Little Miss Muffet when this critter dropped in. I don't know about Bill and the others, but I had a very uneasy time about getting to sleep that night. Much as I dislike sleeping in the hammocks, I deserted my sleeping bag on the floor that night, and opted for the relative safety of the suspended bed.

The following day, we were returning to Leticia and I was eager to get back to its limited degree of civilization. There was a pharmacia in that little town and I was eager to see if they had any calamine lotion to relieve my itching chigger bites. To my joy, they found one small bottle of Caladryl lotion, which was even better. I took this bottle back to the stucco house where we were headquartered and went about my task of applying this lotion to my chigger bites.

Back, legs, buttocks and groin areas had the majority of these annoying bites. I liberally applied the lotion to every area of my naked body that needed the medication. Due to the very high humidity, the lotion was not drying very fast. To expedite the drying time so I could get dressed for supper, I placed an electric fan on the stand near the end of the bed. Then, I knelt on the bed, supported by my hands, with my bare buttocks aimed toward the fan so the flow of air would dry the caladryl on my rearend.

This was the image that presented itself to Bill Flynn when he opened my bedroom door to inform me that supper was ready. He took one look at my naked body, atop the bed in that awkward kneeling position, and with his Brooklyn-type dry sense of humor remarked, "Hey George, I don't know how to tell you this, but somebody stole your girlfriend." We howled with laughter at the ridiculousness of the situation. His remarks became an unwritten punch-line for the remainder of the trip. Humor, however, was not the watchword for the final week of the expedition. Although many fish and other jungle creatures had been accumulated and held for the trip home, the highlight of the trip, the search for the pink porpoises, was proving fruitless. To add to the frustration, there was a personality conflict between Ed Magee and Cochu and his agents. That was making the work even harder.

The completion of a successful documentary film was my principal objective, and the pink porpoises were a key factor in my film story. So I went out on a limb. Even though I had no authority, I personally offered a 100-peso reward, out of my own pocket, to the first native who brought in a live porpoise. Word quickly spread and the Indians and natives intensified their efforts at the nets. The river water was falling more rapidly now and there was better hope that they would have some success.

Since our own expedition had ground to a standstill, with the friction of the two leaders hindering further efforts at collecting, I decided to mount a side expedition of my own.

The natives had told me of a stone-age Indian tribe, the Yaguas, who inhabited an area of Peru in the vicinity of the El Tigre River. It was estimated that their location was about one day's trip up the Amazon and the El Tigre tributary if we used a fast boat. I was sure that a portion of the documentary film should include a look at these people and their primitive way of life.

Jose, the owner of the fast boat that had pulled me on water-skis, had become friendly with me because of our mutual love of the water. He agreed to take me up the El Tigre River to try to find the Yagua Indians. I hadn't much time and this expedition was hurriedly organized (or dis-organized), and we set out for a day's trip up river.

I had presence of mind enough to ask Jose about fuel consumption on the trip. He advised that he carried three six-gallon tanks for his outboard motor. He further advised that we could purchase gasoline from the border guards when we checked-in at the patrol station as we entered Peru from Colombia. So off we went on a fast-paced trip up river to photograph the primitive Indians.

After using almost two tanks of fuel, we arrived at the Peruvian border station. Imagine our shock and disappointment when the border guards asked us to sell them some of our gasoline because their supply was exhausted. We had been counting on them for our return supply. They advised that there was a supply boat somewhere along the river nicknamed "Amazon Queen." This boat had 55-gallon drums of fuel aboard and would sell us some for our return journey. All we had to do was find them.

Hell, we couldn't make it back on the fuel we had left, so we might as well try to find the Indians and also look for the Amazon Queen. Finding the Indians was a little difficult. They had abandoned their living quarters because a woman had died there. Their custom is to move away from any place where a death occurs, build elsewhere, and start all over again.

After further searching, the Yaguas were located. They were in the process of building a dwelling out of palm logs and vine rope. They were truly primitive. Some were naked as jaybirds and others wore clothing because a missionary had come by and given it to them. Neither cared about the nakedness or clothing of the others.

I could have made an entire documentary about this tribe. The Indians who were constructing the framework of the new dwelling were as agile as monkeys. They climbed the log framework with hands and bare feet, shimmying up the poles with no support or other assistance. Their sense of balance was remarkable also. Gripping the cross log with their curled toes, they worked with reckless abandon two stories above the ground.

Their work was soon interrupted, however, when hunters came in from the jungle with fresh meat. Their hunting was done with a long blow-gun and poison darts. These young Indians were extremely proficient with the blow-guns. They demonstrated their deadly aim on a piece of yucca root into which they shot the needle-like darts from a distance of about 50 feet.

The blow-gun fascinated me and I attempted to purchase one from the Indian owner. My money meant nothing to him, so now it was bargaining time. I spoke no Indian dialect. My knowledge of Spanish was quite limited. Jose' spoke a little English and a small amount of Yagua dialect. I think the Indian also understood a limited number of Spanish words. So we had a three-language bargaining session in progress. English to Spanish to Indian and back again the same way.

Pesos and dollars meant nothing to the Indian. Neither did he want any kind of pocket knife or camping gear. My cameras were not even considered in the bargaining. My final bargaining chip was my wrist watch, which was hidden under the long-sleeved nylon jacket that I wore to protect me from the malaria-bearing bite of the ever-present Anopheles mosquito. I had two wrist watches on my arm underneath that jacket sleeve. One was a gold, waterproof diver's watch. The other, my back-up watch, was an ordinary Timex.

The Indian never got to see the gold watch. I kept it under my sleeve and only produced the Timex. This was enough to arouse his curiosity and interest in making the trade. With Jose's persuasive assistance, I finally got him to trade me his six-foot blow-gun, a quiver of needle darts, a piranha jaw with teeth to use as a dart sharpener, and a pouch filled with kapok to attach to the rear end of the darts, all for my ordinary Timex watch. I tried to make it clear to him in the three-language conversation that it was necessary to wind the watch every day. I don't think this part of the conversation was completely understood. There's probably an unwound Timex in the Amazon jungle to this day, serving only in an ornamental capacity.

In the extra time that it took us to locate the Yaguas, we had overextended our food rations. The Indians invited us to share a meal with them. To refuse their hospitality could have provoked some unpleasantness, so we joined them in a meal. The hunters had killed a large river rat, a pacca. This rodent is about as large as a medium-sized dog and is regularly hunted by the Indians for food. They find many pacca along the riverbanks.

The thought of eating a "river rat" was totally unappealing, but I figured if the Indians could do it, so could I. I put away my repugnant ideas and set my mind to eating without prejudice. Bob Horvath had come along on this trip and was not so easily appeased. He had just gotten over a bout with dysentery. (He had forgotten that ice cubes served in a drink in the cantina were made from river water.) Bob was repulsed at the idea of eating a river rodent.

To try and brighten things up and perhaps interject a little humor into the situation, I joked about our meat. We had been in the jungle about three weeks now, and our beards had grown to a moderate length. I noticed that the pieces of the meat that the Yaguas served to us were roughly cut. The meat still contained the animal's outer layer of protective fat with his hair bristles jutting up through it. As I took out my hunting knife and cut away this layer of fat and hair, I casually remarked to Bob that our meat had almost as much of a beard as we did. It sort of resembled a hairbrush.

He did not take kindly to my feeble attempt at humor. His poor stomach had more than it could take. Leaving the eating area, Bob retreated in misery to partake of some dry crackers that we had in the boat. I managed to repress my mental repugnance and got through eating the piece of meat. Actually, it wasn't bad. It tasted a bit like fatty pork chops that had been poorly cooked. It was an experience that I wouldn't choose to repeat, but I survived.

Another Indian later arrived playing a "pan flute." One of the original tribe produced a drum made from dried animal skin that was stretched over a frame. They began some ritual type music and the unclad girls participated in a tribal dance which I filmed with diplomatic aloofness. Right in the middle of all this ceremony, we spotted the Amazon Queen passing by the encampment. It was necessary to cut our visit short in order to catch up with the river boat and purchase the vital fuel that we needed for our return trip.

Somewhere before in this book I mentioned that I'd rather be lucky than good. It happened again here.

Thank goodness the Indian had not wanted pesos for that blow-gun. I needed every peso that I possessed to purchase enough gasoline to make the trip back. The Amazon Queen would not stop or even slow down to do business with us. We had to match speed with her while running alongside. First they wanted the pesos, then they took our gasoline cans, filled them from their 55-gallon drums, and handed the full tanks back to our moving boat. Sure hands were needed or we were out of luck. We held on to the tanks and said goodbye to the Amazon Queen and the Yagua Indians. After an overnight stay at a missionary camp several miles farther down river we made it safely back to Leticia the following day.

The overnight in the missionary camp was an experience too. The missionary was quite a hunter and had trophies across the wall in his hut. One of the more graphic trophies was the stretched-out skin of a 14 foot black cayman alligator, mounted with mouth open and teeth clearly showing. It was an ominous sight and prompted a nightmare in my dreams that night.

I had gone out with the natives on expeditions at night to catch the smaller cayman alligators with a flashlight and a noose as I described earlier. In my dream, we were engaged in catching the smaller alligators when this 14-footer caught us in the process of trapping her babies and attacked with ferocious grunting sounds, jaws and teeth gnashing angrily. She was heading directly towards me with her huge mouth open, ready to tear me apart, when I awoke in a cold sweat, shivering with fear. Sleeping in the Amazon can sometimes be very difficult for a newcomer. I had to get a good look at that 14 foot skin mounted on the wall to assure myself that this was only a dream. The gator in the dream looked just like the wall mounting, open mouth and all.

While I'm on the subject of dreams, there's one other animal that I came across in the Amazon that deserves mention here because of its dreaminess. While we were on the trip into the Yagua Indian camp, I spotted and photographed one of them high up in a balsa tree. It was the South American sloth, easily one of the ugliest animals I have ever seen. Its movements are so languid, its like watching a movie in slow motion, only slower. The film sequence that I shot is fascinating because of its tranquility. This creature wouldn't hurry if her life depended upon it. We couldn't bring the sloth back to Pittsburgh because she will only eat the leaves of the balsa tree.

When I got back to Leticia from my impromptu side trip, I got word that some of the natives had captured a porpoise and were on their way down river with the pink mammal in a dugout canoe. Everything became exciting again. The porpoise was the highlight of the expedition. I immediately got into one of the faster boats and rode upriver to intercept them and film the arrival of this treasured catch. Dramatic on-the-water scenes were obtained as they brought the creature to our larger boat and transferred it into our holding crate for transportation back to Leticia. It was necessary to continue moistening the porpoise's skin with fresh water to prevent dehydration from exposure to the hot sun.

Once in Leticia, everyone gathered excitedly around the boat to get a look at this special catch. Bill Flynn was overjoyed. This would be a feature attraction at the Aquazoo. Then, just as suddenly as news of this first catch, word came down river that the Indians had captured two more, a mother and still-nursing baby porpoise. Once again, I hurried to the fast boat and intercepted them along the way for action scenes of the care of these porpoises enroute, and the transfer, over the water to the larger holding crates.

So, back in Leticia, we had the problem of housing these large aquatic mammals until it was time to put them onto the airplane. In front of the town church there is a reflecting pool, about the size of an Olympic swimming pool, maybe a little bit larger. It was decided that this would be the best place to store the porpoises until departure time. Permission was obtained to put them in that pool. A gasiosos truck was commandeered at the docks and used to transport the crated porpoises to the reflecting pool. "What's a gasiosos truck?" you ask. It's one that is used to deliver cases of soda pop. The driver was most cooperative after we purchased a few cases of pop to distribute to the volunteers who lent a helping hand.

Once the porpoises were safe in the reflecting pool, wt went about the task of collecting all the remaining fish and wildlife and loading them all aboard that old C-46. Crate after crate of marine creatures, all needing substantial amounts of water for survival, were hoisted aboard that airplane. It took the straining muscles of eight men, myself included, to hoist the porpoise crates, with all their necessary water, into the belly of the plane. We began to worry about the ability of the plane to carry all this weight.

Once all the creatures were in place, the members of the aquafari were the last to board. The lumbering old C-46 rolled down the runway and, straining with all its might, left the ground and barely cleared the tree tops of the adjacent jungle. We were airborne, but that was all. We watched for what seemed to be an eternity as the big plane flew almost wingtip to treetop as the twin engines seemed to be roaring in protest to the strain being put upon them.

We all knew how heavy our cargo load was, especially with the need for all that water to keep the creatures alive. We we re all holding our breath and praying that we wouldn't go down in that endless jungle so close below.

What we didn't know was that Captain Brown was using all his aviation experience to assure our maximum safety. He informed me that he used all that low flying time to build up airspeed. He explained further that, should anything happen to either one of the plane's twin engines, he could return to the airfield and land safely. However, if he sacrificed airspeed in an attempt to gain altitude and something happened to an engine, he would have no control of the plane and we would crash into the jungle.

Once I understood that basic principle of aviation, the long period of low flying made sense and my cold jitters went away. We weren't going to crash into the jungle after all. Now we could pay more attention to the care and moisturizing of our precious porpoises. The trip was going to be long and difficult. It was necessary to continuously scoop water from the crates and pour it over the exposed half of the creatures to prevent dehydration. Because of the conservation of weight aboard the plane, it was not feasible to fill the porpoise crates with water. They only had the minimum amount for survival, a layer about two fee deep to cushion their weight and keep them wet. We worked in shifts to continuously pour this water over the upper sides of their bodies.

We landed in Curacao and again in Miami, where the fire departments drove their water tanker trucks out to meet the plane and supply us with fresh water to replace the polluted contents of the crates. The old water had become pretty foul-smelling after all those hours of travel. Porpoises are mammals and they have excretion and toilet functions the same as humans. We all welcomed the supply of fresh water as the odor in the confinement of that plane was anything but pleasant.

During the flight back, I was sitting atop one of the crates when Bill Flynn suggested that I might want to seek a better resting place. I had chosen to relax on top of a crate of 13 electric eels. Each eel is capable of discharging an electrical charge equivalent to 600 volts of household current. Contact with these creatures could be quite a "shocking" experience. I needed no further encouragement to move to another location. I fell asleep on a 100-pound sack of peanuts. When I awoke, I found that someone had pinned a tag to my chest. It identified me as a rare zoological species, "homo sapiens." They had also taken some pictures of me with the tag attached. I was asleep and unaware of these pictures. They surprised me with the photographs at a later date when we got together and laughed about some of our experiences.

What seemed like eons later, we were over Greater Pittsburgh Airport and prepared our cargo for the shock of landing. The mother porpoise had spent the entire trip with her flipper around her baby in a loving embrace. It was a tender sight to behold and I captured this tenderness in a treasured sequence of film just before we landed.

Once we were on the ground, pandemonium reigned. Our landing was a media event. Advance publicity had brought a large crowd of people to witness our return. A band was playing South American music and a motorcade of convertibles was waiting to parade us through downtown Pittsburgh and out to the Highland Park Zoo, where a fleet of moving vans would carry all the crates of our specimens and creatures to the Aquazoo.

The final part of my documentary included the return, the motorcade parade, and finally the safe transfer of the fish, alligators, snakes, and other marine creatures into their proper places within the aquarium. But the highlight was again with the porpoises. Scuba divers from my diving club volunteered to get them safely adapted to their tanks. When the divers signaled that everything was OK, we breathed our final sigh of relief. The aquafari was complete.

For many of the members it had been a rough trip, for some, downright miserable. But our experience gained for us a new knowledge of man's adaptation to his environment. Besides being a working expedition, it was extremely educational. And now the real work for me was about to begin. Thousands of feet of motion picture film had to be processed and edited. Workprints were reviewed and then adapted to Lee Nestor's script. Narration and special music were recorded and synchronized to the film. All was prepared for a special program on Channel 4 and for a large-screen premier showing at the opening festivities at the new Aquazoo.

The documentary entitled "Amazonas" was a big success. It won a Golden Quill award that year and many other honors were bestowed upon it in subsequent showings. A dozen copies of the film were made and shown to schools clubs, church groups, and civic organizations throughout all the surrounding area. Each time I personally show this film to a community or school group, I bring along the blow-gun that I obtained by trading my Timex watch. When I shoot the needle darts into a target, it really piques the interest of the audience. I also brought back a stuffed piranha. They like to feel his razor-sharp teeth. It makes the film seem more real. The promotional value to the zoo is tremendous.

I was particularly impressed by seeing my work projected on a full-sized theater-type screen. Call it ego. Call it vanity. Call it whatever you like. I can't fully explain the feelings that I got seeing my film acclaimed by masses of people when it was presented to them in bigger-than-life projection. I felt an unexplainable desire to produce a full-length film for movie theater exhibition. My efforts became channeled in this future direction. That should probably be covered in a new chapter. I'll call it "Around the World Beneath the Sea." You'll learn why when you turn the page.

CHAPTER NINETEEN
AROUND THE WORLD
BENEATH THE SEA

Author with self-built underwater camera prepares to film Around The
World Beneath The Sea.

Picture, if you will, shiny silver bubbles of air, glistening in the sunlight as they rise from the depths of the deep blue Caribbean Sea. The sound you hear is music from a synthesizer that subliminally causes you to question the origin of these rapidly expanding silver discs. As the camera descends toward the source of the bubbles, two figures come into view. A dark-skinned native man and a fair-skinned girl with long, black hair. They are sitting on an outcropping coral ledge, 100 feet down in the crystal clear Caribbean, totally enchanted by the beauty of the surrounding coral reef and the brilliantly colorful tropical fish that are their silent companions in this fantastic world beneath the sea.

As the camera draws nearer to the couple, it becomes obvious that they are sitting on a ledge above a deep-blue, bottomless abyss. The bubbles are coming from SCUBA gear (Self Contained Underwater Breathing Apparatus), which they both are wearing. As the camera moves closer to the face of the girl, her innermost thoughts can be heard above the sound of the synthesizer music. "Never in my wildest dreams," she wonders, "did I ever imagine that I'd be sitting here in this underwater paradise and feel so much a part of this hidden world. If Chuckles could only see me now. My little pet porpoise would probably be very happy for me. After all, it was my interest in him that got me started into diving in the first place. Who would have believed that it would lead to a trip 'Around the World Beneath the Sea'?"

As the girl and her native diving companion move off along the width of the reef, the camera stays on a particularly picturesque section with colorful coral and tropical fish. The title zooms up to full screen from the background.

Now the stage is set. In the first two or three minutes of the film, the audience is immediately exposed to some of the most colorful and exotic scenes of a world that is totally new and foreign to all but the diver who would venture into this hidden part of our universe. Questions are now posed. Who is this girl? Who is Chuckles? How did she arrive at this obvious state of bliss that she is enjoying on the reef?

Following the titles, the film takes the form of a flashback. It will show the life of the girl as she evolves from a teacher at a girls' school, through a volunteer program at a local zoo aquarium, where she becomes a daily swimming companion to an orphaned baby porpoise. His name is Chuckles. This association prompts her interest in marine life and creates a desire to become more involved through a course in scuba diving.

Without becoming too technical, the film will skim over her advanced underwater education and associations with various experts in marine biology and undersea exploring. Now fully trained, she sets out to explore this hidden world beneath the sea. With a minimum of contrivance, the film will have one diving experience pave the way and set the stage for the next undersea location. By introducing her to others in the field, each of her dives will bring invitations to continue on to some other exotic dive spot.

All the famous locations of the world can be covered using this format. Florida, California, Hawaii, Tahiti, Japan, the Mediterranean and Red Sea, Australia's Great Barrier Reef, Bermuda and the Bahamas can all be covered in this method. The final scene brings us back to the area filmed in the opening of the show, the shelf of the ocean off Montego Bay, Jamaica. There, the ultimate in picturesque reef and tropical fish abound. The viewer will be left with a pleasant feeling of an experience long to be remembered.

It is anticipated that 50 percent of the film will be produced underwater with the primary purpose of exposing this hidden part of the world to the inquiring eye of those who have a desire to know its secrets and share its beauty, but, for whatever reason, cannot themselves venture into the underwater world.

The basic idea of this film is not new. A trip around the world to pursue a sport or avocation. Just a few years ago, a novice film producer had a similar idea about his particular sport of surfing. With a limited budget, he set off on a search for the best waves. He and his companions took surfboards to all parts of the globe to find the best waves available and film the rides that they provided. The resulting film was a great success at the box office. The first year's gross receipts greatly exceeded the cost of the production.

I am stealing the basic idea from the producer of the surfing film. I feel that the underwater world has much more scope and a greater overall appeal to an audience than just following a big wave. As a matter of fact, as the interest in the girl increases, I anticipate that the appeal of this type of movie will generate enough attention to promote the filming of a sequel. There is certainly enough material available to make any number of films, once a trend is established. So I propose that the necessary investment capital be provided to make this proposition become a reality. Respectfully submitted etc.

That was the proposal I presented to an investment broker who specialized in tax shelter programs for his clients. The idea was to produce my long-desired, full-length theater film. It would be financed by a tax shelter program engineered by this broker. The proposal was met with favor by many of his clients and I got the green light to produce a pilot film for their approval.

The girl who would star in the film was actually swimming with the little porpoise that we had brought back from the Amazon. She was a Zoo volunteer who gave him the companionship that he needed after the death of his mother. She really did take scuba lessons in order to better perform her aquatic duties.

We traveled to St. Croix in the U. S. Virgin Islands. There, I produced an underwater pilot film amid the gorgeous tropical reefs that surround this Caribbean paradise. The film closely approximated the proposal. I was extremely pleased with the results and so were the investors. They heartily approved the pilot film and were eager to finance the entire production. I thought I was finally on my way to producing my big project, a full-length theater movie.

Enter the IRS. Yes, the Internal Revenue Service. Their timing couldn't have been worse. Just as this group was about to invest big bucks into my movie, the IRS changed its regulations allowing tax shelter benefits for investment in motion picture production. the clients could no longer derive the tax deferments that they needed from this investment.

I had spent a considerable amount of time and my own money in the production of the pilot film. They liked it very much, but apologized for not being able to invest their money as had originally been planned. They had elected to go with another program that would provide them with the desired tax shelter. I was left holding the bag. At least the pilot film had given me a glimpse of my dream. The conditions under which it was shot were pleasant. Nevertheless, there was an empty, unfulfilled feeling deep inside my chest that needed to see something on the big theater screen.

That need was going to be gratified somehow.

In previous years, I had produced a number of films for the Norwegian Caribbean Cruise Lines. These were publicity promotions and television features that I created for them in exchange for a Caribbean cruise. I had an idea of how to fulfil my need to see a production of mine on the big theater screen. The cruise line would provide my means to this end.

Through my association with Variety, it was possible to get a committee from the major theater chain owners to exhibit a short feature about cruise activities in all of their theaters. In return, a percentage of the profits from any cruise booked through this theater promotion would go to Variety Club Charities.

With the promise of theatrical exposure, Norwegian Caribbean Lines agreed to underwrite the production of a promotional film aboard their flagship "Southward". This "Cruise For Variety" feature would ultimately be produced on 35mm reels for theater use. A portion of my dream was being fulfilled.

"Never Let Your Work Interfere With Your Fun" was never more appropriate. The cooperation of the ship's officers and crew was marvelous. Many of the passengers were eager to assist in the production as well. Since the ports-of-call on this cruise included some of the most exotic dive sites in the Caribbean, I naturally included a lengthy sequence of underwater scenes in the final production.

The timing of the completion of the Cruise For Variety featurette coincided with the announcement of the annual Academy Awards. My film was released that same day and shared theater screens all over the area with the Academy Award films. I am having difficulty in explaining the feeling of pride that I experienced each time I visited a theater and watched my production on the big screen. I would match the quality of my film against that of the Hollywood prints and I was pleased with the favorable comparisons.

Another thing that I did was to situate myself in the midst of a group of patrons of all ages. I would carefully listen to their comments as they viewed my featurette. Movie patrons are different from television viewers. People who go to the theater have paid money to see the feature. They are not distracted by household interruptions and generally pay close attention to the screen. Their praise or criticism can be taken with more validity. They make better critics than television viewers. I didn't eavesdrop on their comments merely for ego satisfaction, I wanted to learn from their comments. I must admit, I did need to feel the boost that I got from hearing good things about my work. The pressure to produce a theater movie was finally brought under control and I was free to move on to other film projects.

This final chapter is going to cover one of my most spectacular film challenges. We're off to Venezuela and a look at "Angel Falls".

Aerial view of the first 3212 feet of Angel Falls as it breaks from George's Gorge and falls over the sheer cliffs to the skirt montain below.

CHAPTER TWENTY
ANGEL FALLS

These falls are so high that, by the time the water reaches the
ground, it has expanded to 10 times its diameter

The telephone rang unexpectedly one evening. The caller was Ed Magee, president of the Zoological Society. They were about to launch another extensive expedition into South America and, since I had done so well for them in the Amazon, would I please consider accompanying them on this trip to "The Lost World of Angel Falls?" Also, would I be so kind as to quote a price for my services in producing another documentary film?

Angel Falls, I was informed, is the highest waterfall in the world. If falls from a mysterious plateau called Ayantepuif which rises ominously from the jungles of Venezuela, about 600 miles inland. Sir Arthur Connan-Doyle had used this unexplored mountain plateau as the setting for his novel The Lost World. In his book, pre-historic dinosaurs and other weird creatures had been preserved from the rest of the world by the isolation of sheer cliffs that surround this austere tepui. In case you are asking yourself, "What's a tepui?" I probably had better mention that it's the Indian word for a flat-top mountain.

Back to the jungles of South America? My memory flooded back to the Amazon and the misery that accompanied that trip. I was not anxious to return to some unexplored area, 600 miles into the Venezuelan jungle for a search of the unknown Ayantepui. Still, the spirit of adventure has always been a strong force in my life. I couldn't resist the challenge. One thing I did do, however, was quote a price that was much higher than the cost of the Amazon trip. This, I figured, would compensate me for the anticipated miseries. My reputation from the past documentary was like money in the bank. They accepted my price and preparations were made for another South American expedition.

I did some research before we left. I found out that Angel Falls had not been discovered until the mid-1930s. Prior to that time, the world thought that Victoria Falls in Africa was its highest waterfall. Then an American adventurer and soldier-of-fortune, Jimmy Angel, made a discovery that would correct all the geography books.

Angel was a bush pilot who flew all sorts of free-lance jobs back in the '30s. He stationed himself around the area of Panama. One night, in a Panama City bar, an old prospector struck up a conversation with Angel and asked him if he would take on a mysterious flying assignment. Jimmy agreed and piloted the old-timer down to Venezuela where, without the aid of any maps or charts, the old codger guided him on a curious flight. He followed river paths and landmarks that only he knew, until they arrived at the massive plateau mountain that today is known as Ayantepui.

Instructing Angel to land on top of the plateau, the old prospector disappeared for a couple of hours. He returned to the plane laden with bags of gold nuggets and raw diamonds. Angel returned the man to Panama and was paid in gold nuggets for his flying services. The old man never explained any more about the source of his treasure. The knowledge obsessed Angel and he returned to Venezuela several times to retrace his steps and try to locate that mysterious plateau once more. He finally found it, but when he landed his plane on the top of the tepui, the field that he chose turned out to be a marshy swamp. His plane bogged down in the soft ground and he was unable to take off again.

Before landing, Jimmy Angel had flown around this massive tepui, trying to locate the spot where the old-timer had set him down. While he was circling the mountain, he was treated to a vision that no one except the primitive Indians of the region, had ever seen before. The parting clouds revealed a magnificent waterfall, cascading from the face of the plateau, 3,212 feet down sheer cliffs to the skirt mountains below. There it formed a white-water rapids and descended the remaining 4,000 feet to the river at the plateau's base. This waterfall was 19 times higher than Niagara.

What good was this discovery going to do Jimmy now ? His plane was hopelessly stuck in the marsh. Take-off was impossible. He had limited supplies and was trapped on a plateau some 300 square miles in area. It was isolated from the jungle below by over 3,000 feet of sheer cliffs. He was also 600 miles inland from any civilized area,

While Jimmy was circling the mountain looking for a place to land, he noticed that an area on the South face of the tepui , away from the falls area, had less of a sheer cliff and somewhat of a "V" cut in the plateau that might provide some kind of a descending slope to the jungle below.

He set out for the South face. It took several days to negotiate the harsh terrain. He had exhausted himself physically and was out of food supplies as he located the crevasse in the mountain and made his way down. There is no record of the time spent descending. The only thing that is known is that Angel somehow made it to the skirt mountain area and was miraculously found by a tribe of primitive Indians who were foraging for food in that area. He was emaciated and near death when they found him.

One of the principle staple foods of these Indians was the meat of the huge spiders that inhabit that area. Angel was fed this spider meat along with other food concoctions. After a considerable amount of time, he was nursed back to health. Somehow he made his way back to Panama and made known his discovery of the world's highest waterfall. Shortly thereafter, he engaged in a barroom brawl and died as a result of injuries sustained in the fight. He never got a chance to return to Ayantepui and recover his 1936 Pairchild Flamingo airplane that remained on the top of the plateau.

Other pilots flew into Venezuela to substantiate his claims. When the clouds cooperated and did not obscure the view, they were treated to a spectacular sight of water cascading from the top of these multi-colored cliffs and falling so far that the flow disintegrated into a vaporized mist by the time it struck the bottom. Surveyors on jungle expeditions later verified the height, and a waterfall 1000 feet higher than Victoria went into the geography books as the new record-holder.

The unexplored area of the plateau atop the falls was the target of the zoological society's intended expedition. This would be different from the Amazon. This safari had more people involved. It also had different objectives. The Idea for this expedition had a different initiation.

Larry Wolfe, the architect who designed the Aquazoo, had been with the Zoo Society on the Amazon trip. Larry was also a mountain climber and a member of the Explorer's Club of Pittsburgh. The Angel Falls expedition was originally the concept of the mountain climbing members of the Explorer's Club. They wanted to climb the face of the world's highest waterfall and they brought their plan to Wolfe's attention.

Larry approached the Zoo Society on the basis that an exploration of this "lost world" might lead to the discovery of some unique species of animals that have been isolated from the rest of the world. Such a find would be of great promotional value to the new zoo image in Pittsburgh. The proposal mushroomed into interest from the academic and scientific community. Like "Topsy" from Uncle Tom's Cabin fame, it just grew. The plan for a small group of mountain-climbers to attack the face of Angel Falls grew into an 18 man expedition. Ivan Jirak, Explorer's Club president was in charge of all the arrangements.

A staunch supporter of the zoo's activities was the Gulf Oil Company. Through their Venezuelan subsidiary, Mene-Grande Oil, they were instrumental in obtaining the assistance of the Venezuelan government. Larry Wolfe traveled to Caracas and spoke before the Venezuelan Parliament to advise them of the scope of the exploration and secure their cooperation. Units of the Venezuelan Air Force were placed at the disposal of the expedition, including a large cargo plane and a jet helicopter.

Three groups comprised the expedition: six mountain climbers, six parachutists, and six scientists. I fell into the scientific category as the documentary cinematographer. We gathered in Caracas and then transferred all our gear to the Air Force cargo plane for the flight to a jungle outpost named Canaima. From this headquarters we prepared for our onslaught on the mountain.

As we flew from Caracas to Canaima, the pilot circled Ayantepui. I was able to shoot some aerial films from the window of the plane and get some idea of the magnitude of this massive eruption from the floor of the jungle. It is huge and most impressive. The dense green foliage of the 4000 feet of skirt mountain abruptly ends as 3500 feet of sheer rock face rises up on all sides to a massive plateau.

The plateau is not just a flat surface. It contains hills, valleys rivers, lakes, waterfalls and swamps in its mountaintop terrain. The area of the plateau is about 300 square miles, roughly about the size of the entire city of Pittsburgh. It is like an island in the sky, isolated from the rest of the jungle below by these steep sandstone cliffs. The face of the cliffs is formed from multi-colored layers of rock. Pink, salmon, tan, orange, and yellow blend into an impressive, eye-pleasing view.

But where are the falls? I wanted film of my first view of nature's highest water spectacle. All around this massive protrusion, wispy clouds drift into the high cliffs. They merge into each other until they form massive cloud formations that obliterate much of the mountainside. They also cover the area around the falls. They frustrate photographers with their hide-and-seek tactics. There would be no filming of the falls today. The clouds had won this round. I began to understand why they had not been discovered until the 1930s.

Once we got organized in Canaima, the first order of business was to get the climbers started at the bottom of the mountain. The jet helicopter was employed to bring the six climbers and all their gear to the riverbed at the bottom of the falls. They set out to climb the skirt mountain and then begin their assault on the sheer cliffs. I filmed their departure and then entrusted one of my cameras to the lead climber. He volunteered to shoot some footage from his point of view during the climb.

With the climbers in position, the next group to be accommodated was the six parachutists. Their job was to drop onto the plateau in the area where Jimmy Angel's plane was situated, and investigate the remains of the aircraft. Then they were to prepare a safe landing location for the helicopter to bring in the final group, the six scientists.

Filming the parachutists was a thrill. With a parachute strapped to my own back for safety, I was able to lean out the open door of the cargo plane and film each man as he jumped. The temptation to follow each man down into the void was extremely great, especially knowing that I had my own chute. But remembering the broken ankle from the motorcycle wreck in Bermuda dispelled any idea I might have had to try a parachute jump.

All six of the jumpers landed within a few feet of Angel's plane. They explored and photographed this historic relic. It was made of corrugated aluminum and was amazingly well preserved. It withstood exposure to the elements for all these many years without showing too much evidence of deteriorization. Maybe the unique climate on top of this mountain had something to do with it.

Returning to the base, I transferred into the helicopter and was transported to the parachutists' jump site. They had cleared a safe landing place for the chopper just a few hundred feet from the antique plane. The area directly around the plane was a swampy marsh, covered with bromeliads. These huge plants were rooted in the muddy soil. The parachutists had slopped through the marsh until they found a safe place, on higher ground, where the copter could land without any chance of getting bogged down.

I had to mush my way over to Angel's plane using the bromeliads as stepping stones. That only worked some of the time. More often than not, I would slip into knee-high, even thigh-high mud. The reward was worth the effort. I was able to shoot some exclusive, close-up footage of this historic aviation relic and make a film record of its excellent state of preservation. A little humor was also added as some of the parachutists sat at the controls and played pilot.

The next thing to do was locate a safe and suitable location for the main encampment. We set out for a site about half a mile from the brink of the falls. Here, the river that forms the falls makes a 90-degree bend and cuts into a deep gorge for its final run to the face of the falls. By cutting away the brush from a flat rocky area, a safe landing place for the helicopter was prepared. The remaining scientists were brought up to the plateau to begin their explorations.

Besides me, the scientific party included Ed Magee, Zoo president; Larry Wolfe, Zoo architect; Dr. Ralph Buchsbaum, professor of ecology at the University of Pittsburgh; Dr. Ernesto Foldats, director of the Institute Botanico, University of Caracas; and Dr. Roger Latham, naturalist and outdoors editor for the Pittsburgh Press. Each brought along equipment, supplies and instruments to study this heretofore unexplored area.

Dr. Buchsbaum set up shop immediately, unfolding a collapsible table and loading it with all the various instruments of his profession. To look at him, you'd think he was back home at the university instead of 600 miles deep into the Venexuelan wilderness in an area no man had seen before. He settled in nicely to his tasks of examining and evaluating everything that was found in this strange place.

Magee and Wolfe were more interested in the animal or marine life of the mountaintop. They set out on various expeditions from the main camp in search of any kind of animal life. Dr. Latham, a naturalist and writer, pursued a study of the total environment of the plateau.

Dr. Foldats, the botanist and orchid specialist, was in seventh heaven with the discoveries that he was making. He found many new species of plant life growing in this special climate. I spent time with each scientist and filmed the highlights of their findings.

On one excursion with Dr. Foldats, into the undergrowth surrounding our camp, he came upon a species of orchid that had not been previously known. It was not yet named or classified. He was extremely jubilant and, as I was filming his discovery, he asked me the name of my wife. When I told him her name was Mary Regina, he exclaimed, "Good ! 'Orchedia Maria Regina,' I name it for her." I was greatly impressed by this honor he had bestowed upon my family. this was certainly an unusual experience for me.

The whole trip was a continuous chain of unusual experiences. My first night atop the plateau was a combination of fascination and terror. Then the terror turned back into fascination again. Because this huge mountain extrudes from the floor of the jungle like somebody had squeezed a giant tube of toothpaste, the weather patterns are extremely different from any of the surrounding areas.

Imagine a massive obstacle, 7500 feet high, with 3500 feet of solid sandstone walls extending for miles in either direction. Small clouds drifting along at 3000 or 4000 feet above the jungle and savanna suddenly bump into this huge barrier and adhere to its surface. Other clouds drift along and join-up with the ones already stuck to the mountainside. Individually, they don't carry enough moisture to produce any rain for the jungle below. Collectively, however, it's a different story.

You could almost set your watch by the regularity of the weather pattern. All during the day, the clouds would gather around the sides of the cliffs, building in intensity and size. They gradually rose with the updrafts of air along the face of the mountain. By late afternoon or early evening, the big clouds would finally drift across the edge of the plateau and envelop the area in a damp, foggy mist that resembled London on one of its worst days.

These huge clouds would swirl uneasily overhead until sunset. Then, with the cooling of the night temperature, all hell would break loose. Torrential downpours accompanied by lightning, thunder, and fierce winds replaced the calm of the daylight hours. It's no wonder that the superstitious Indians worshiped this tepui and were afraid to venture close to it. These massive storms convinced them that an angry god dwelt in this place and they gave it great respect.

I gave it great respect too. The first night sleeping (or trying to sleep) in a tent that was staked out near the edge of the gorge, was an unnerving experience. None of us had expected the fury of these storms. The force of the sudden wind changes whipped the canvas of the tent and threatened to blow us into the gorge. Lightening continued to crackle all around us and added to our fear. We just held on for dear life and waited-out the storm's violent life.

Then, with no further fanfare, the storm abruptly stopped. The winds became calm and the heavy rain just quit. Going out to inspect the damage that was done to the tent, my earlier terror turned into fascination again. It was an unbelievably beautiful panorama that presented itself to me. The sky was crystal clear and black as ebony. the storm had completely cleansed the atmosphere. No clouds remained and the stars of this midnight sky were the brightest and clearest that I have ever seen.

It was breathtaking. We were 7500 feet up in the thin air. there was no extraneous light for hundreds of miles. the area was completely devoid of any distracting illumination. The stars looked like big pieces of fluffy popcorn, just waiting to be picked out of the sky, if my arm were a little bit longer. I tried to capture this spectacle on film, but the camera just can't reproduce the scope and magnitude of the entire sky the way the human eye can encompass it. In order to share my appreciation of this spectacular sight, the best I can do is explain the experience the way I just did.

With the storm past and the night so beautiful, I didn't want to return to the tent just yet. Wandering about the area near the campsite, I got the urge to look around using a powerful flashlight. Maybe I could find some kind of nocturnal animal that the others might have missed in the daylight hours. As I ventured farther from camp, my initial curiosity was gradually replaced by a cautious fear. What was I doing out here by myself? Visions of Connan-Doyle's "Lost World" creatures invaded my fantasy. Maybe there was some kind of dangerous animal lurking just beyond our camp. I wasn't going to be a hero and find out. Returning to the relative safety of the tent, I finally got a good night's sleep.

The next day dawned bright and sunny with a delightful temperature that held somewhere in the 80s. The sun dried everything that had been soaked by the evening rainstorm. After a hearty breakfast, we set about the task of reaching the area at the brink of the waterfall. Our camp was only about a half-mile from the edge of the falls, but this final distance was rugged terrain. Swampy marsh land blocked a straight-line passage. Detours were necessary around eroded and dangerously undercut surfaces. There were wide crevasses that required jumping across. Some of these crevasses showed no bottom. The journey to the edge of the falls took almost half the day. Jumping across these bottomless crevasses , while protecting the movie camera and equipment, became quite a feat. Especially when the landing areas on the other side were sometimes rocky sections that contained slippery, damp moss. This was some of the most inhospitable terrain that I have ever encountered.

Once I slipped and fell, cutting my hand on a rough rock while trying to protect my camera from damage. First aid and a quick bandage quickly put me back in business. I could now see the rainbow arching above the mist that drifted upward from the falls. We were approaching the brink.

As official photographer for the expedition, I was permitted to go to the brink ahead of the rest of the party in order to film their arrival and the display of the expedition's flags over the face of the falls. Thus, merely by circumstances of my profession, I became the first human known to stand at the brink of the world's highest waterfall. This honor almost cost me my life.

Impressed by being the first to stand at the brink of Angel Palls, I wanted to make a record of this accomplishment, in writing, upon the rock surface at the edge of the cliff. Giving my camera to another expedition member so that he could film my inscription on the rock, I cautiously made my way to an undercut section. I wanted to write on an area that would be protected from the weather and keep my message preserved for posterity.

In order to write on the underside of this rock projection, I was forced into an awkward position. It required bracing my feet against rocks at the edge of the cliff. The next stop down was 3212 feet below. As I inscribed my name and address, the date, and a brief message, with magic marker on the undersurface of the rock, I could feel my left foot gradually slipping along the damp rock that supported it. Something stubborn in my attitude refused to recognize the threat to my safety. I persisted in writing until the message was complete, even though my foot continued to slowly slide toward the edge of the supporting rock.

I'm glad I have a relatively short name. I finished my message and backed off from the cliff edge before my foot slipped completely. Probably no one will ever see that message up there at the top of the falls, but I know it's there and I was willing to take the risk of writing it there for the sake of that knowledge. I also placed four coins in an indentation at the face of the falls, a penny, nickel, dime and quarter of U.S. mintage. They will attest to any future explorer that Americans were here first.

As I mentioned previously, the expedition carried various flags representing the United States, the City of Pittsburgh, the Explorers' Club, and the Zoological Society. One of the key shots that I needed for the film documentary was a display of these flags over the rim of the falls. An interesting phenomenon occurred during my attempt to shoot this piece of film.

Pat Lawton, leader of the parachute-jumping team and president of the Pittsburgh Sky Divers, was holding one of the flags over the edge of the falls. Updrafts were blowing the flags back along the arms of the holders. They were difficult to hold straight due to these backward drafts. I naturally wanted one scene with all the flags showing clearly and in full view. As I waited for a lull in the updrafts, Pat suddenly admonished me that I had better get this picture quick. He said he was "turning green" and getting sick from the effects of looking down from this extreme height.

I couldn't imagine that a man who had fearlessly jumped out of the open door of airplanes in more than 2000 parachute jumps would be affected by a mere 3212 feet of cliff height. The difference, it seems, was that he didn't have a parachute strapped to his back. He jokingly suggested that, if he had a parachute, he could leap from these cliffs, free fall, and be able to track away from the face of the rocks, open his chute and drift safely to the jungle below. I said that if he wanted to risk doing that, I would be happy to film it. That's called a "Mexican stand-off" Nothing further was said about such a foolhardy jump.

I provided one other service for the expedition members while we were at the brink of the falls. A huge boulder at the edge interfered with a completely panoramic view from this magnificent vantage point. Climbing on Larry Wolfe's shoulders, I was able to "belly-hunch" my way up to the top of this boulder for an unobstructed, wide-angle view of the entire area. One by one, each member handed up his camera and I was able to shoot panoramic pictures for everyone from my exclusive perch.

A description of the top of the falls wouldn't be complete without the mention of the lack of a roar. Anyone who has visited Niagara or any other major waterfalls, can vividly recall the sound of the rushing water, rumbling and roaring as it tumbles over itself at the foot of the cataract. Not so with Angel Falls. There is a deadly silence as the cascade of the river plummets over the brink and takes that breathtaking drop to the skirt mountain below. The only noise you can hear is a slight "whooshing" sound as the flow leaves the edge of the gorge.

Speaking of the gorge, by the way, the other members of the expedition decided to name it after me. The name just seemed to fit: "George's Gorge." There may not be any official Venezuelan record of this dedication, but I'm nevertheless proud that my fellow expeditioners put my name to the final half-mile of river gorge that cuts its way to the brink of the falls.

As for some of the other expeditioners, we hadn't heard from the mountain-climbers for several days. The lack of radio contact had expedition leader Jirak a bit concerned. We had gone out each day in the helicopter to scout their location, but cloud cover along the mountain had been too thick to permit us to spot their position. On the fifth day that I went out with the helicopter crew on this reconnaissance flight, we spotted their orange marker, about one third of the way up the sheer face of the cliffs. This was considerably less progress than they had anticipated. They were way behind schedule and there was some unknown problem. Further attempts to contact them by walkie-talkie radio were to no avail.

In the meantime, other branches of the expedition were continuing their explorations with mixed results. The zoologists Magee and Wolfe, with assistance from Lawton and other members of the parachute team, had made exhaustive searches in every direction from our main camp. Their attempts to find some evidence of animals of any species were meeting with no luck whatsoever.

The ecologists and botanists, on the other hand, were making discovery after discovery. In this "Land That Time Forgot," they were amazed at the methods that nature manufactures for plant survival in unfriendly climates. One of the things that they discovered was a gelatinous material that some of the plant life produced to provide nourishment. This jelly-like substance is not found in similar species elsewhere in the world.

They also had an opinion as to why the zoologists were not finding any animal species on the mesa. The soil is very poor and lacking in nutrients. Also, this is the only large area of vegetation in a tropical climate that does not have a dry season cycle similar to other jungle areas. Vegetation does not dry up and lose its leaves and foliage up here. It becomes very dense, but lacking in nutritional value. It would make poor foraging material for any leaf-eating animals. It was not going to be a good trip for the zoologists.

Dr. Buchsbaum's scientific set-up was unique. All his instruments and meters were in place on his folding table and he had a clamp-on umbrella attached to his chair for protection from the sun. The only thing that he forgot was that, while he had the umbrella for protection of his body, his hands were exposed to the sun for long periods of time while he used his microscopes and various meters. As a result, he got a painful case of sunburn on the back of both hands.

I took a lesson from his mistake and protected my hands and the rest of my exposed skin with suntan lotion. Continuous use of the camera left my hands exposed to the unfiltered rays of this blistering tropical sun. I'm sorry the doctor got burned, but I'm grateful to have learned from his mistake. I also overcame my reluctance to wearing a hat. Up here, at an altitude of 7500 feet above sea level, the air is thin and the tropical sun is not filtered by any pollutants. The skin gets the full effects of the infrared and ultraviolet rays. It can cook an unprotected head in a few hours.

As the days passed, we made another check of the mountain-climbers with the helicopter. They were still less than half-way up the cliff. It was obvious that they were not going to make it up to the top in our allotted period of time. The helicopter spent so much time searching for them, in and out of the clouds, that by the time we found them, the plane was low on gasoline. I had to accompany them back to Canaima for refueling. The support plane with their gasoline supply was one day late arriving at Caniama and I was treated to a one day vacation away from the expedition while the crew awaited the fuel. We were given the hospitality of Jungle Rudy's Camp Uciama. This is a primitive tourist camp at the base of Hacha Falls on the Caroni River. Hacha Falls are like a miniature version of Niagara with tea-colored water cascading over two major cataracts.

Below the falls are sandy beaches and excellent swimming areas. I enjoyed the swimming break and the companionship of a girl from California who was vacationing there with her aunt, a lady who liked to visit out-of-the-way places. Rena and I discovered that we could take a piece of driftwood log from the bottom of Hacha Falls and ride the current with it all the way to the end of the beach. A little feminine companionship was a welcome break to the all-male associations I had been confined to for the past couple of weeks. I would have liked to dine with Rena and her aunt that evening, but I had commitments with the helicopter crew and they had priority.

Early the next morning, the fuel supply arrived and we returned to Ayantepui for a rescue mission to retrieve the climbing team. They had experienced multiple difficulties. The unusual rainy periods forced unexpected detours due to high-water problems. Their food supply was running out, and repeated minor injuries from falling through rotted vegetation had exhausted their strength and energy. Their walkie-talkie had been damaged in a fall. When they finally got it repaired and communicated with expedition leader Jirak, a

Author prepares to photograph at edge of 3,212 foot brink of Angel Falls.

decision was made to abort the climb. They descended to the riverbed where we picked them up in the helicopter for transportation to the summit.

As we left the riverbed with the disappointed and weary climbers, mother nature gave them -- and me -- an unexpected break. As if in a gesture of good will, the weather cooperated to eliminate all obscuring clouds from the face of the cliffs adjacent to the waterfall. A magnificent view was provided as we ascended in a flight over the skirt mountain and across the face of the cliff.

The captain of the helicopter was an excellent pilot. He flew as close to the falls as was safely possible. I was able to get several excellent sequences of film as he flew in from every angle to give the mountain-climbers a special visual treat. Then he circled our camp and, at my direction, flew along the half mile of George's Gorge, allowing me to hang out the open door of the helicopter as we flew directly over the brink of the falls for the most spectacular and dramatic shot of the entire trip. Suddenly, the river and the gorge below vanishes from sight at the edge of the cliff. The enormity of the length of the falling water boggles the mind. As he flew out beyond the falls, he circled the plane and gave an even more breathtaking angle to the view. The impact of that sight literally took our breath away.

Now that the climbers were back together with us at the main camp, we got them a good, hot meal and a decent night's sleep. Next day it was time for one final expedition out from the camp and a two-mile trip up the Angel River to a lake at its headwater. Having only two snakes and a few frogs to show for all their searching, the zoologists at least hoped to find some aquatic life in the upper lake. I was about to serve in a dual capacity, as both cinematographer and skin-diver.

Water and photography still shaping my career.

After a difficult journey upstream against white-water rapids and strong currents, we arrived at the lake. I donned mask, snorkel, and flippers and began diving the length and breadth of the pool. Had this lake been in Pennsylvania, there would have been an abundance of fish and marine life populating its waters. The underwater visibility was good, even though the water was the color of iced-tea from the staining effect of decaying hardwood, it was still extremely clear. I really wanted to find some kind of fish or marine life here, but tadpoles and frogs were the only aquatic creatures that all my diving and searching revealed.

Ed Magee desperately wanted to find some species of fish for the Aquazoo. He was down to his last resort, dynamite. Two separate charges were set in the middle of the lake, one at the bottom and the other a few feet below the surface. The intent was to stun any fish or marine life with the force of the underwater blast. After each explosion, I again dove all around the area in search of any marine creatures, all to no avail. This was certainly a most disappointing conclusion for the zoologists.

The trip back down the river to the main camp went much faster because we could shoot the white-water with our air matresses. The only problem was that I drowned one of my cameras. Although I had it triple-wrapped in heavy duty plastic bags, a spill over one of the rapids and a landing on sharp rocks played havoc with the plastic bags and filled the camera with water. I had some intense salvage and maintenance work to do when we got back to camp.

The ecologists and naturalists offered some explanation to the lack of fish in this lovely lake. Once again, the climate atop the mesa is unique to the rest of the world. Clouds too small to provide rain to the jungle below leave a dry season down there. Up on the mesa-top, clouds that have collected against the cliffs all day are now big enough to contain significant moisture for the daily rain that comes in the form of the violent storms after sunset.

Being in a tropical location and having no dry season, plants and trees don't loose their leaves. There is insufficient supply of decaying vegetation on the ground to be washed into the streams and rivers. This decaying plant material is the beginning of the life-chain and nutritional source for the tiny marine creatures that are at the base of the aquatic food cycle.

Without the tiny creatures, there are no little fish. Without little fish, there is no food for the bigger fish. The entire food chain is thwarted by the lack of decaying vegetation. this left only a beautiful, empty lake and nothing to take back to the Aquazoo. Their hope of finding some species of fish that had been isolated from the rest of the world for eons became a pipe dream.

The helicopter returned the next day to begin taking supplies and expedition members down from the mountain. They brought an envelope addressed to me. It was a letter from Rena, expressing her regrets that we hadn't been able to have dinner together in Canaima and inviting me to visit in California, if I ever got the chance. Larry Wolfe was with me when the pilot delivered the letter and I showed him its contents. "I'll be damned, George," he exclaimed. "Here we are in one of the most isolated spots in the world, making an exclusive exploration of virgin territory, and you get a special-delivery air mail letter, hand-delivered by the Venezuelan Air Force. And from a female, no less." I could only reply, "Larry, I'd rather be lucky than good."

The departure from the mountain seemed routine until we got back to Caracas and learned that we had been the source of headlines in the daily newspapers. The El Nacional newspaper of Caracas boldly displayed the following:

ANSIOSA EXPECTATIVA POR LOS 18 CIENTIFICOS Internados en la Selva PERDIDA EM CANIAMA

They thought that we were lost in the jungle and in danger. In translating the accompanying story, we learned that our radio broadcasts back and forth to the mountain-climbing team had been overheard by amateur radio operators somewhere in the area. They had been misunderstood for emergency distress calls. The U.S. Ambassador in Caracas had been informed and he asked the State Department of the Interior in Venezuela to initiate a rescue search for us.

We had arrived in Caracas too late to squelch the newspaper stories, but we immediately contacted the Venezuelan authorities to terminate the rescue search activities. Then it was necessary to telephone the United States and put our worried families at ease. This had been a nasty piece of misinformation and I'm glad we were able to stop the rumor before anyone at home got panicky.

We returned with happy botanists, ecologists, and naturalists, but dejected zoologists and mountain-climbers. I had thousands of feet of spectacular film and interesting coverage of the expedition. There was no happy ending, however, for the Zoological Society, who was paying the bill, now refused to further finance the editing and production of the final documentary. The impetus to spend additional money on the final production lost its steam. The documentary had never progressed beyond the work-print stage when the Zoological Society was disbanded due to a political controversy with municipal officials over the operation of the zoo. I am left with reels of unproduced film and no sponsor.

Just recently, I projected the edited Angel Falls work-print for a select group of professors at Penn State. I narrated the film while it was being shown and held a question and answer session afterward. They were all favorably impressed with my presentation and a copy of the film was left with them for further evaluation. If my luck holds up, they may find funds from one of the departments of the university to finance the completion of this interesting documentary.

Author, with trusty Bolex in hand, is photographed at the head of "George's Gorge" where the Angel River cuts is last half mile before plunging over the sheer mountain cliffs to create the world's tallest waterfall. This Gorge was named after the author by his fellow expedition members.

I've projected this workprint several times to various groups. I love to hear the reaction of the audience when the film comes to the place where the helicopter flies along George's Gorge and out over the drop-off of the falls. I can actually hear people sucking in their breath in astonishment at the visual thrill this scene brings to the viewer. I hope to put it together with music and narration to match its spectacular beauty. The film is good, but I need that little bit of luck - again - to bring it all together.

Meanwhile, my wife, three daughters, my mother, god-mother, and mother-in-law, are all wearing solid gold pins in the shape of South American orchids. I spent the bulk of my extra profit in Caracas, buying these gold pins to honor my wife on the occasion of the new species of South American orchid that now bears her name. I only regret that, as of this writing, my lovely wife cannot appreciate this honor or anything else, for that matter. Alzheimer's Disease has reduced her physical and mental capacity to almost nothing. She did have some good years, prior to the onset of this disease, when the recognition, the gold orchid pin, and the name "Orchidia Maria Regina" was appreciated and enjoyed. I'm fortunate to have shared this enjoyment with her while she still had her health.

Author poses with wife Mary Regina (Jean) on the occasion of their 25th Wedding Anniversary at a time when she still enjoyed good health. The children surrounding them are, from left to right: Jim, Rosemary, George III, - Patti, Barb and Tom

Mary Regina's (Jean's) bout with Alzheimer's placed me in the role of caregiver and literally put an end to any future efforts at exotic travel filming. Funny how things sometimes come full circle. I've spent the interim years shooting coaching films again, this time for the University of Pittsburgh football team. Not very glamorous by comparison with the travel films, but something I could do and still remain close enough to care for her needs as the disease progressed.

That doesn't leave me with much more to write about, so, I think I'll close with a brief look at where we might be going with photography.

As an officer of the News Photographers Association of Greater Pittsburgh, I was recently privileged to sit in on a seminar and demonstration of making photographs without film. Microchips are taking over most of the world. They have invaded the field of photography with a dramatic impact. The camera of the future, with prototypes already available, uses a floppy disk, just like a computer. This disk can hold up to 50 pictures and can be erased and reused. The technology has far-reaching photo and video applications. There's the capability for instant transmission via telephone lines or satellite broadcast to meet production deadlines. Picture quality with fine-line resolution is rapidly improving.

No more will a 10-year-old boy experience the thrill of the magic development of the photographic image onto that plain piece of white paper. The 10-year-old of this upcoming age will probably treat photography like just one more video game or computer process. Electronic imaging, as the new photography process is called, will probably catch up with the quality of photographic film by the turn of the century. Picture-taking, as we have known it, will become a thing of the past. The technology is unique and is a natural by-product of the space age. I was tremendously impressed by the demonstration and the applications that will probably replace basic photography.

My last couple of years as a news photographer were spent with a new title "videographer." The video camera and videotape recorder have almost universally taken the place of the motion picture camera and film in the television industry. They do the job more efficiently than the movie camera and soon they will be able to do it more economically too. Videotapes that are no longer needed for their content can be magnetically erased and re-used. The image quality that video tape produces is rapidly approaching the level that had been achieved by the motion picture film.

Newspapers like U.S.A. Today, are using video still-pictures more frequently to make deadlines and scoop competition. They still appear to sacrifice something in quality when compared to standard photography but technical improvements are continuing to be made. Experts predict that their visual quality will soon match the photographic level. Apparently the filmless camera is here to stay.

Perhaps I'm a dinosaur. At least I know that I hold a nostalgic grip on things of the past that I knew as good. Basic photography is one of these good things. I hope its magic will continue to inspire young people the way it did me. There's still a thrill each time I see a picture come to life in a developing tray and I know that my skill and experience have been employed to make it a good photograph. Technology ... don't do me any favors. We all want to leave the world with some kind of legacy. Mine is photography, and I pray that it will endure through this electronic intrusion.

I'd like to express my thanks to all my comrades who shared in the adventures in these latter chapters. This is not just my book, it belongs to all of us. I hope when you read these stories you will enjoy and re-live our experiences almost as much as I have enjoyed and re-lived them during the writing.

The stories and chronicles related in this book are factual accounts of true events and happenings. All the people mentioned are real. Some names and localities have been altered to protect privacy.

I have trusted my memory for some of the minor details and statistics. They are correct to the best of my recollection.

POST-SCRIPT

I have my grandson Stephen to thank for this final idea. He overheard me discussing the book and the various stories contained herein. He pondered for a minute and then asked, "Grandpap, why don't you transfer your films onto DVD and make copies available to your readers? When people read about these films, they are going to want to see them."

I'm taking his advice and producing copies of Amazonas onto DVDs. I'm further considering completing the Angel Falls production into a presentable feature and making that available also. if I get sufficient inquiries and/or orders for these cassettes it will make my efforts in producing this documentary worthwhile.

By the time this book is completed, I will have information on the price of the DVDs including shipping and handling. The number to call for phone-in orders is (724) 274-8501.

After we discussed the DVD project Stephen asked me if I would show him how to print a photograph. I took him to the darkroom and gave him the basic instructions on how the enlarger operates. Then I left him on his own to experiment with the process. As I looked on from the background I realized:

The room was dark, the only illumination was coming from a dull amber bulb, hanging some distance from the activity below. The young boy slowly slipped a sheet of white paper into a tray containing a liquid chemical formula. He waited patiently, concentrating on the miracle that was about to occur.

We had come full circle..

by George

POST-SCRIPT TWO

Captain George (Author), with crew, after dramatic rescue
on Allegheny River.

Time waits for no one and I am no exception to that rule.

Many years have passed since our trip to Angel Falls in Venezuela. As a matter of fact, Venezuela now has a ruler who would not be so cooperative with Americans as was the government who gave us the helicopter and transport plane to support our expedition to Anaytepui. I've learned that the Venezuelan government has brought Jimmy Angel's Fairchild Flamingo airplane down from the plateau via powerful "sky-lift" helicopter, and has displayed it at an air show in Caracas.

Time has also changed my focus on life. As a matter of fact, my focus, in my right eye, was changed by replacement lens surgery that resulted in the tearing of my iris that made my photography work a little less than the perfection that I had achieved in the past, so I turned my interests to my companion passion and got more involved with water.

After a period of intensive study and sea service time, I obtained my Coast Guard Captain's License and became a Merchant Marine Officer with a Master's License to operate a vessel commercially. My past connections with the Gateway Clipper Fleet allowed me to spend some time on their vessels learning the commercial side of boating, and subsequently got me involved with Captaining local vessels like the Carnegie Science Center's "Voyager" and "Discovery", floating classrooms for local students, with laboratories set up aboard to allow the students to study the microscopic marine life that abounds in Pittsburgh's Three Rivers.

I also spent a tour as Captain of the "Just Ducky Tours", a flotilla of World War II amphibious vessels that also travel on land. It is quite an experience to drive 7 tons of steel vehicle/vessel down a launching ramp and into the water with three dozen passengers wondering if this contraption really will float. I've always had my eyes on the water, but I'd like to have been able to watch the expressions on some of the faces of passengers as I split the water with the bow of the "Ducky" and it actually did float and sail away on the water-bourne half of its tour.

I've had a couple of other Captaining positions, running water taxis and cruise vessels, and also as Captain of the "Baywatch" vessel, owned by Channel 53 Television, who used it to entertain advertising clients as a sales enhancement incentive. The "Pamela Anderson" look-alike contests were never dull.

All this current interest in the water resulted in my joining the United States Coast Guard Auxiliary and spending the past 20 years involved with safety patrols and training sessions for new members.

One of these training sessions was particularly intense and resulted in the rescue of a 25 ft. cruiser that had experienced engine trouble and was caught in a strong current on the Allegheny River and was in imminent danger of being swept over a low-head dam, to the peril of a man, woman and 3 year old little girl who were aboard.

My 50 ft. Cabin Yacht was offered for use to the Coast Guard as an operational facility and I was on a training mission with several new recruits and three instructors. One of the points of instruction for new recruits was the procedures for transiting the navigational locks at the dams in the Allegheny River. My crew and I were waiting above Lock #2 Allegheny River for our turn to proceed down-river. A commercial towboat was in the lock and we tied-up to the upper wall awaiting his departure.

The above mentioned 25 ft. cruiser was also awaiting transit through the locks and the operator had ignored my warning to him not to wait in the area in mid-river beyond the safety of the lock walls, due to the swiftness of the current because of recent heavy rainfall. After my warning, I watched him go out to the danger area and drive his boat around in circles waiting for the lock doors to open. As there was nothing further that I could do about his ignoring of my warning, I turned my attention to my trainees and proceeded to instruct them about the protocols of transiting the locks. My back was turned to the circling cruiser.

All of a sudden, one of my trainees yelled, "Captain George, that boat is in trouble out there". Sure enough, when I turned, I saw that the cruiser was no longer circling. Its engine had stalled and he was unable to get it started again. The vessel was turned sideways in the river and was drifting swiftly in the strong current and heading for the brink of the dam.

Lucky for them, my vessel was equipped with twin 454 hp. V-8 engines that had the power to negotiate a rescue under these circumstances. I calculated that I had just enough time to untie from the lock wall and get out in the river, between the cruiser and the dam, tie him alongside my vessel, and tow him out of danger.

Had my trainee seen this peril just a minute later, I would not have had enough time to negotiate this rescue and three lives would surely have been lost, not to mention the two little dogs who were also aboard. These people were about 2 minutes away from death and were fortunate that fate had put my vessel in the right place at the right time, because, in one more minute, I would not have made the decision to risk my vessel and crew in this perilous situation.

Author receives Coast Guard award following river rescue.

Captain George and crew, group photo at award ceremony.

As an added highlight to the rescue, I later learned that the woman has since given birth to a baby boy and that makes 4 souls who were saved that fateful evening. Oh yea, as well as the two little dogs.

Captain George (at helm) and crew of Blue Heaven IV, after rescue mission.

Maybe the fact that, as a member of the Pittsburgh Safe Boating Council, I instituted the annual "Blessing of the Fleet" ceremony and have been involved for the past 20 years with providing local boaters with the blessings of various clergy from the Pittsburgh religious community at a gathering of the boats that occurs each June on the Sunday following Father's Day. Some of that blessing rubbed off on those boaters in the cruiser on that particular June evening.

Still in association with my love for water, for about 10 years, I wrote a column for a local boating magazine entitled "Ask Captain George" wherein I tried to assist the local boating community with information and answers to the many questions they had concerning their usage of our waterways. I also founded an organization known as "Boaters Are Voters" from which I lobby local, State and National politicians on behalf of recreational boating. The water-involved half of my career continues.

As I write this Post-script, I am preparing for two final safety patrols on the Allegheny River to protect boaters from the dangers of fireworks that will be shot from barges on the river to celebrate local events. That has been my principal contribution to boating safety and I hope to continue in this capacity as long as my physical stamina and health will permit.

ASK CAPTAIN GEORGE
by Captain George W. Boyle

My publisher just sent me an email to advise that my column is due and he wants it ASAP. I had no idea what to write this month and I went for a boat ride to clear my mind and see if a good topic would crop up.

Traveling down the Allegheny River at about 7:30 pm, as I rounded a curve in the river, I found that I was headed directly into the setting sun and it was reflecting a brilliant golden orange across the entire length of the river and casting twinkling and sparkling gems of gold right into the bow of my boat.

The sight was so spectacular that I just shut off the engines and let the boat drift while I relished in the view that nature was providing for my enjoyment. This golden path was extending the full length of the waterway and, when the wake of a passing boat crossed the sunlight path, the golden reflection wriggled like a giant sea serpent.

As other boats passed by, obviously in a hurry to get somewhere important, I felt sorry for them as they were not aware of the special treat that nature was providing, right here on the Allegheny River.

I turned on a good music station, poured a refreshing beverage, and just sat back and enjoyed the view.

At first, my concentration was on the sun itself, a giant, golden globe that was slowly descending into the distant hills at the far end of the river and casting his golden rays across the water to entrance me.

Then, when the last section of this golden globe had disappeared behind the hilltop, I began to notice other special treats.

The wispy white clouds that crisscrossed the sky began to take on hues and shades of soft pink and peach colors that began to enhance the soft blue of the evening sky.

Little by little, those soft shades increased in intensity and the entire panorama of the sky blossomed into a colorful pageant that no artist could capture with complete authenticity.

While the entire sky was being colored from peachy/pink to deep rose, the pale blue background was intensifying into a deeper and more robust royal blue and the area in the Western sky where the sun had recently descended had turned to a combination of bright crimson and glowing orange.

This spectacle in the sky was also reflected across the expanse of the water, creating a double appreciation of nature's splendor.

It took 15 or 20 minutes for this changing panorama to unfold and, as I was privileged to witness it in all its glory, I took time to reflect on the good fortunes that we have in our uses of the waterways.

When you leave the land and depart on a boat, no matter what the size or

Allegheny Sunset – The photo above, taken by contributing photographer Alex Dehesa, is similar to the one described by Captain George.

manner of propulsion, your entire perspective changes. Boats are special vessels and the water that carries them is unique to anything in the world.

A wise creator gave us water for our use and I gained a little more appreciation of it this evening as a little prayer of thanks whispered from my lips as the lingering colors slipped away into grey and black.

I couldn't help but notice how crisp the silhouettes of the trees along the shore stood out against the darkening sky that soon will be filled with stars.

Treasure these special moments, fellow boaters. We take too much for granted and the good things slip away in the rush of our hurried world.

I never thought I would be writing a column like this, but I'm glad I had a chance to share this beautiful experience with you and suggest that, next time you are out on the water at sunset time, take time to stop and enjoy what nature gives us every evening.

You'll fell better for the experience. I know that I do.

(If you have a boating question, write to "Ask Captain George," c/o Anchors Aweigh, 548 Juniper Court, Mars, PA 16046, or fax it to 724-779-7003, or you can email Captain George at: anchor@zbzoom.net.)

One of Captain George's (author's) favorite columns in "Anchors Aweigh Magazine"

It has been my privilege to share some highlights of instances and circumstances that have occurred in my career that were indeed unique, interesting, at times exciting and sometimes terrifying, but never dull.

Captain George (Author) attends booth at Pittsburgh Boat Show
for his "Boaters Are Voters" organization.

I hope, dear reader, that you have enjoyed reading of my adventures as much as I have enjoyed writing about them for you, because, just as surely as I am writing this now, each time I tell someone one of the stories contained in these pages, someone will invariably say to me 'YOU OUGHTA' WRITE A BOOK"

And I just did . . . by George

WA